"To truly gain internal and external success in sport at any level, you have to understand how the greats did it. *The Other Talent* is a beautiful, compelling, and essential dig into how the sausage is made for those at the top and therefore is invaluable for anyone wanting to keep striving upward!"

—Lesley Paterson, author of *The Brave Athlete: Calm the F*ck Down and Rise to the Occasion*

"In *The Other Talent*, Matt Fitzgerald offers a captivating look into the psychology of elite athletes, revealing the traits that drive success. It's a valuable resource for athletes, coaches, and anyone striving for excellence in their endeavors."

—Jim Afremow, author of *The Champion's Mind*

"Matt Fitzgerald has done it again, taking a complex concept and explaining it in the most layman of layman's terms. He's certainly convinced me that having a 'screw loose' and getting your 'shit together' are requirements for being a world-class athlete."

—Ben Rosario, executive director of HOKA NAZ Elite

"As I am a retired Navy SEAL, combat veteran, and gunshot wound survivor, people marvel at my physical strength to excel in my special operations career and overcome life-threatening injuries. What I always tell them is it had nothing to do with my muscles and everything to do with my mind and heart. Matt Fitzgerald's new book, *The Other Talent*, captures this in amazing detail. So many athletes put in tremendous physical training effort to achieve super-human results but frequently fall short of their performance goals. They fail to recognize so much of our ability to operate at the highest levels resides in our minds with strong mental health. If you are an athlete, CEO, first responder, military member, or even someone looking to level up your mental fitness, I highly recommend this book!"

—Jason Redman, retired US Navy SEAL, *New York Times* bestselling author of *The Trident* and *Overcome*, and mental performance coach

"I was at school, maybe thirteen or fourteen years old, when a fellow pupil told me I was weird for disappearing off to go running every lunch hour. My retort was, 'Maybe so, but tell me who's normal?' Since then, that same passion, obsessiveness, drive, craziness, weirdness has been the bedrock to everything I've been lucky enough to achieve. Matt's book reminds me that we all have our quirks and finding the correct outlet for them is a key component of, I think, what we call success. And endurance sports are perhaps one of the pursuits in which success most directly correlates with effort. You'll have to read it yourself to decide whether you think it's crazy that some of the toughest sports around find you, or more crazy when you find them. Enjoy!"

—Alistair Brownlee, two-time Olympic gold medalist

Also by Matt Fitzgerald

The Comeback Quotient
Running the Dream
Life Is a Marathon
How Bad Do You Want It?
The Endurance Diet
80/20 Running
Iron War

THE OTHER TALENT

THE OTHER TALENT

The Curiously Complex Role of *Mental Health in Athletic Greatness* and Why It's Never Too Late to Harness Your Potential

MATT FITZGERALD

BenBella Books, Inc.
Dallas, TX

BenBella Books, Inc.
10440 N. Central Expressway
Suite 800
Dallas, TX 75231
benbellabooks.com
Send feedback to feedback@benbellabooks.com

BenBella is a federally registered trademark.

Printed in the United States of America
10 9 8 7 6 5 4 3 2 1

Library of Congress Control Number: 2023059708
ISBN 9781637745458 (trade paperback)
ISBN 9781637745465 (electronic)

Editing by Rachel Phares
Copyediting by Scott Calamar
Proofreading by Lisa Story and Rebecca Maines
Text design and composition by PerfecType, Nashville, TN
Cover design by Faceout Studio, Elisha Zepeda
Cover images © Shutterstock / namtipStudio (sweat) and El Nariz (woman)
Printed by Lake Book Manufacturing

Special discounts for bulk sales are available. Please contact bulkorders@benbellabooks.com.

In memory of Laurie, great in love

Do I want to tackle a 230-pound guy who's running like a deer? Heavens no, no one in their right mind would. But there is something that drives me and compels me to stick my head in there and give it my best shot.
—HALE IRWIN

CONTENTS

FOREWORD

I first "met" Matt Fitzgerald as a guest on his *80/20 Endurance* podcast. I'd come on the show to discuss my book *The Tyranny of Talent*, about the challenges of identifying and developing talent in sport, and we hit it off right away. We had a great discussion and many of the points I made in my book are made, often more succinctly and definitely more passionately, in the book you're about to read.

I read a lot of books. Normally two to three a week. Everything from scientific textbooks to the latest fluffy fiction. *The Other Talent* belongs in a category I call "fun science"—books that stretch my brain in an area by looking at issues and problems from a perspective that's different from my own. This book is part sports history and part thesis about the psychology of athletic greatness. If Matt has a singular "talent," it's writing sports history in a way that immediately engages the reader with the subject.

I was equal parts honored and nervous when Matt asked me to write the foreword. Honored because of Matt's background and pedigree; nervous because of the content and never having written a foreword before.

This foreword was frustrating to write!

Not because the writing isn't compelling or interesting . . . It is.

Not because the arguments aren't persuasive . . . They are.

It was frustrating because after spending a quarter of a century of my life trying to find the reasons some athletes succeed and others don't, I've realized the problem is even more monstrous than I initially thought. *The Other Talent* reminds me of how far we need to go to understand the psychology of athlete development and performance. Even more important is Matt's point (supported by the latest research) that the area we may know the least about is likely the one that's most significant for understanding the secret to success.

We see ourselves in sports biographies. Even the most accomplished athletes are humans, after all, and they provide models of achievement and performance that reflect the capabilities of our species. As Matt notes near the end of his book, and a position I agree with completely, athletes who have achieved greatness in sport can be role models illuminating the process of greatness in any domain. From this viewpoint, sports stories remind us of our own potential.

Matt's original title for the book was *Screw Loose, Shit Together*; I'm not sure which one better captures the essence of his message. Certainly, *SLST* reflects the "rawness" of Matt's language and approach, but may not have the same popular appeal as *The Other Talent*. Regardless of the title, make no mistake: this isn't a book for the faint of heart, or those looking for the safe and sterilized language typical of most popular sport science books.

I have to admit, there are things in the book that didn't sit well with me. I wasn't particularly surprised by this. Conversations and interactions with coaches, policy makers, and athletes have reinforced to me that I'm lucky to be able to look at the world from the sheltered viewpoint of science. This perspective frames the world relative to neat and tidy research questions. In science, we view the world in terms of "things we know" and "things we don't know yet." Understanding the complex relationship between athlete mental health, long-term development, and optimal athletic performance firmly belongs in the "don't know yet" category. In Matt's perspective on athletic greatness, the two defining mental characteristics of great athletes—"screw loose" and "shit together"—are almost certainly an oversimplification of what the scientific research tells us. Except people working with athletes (or trying to raise one) can't be constrained by what research tells us is likely true. Science is always describing a picture whose final image is still being developed. The real world, on the other hand, requires action and gets by through working in generalities (how does this reflect what I see in the world?) and determining usefulness (what can I take away from this to improve my own experience?).

From this utilitarian perspective, this is an empowering book. It focuses on identifying, acknowledging, and taking control of your limitations so that growth is in your future. I think the potential of this book, however, will be determined by your ability to engage with the examples Matt uses to make his case. Try to see yourself in what you read. The diversity of examples undoubtedly means some are going to fit your experience and viewpoint better than others. "I'd rather be impactful than right," Matt writes at the end of the book. This is a laudable and important goal. We learn and advance thinking more when we're wrong than when we're right. Even in scientifically controlled studies, recent estimates suggest most results are "wrong," or incomplete in answering their research questions, but we wouldn't argue such studies aren't valuable. Impact should always be the goal.

You don't have to agree with everything you read in the pages that follow, and it's likely better if you don't. Agreement would reinforce that these issues are simple and easy to deal with. They're not. Leave the simple questions to the physiologists and biomechanists. There are important issues raised in this book, particularly in the current climate of athlete mental health, safe sport, and holistic athlete development. However, we need to have honest discussions about these issues—warts and all. The potential of Matt's book is in engaging people to think about how these issues apply to them and their development . . . and forcing the scientific community to do a better job of outlining what we know and don't know for athletes, coaches, parents, and other sport stakeholders responsible for putting this research into action.

If I were a betting man, I'd predict we'll eventually confirm that there is no simple binary distinguishing "enough" from "too much" relative to most of the concepts discussed in *The Other Talent*. Most research from studies of elite and exceptional performers categorizes athletes into skill or performance groups (e.g., experts compared to novices or non-experts; medalists versus non-medalists; super-champions versus everyone else). However, most of the variables affecting human development, function, and performance exist on a continuum that has greatest relevance to individuals, not groups. Even with a group of performers at the same level, there is considerable variability within the group on most variables.

A greater understanding of this variability would allow us to better construct learning and developmental environments for athletes at all stages of skill and performance—improving the benefits while minimizing the costs. However, to get there we've got some tough questions to answer. Such as:

What is the ultimate value of self-regulation as a process?
To what extent are elements of self-regulation stable or trainable throughout the lifespan?

What is the threshold of mental health that leads to diminished returns? When is a screw "too loose" that a person can never get it tight enough to function at the level of greatness?

Can we manufacture situations in an athlete's development to loosen screws and then tighten them? Do athletes need difficult and challenging experiences in order to develop the types of psychological qualities necessary for greatness? If so, how do we manage the unappetizing cause (e.g., early trauma/adversity) with the desirable effect (e.g., resiliency, mental toughness)?

These questions are incredibly hard to navigate from a scientific perspective. Scientists only ever get the part of the picture that can be controlled, measured, and quantified in strictly controlled research designs. Can we quantify "screw loose" or "shit together" in meaningful ways? What Matt's book does is set us on a course to answers by identifying the problem. But these relationships are going to be subtle, not simple. As Matt discusses in the penultimate chapter of the book, the fact that some of the athletes described here had terrible fathers doesn't mean terrible parenting is a ticket to success. It is also crucial to remember that focusing on those who make it to the end of the journey only provides descriptions of the "survivors" of the systems that produced them, not evidence that these systems are optimal!

Explorations from people like Matt show us the gaps in our understanding that help us get our "shit together" to test the validity of questions raised by those in the real world. Matt's identified the effect, proposed the "cause," and now it's up to researchers to determine the validity of this relationship. Despite the remarkable case studies described in *The Other Talent*, validation of Matt's theory can't come from anecdotes. Even though, as the quote goes, "the plural of anecdotes is data," they aren't very good data. Ultimate validation has to come from empirical assessment, repeated across time and contexts, until we reach the truth.

So, turn the page and enjoy the book. This isn't going to be an echo chamber where you just get to hear ideas you already agree with. What a boring book that would be. The key takeaway from decades of research on athlete development is that the story of human potential is one of variability, not consistency. Some things will work for some and not for others. The stories used to anchor the discussion are just examples; you may see yourself in them, you may not. The key is focusing on the elements of Matt's narrative that are relevant to you. Things like:

1. Whatever your unique psychological strengths and limitations are, they need to be managed in a way that increases your likelihood of success.
2. Being able to self-regulate our own behavior and performance increases our likelihood of success.

Thanks, Matt, for writing a book that gives me a kick in the backside. As you note, frustration can be a great motivator! Time to get back to work.

Joe Baker, PhD
Author, *The Tyranny of Talent*
Toronto, Canada

There is no greater impediment
to the advancement of knowledge
than the ambiguity of words.
—THOMAS REID

I was not the first American to catch COVID-19, but I came pretty darn close. There were sixty—not six thousand, not six hundred, sixty—confirmed cases in the United States as of February 29, 2020, the date on which I unwittingly inhaled a hefty payload of the virus while running the Atlanta Marathon in the company of several thousand other sweaty, half-naked mouth breathers. The actual number of carriers was surely much greater, perhaps in the low four figures, but that's still a tiny fraction of the total population, placing the odds of getting infected on or before that date at roughly one in 33,000. Now, I'm no statistician, but I'd call that unlucky. Alas, worse luck followed.

Most people who get infected with the coronavirus recover fully. Others die. I did neither, landing instead somewhere between these absolutes, in the purgatory known as long Covid, a mysterious chronic illness whose myriad symptoms include crushing fatigue, shortness of breath, and nerve pain, as well as brain-centered complaints ranging from anxiety and agitation to insomnia and depression. I've experienced all of the above, plus weirder symptoms like derealization (a dreamlike sense of separation from the world), rumination (a tendency to plunge down bottomless rabbit holes of unproductive thought), and hyperekplexia (a startle reflex so sensitive that I keep my cell phone muted at all times because I jump like a combat veteran whenever it rings, even when I'm expecting the call).

My wife can relate. She doesn't have long Covid, but she is bipolar, and she knows a thing or two about struggling to control one's thoughts, emotions, and perceptions. Prior to my experience with long Covid, the greatest mental health challenge I faced was supporting Nataki during the worst phase of her illness, a decade of hell-on-Earth marked by seven involuntary hospitalizations, countless 9-1-1 calls, and two suicide attempts (one for each of us).

Why am I telling you all this? Because I want you to know where I'm coming from when I discuss matters of mental health in this book. In particular, I want you to understand that, as cavalier as my use of words and phrases like "screw loose" and "shit together" might seem, I write from the perspective of one who takes mental health very seriously. I just have a different way of talking about it than do some other folks who take it just as seriously.

Some, mind you, not all. In this book you will hear from psychologists who, like me, believe there's no such thing as a normal person, from therapists who profess that none of us has our shit entirely together (using precisely this language), and from neuroscientists who say that addiction isn't always a bad thing. You will also hear from champion athletes who validate these ideas in both word and deed, including

2

Chrissie Wellington, a British triathlete who describes herself as having an "addictive personality," not self-critically but with pride, characterizing her compulsive nature as more of a blessing than a curse. "The word 'addiction' comes with negative connotations," she has written, "but it doesn't have to be a damaging impulse. It's all about channeling your craving into something positive." So, please understand that when I apply phrases like "crazy" and "addictive" to the great athletes studied in these pages, I'm being neither recklessly unscientific nor glibly disparaging. To the contrary, I'm merely describing what I and certain freethinking experts see—and how a number of great athletes see themselves.

Among the many interesting people I interviewed while researching this book was Eric Kussin, a former professional sports executive who suffered a strange and sudden mental breakdown in his early thirties. Eric spent the next two and a half years in a state of almost total incapacitation, but he was eventually able to claw his way back to health. When at last he felt like himself again, Eric founded a charitable organization called We're All a Little "Crazy." Its mission is to normalize mental health struggles, but not in the usual way. Whereas other organizations that embrace the same mission like to point out how one in five people has a mental illness, Eric's message is that *five* out of every five people experience trauma affecting their mental health.

It's a crucial distinction. No matter how many people we choose to classify as mentally ill in our well-intended efforts to normalize the phenomenon, we're still segregating them from those we place in the category of the not mentally ill—still "othering" them, as my woke friends would say. Eric contends, as do I and others you'll encounter in the coming chapters, that all humans belong to a single category, which is the category of people who are working hard to either maintain or regain their sanity. That, indeed, we are all a little "crazy."

"EVERYONE in the world is affected by life's inevitable traumas and stresses," Eric writes on his foundation's website. "We can't escape them, as they are part of the human experience and they impact us on many levels. Mental health exists on a continuum, with some simply experiencing more severe declines than others over varying periods of time in their lives (and/or being more genetically predisposed to such declines)."

Taking a cue from Eric Kussin, I will henceforth place "crazy" between quotation marks to indicate that the word is being used neither diagnostically nor pejoratively but in reference to the "craziness" that is endemic to the human condition. But I won't stop there. For as much as Eric and I agree on the universality of "craziness," I'm not sure we fully agree on the *value* of "craziness."

Here's how I see it: If we grant that mental health challenges are ubiquitous, it follows that our individual struggles to cope with these challenges—our unique flavors of "craziness," so to speak—are defining elements of *who we are*. And if "crazy" is part of who we are, what sense does it make to judge "craziness" as categorically negative, meaning bad in all cases and in any amount? It makes no sense to me. And I'm not alone.

"There is no great genius without a tincture of madness," observed the Roman Stoic philosopher Seneca some two thousand years ago. Modern science substantiates this notion of mental imbalance as a generative force. A 2010 study by Swedish researchers found that teenagers who achieved high scores in a test of intelligence were four times more likely than their less-brilliant peers to be diagnosed with bipolar disorder within the next ten years. At a biological level, researchers have identified overlaps in brain structure between persons with schizophrenia and "healthy" people who happen to be highly creative. No one is saying that mental illness is something we should aspire to, or that mental illness and giftedness are the same thing. But what the evidence *is* telling us is that, to a large extent, our mental health challenges and our gifts spring from the same source.

This book explores the idea that, in the right circumstances, "craziness" can be quite useful—part of the formula for success and fulfillment in life, if not always a pleasant thing to experience. In the following pages I will argue that a certain kind of "craziness," when combined with a particular form of sanity (namely, having one's shit together), facilitates greatness in sports—and can have implications for our nonathletic pursuits. I realize that, in making this argument, I'm opening myself up to potential charges of glorifying mental illness. But I hope to persuade *you*, at least, if not every reader, that "crazy" is more than just a misfortune that happens to certain people. It's part of what makes each of us human, something that can be embraced and harnessed toward useful ends. And for a special few, "crazy" is their superpower.

Well, half of it. I'm focusing here on the "screw loose" side of the psychological recipe for athletic greatness, but as you will soon see, the "shit together" side is equally important. If the former functions as the engine of high achievement in sports, the latter serves as the steering wheel. Good luck reaching a remote destination—say, the Olympic podium—without both.

Another potential criticism I'd like to forestall here, if I may, is that I have conflated the mental makeup of great athletes with the mental health struggles they commonly experience. Studies have revealed alarming rates of anxiety, depression, eating disorders, and substance misuse within this population, a pattern that experts have attributed to the uniquely stressful elite-athlete lifestyle, with its tremendous training demands and extreme competitive pressures. Recent high-profile cases (swimmer Michael Phelps, gymnast Simone Biles, and downhill skier Mikaela Shiffrin, to name a few) have brought increased public attention to the mental health toll exacted from world-class sportspersons, a topic that merits a book of its own but is not the book I've written. The book I *have* written is less about the risks to mental health to which elite athletes are exposed than it is about the oddly two-sided mental makeup that enables certain athletes to achieve greatness in the first place.

If I glorify anything in these pages, it is indeed the greatness of great athletes. But I do so in a way that differs from the average sports fan's shallow idol worship. Displays of physical talent and skill are impressive, but not as impressive to me as the *humanity* required to be truly great in sport. That's the thing we sports nuts so often forget: these world champions and MVPs are people just like us. Imagine what it's like to be *expected* to win a gold medal for your country with a billion people watching on live television and an ailing parent back home you're worried about and a costly mortgage on a new house you'll no longer be able to afford if you fall short of the podium and lose the support of sponsors and a niggle in your right hamstring that just popped up out of nowhere and a younger rival who you're pretty sure is juiced gunning for the same gold medal for which you have sacrificed, risked, and endured far more than most people could even imagine. To hold it together and deliver results in such circumstances demands more than physical ability. The world champions and MVPs might make it look easy sometimes, but it's not. They feel the same way you would in that white-hot spotlight, and the more fully you understand what it takes for them to avoid melting beneath its relentless gaze, the more relatable they become.

Speaking for myself, as a former athlete who wanted to be great but wasn't, I have a special appreciation for what's required, on a human level, to achieve what I could not. And as a student of sport with a mind that, for better or worse, has its own peculiar perspective on things, I believe I have a unique grasp of what it takes for a flesh-and-blood person—not an überconfident action-movie hero but a mortal person who puts their pants on one leg at a time—to be better than anyone at something a whole hell of a lot of people try to be good at. All this to say, when I call great athletes "crazy," I mean it as a compliment.

CHAPTER
ONE

Talent, Early and Later

Nothing is more common than unsuccessful men with talent.
—CALVIN COOLIDGE

On April 15, 2018, Scottish runner Callum Hawkins joined twenty-three of his elite peers at the start line of the Commonwealth Games marathon on Australia's Gold Coast. The weather that day was inconducive to prolonged exertion, the surface temperature already approaching eighty degrees Fahrenheit on the sunbaked Southport Broadwater Parklands when the race began at ten past six in the morning. Callum, however, saw the ovenlike conditions as an advantage. Confident in his ability to outsuffer all rivals, he set an aggressive early pace that wrought

9

a rapid attrition. By mile twenty-four, the young Scotsman held a commanding two-minute lead over defending champion and host-nation representative Michael Shelley.

Under normal conditions, it is almost impossible for an athlete to exercise himself to death, the human organism being equipped with various fail-safes to forestall exertional self-annihilation. An exception is hot weather, when it is possible for the highly motivated athlete to push through warning signs such as dizziness and blurred vision to the point where the primary seat of these fail-safes—the brain—overheats, and then all bets are off. And that's precisely what Callum Hawkins did a mile and a half from the finish line of the 2018 Commonwealth Games marathon.

Spectators lining this part of the racecourse watched in wide-eyed bemusement as the sweat-basted leader began to reel from one side of the road to the other like a blindfolded drunk in a windstorm. Seemingly oblivious to his predicament, Callum pressed on, the spastic movements of his flailing arms and wobbly legs belying the slackly impassive set of his facial features. It was only a matter of time before he went down, and lucky for him he was at the very edge of the road when he did, toppling unharmed onto a grassy verge as onlookers inexplicably applauded, as though the stricken athlete at their feet had just performed a difficult trick and scored significant style points.

It seemed a good time to quit, but Callum did not. Like a flattened welterweight trying to beat a ten count, he peeled himself off the turf and onto his hands and knees, only to buckle and kiss the tarmac. As the unwitting Michael Shelley loomed closer, quitless Callum gathered himself and tried again to regain his feet, buckled again, and gave it one more go, this time succeeding, if one can call it that.

Still leading the race, Callum lurched along the tarmac in a grotesque approximation of bipedal locomotion for another couple of hundred meters before taking another digger, this time smacking his head against a metal railing and staying down. After an unforgivably long delay, medics came to the fallen runner's aid, ending his race officially. Upon waking in the back of an ambulance, hyperthermic but past the worst danger, he croaked out three words expressing his only concern.

"Did I win?"

Close brushes of this sort are not uncommon at the highest levels of sport. Another happened at the 2022 FINA World Championships in Portugal, where American artistic swimmer Anita Alvarez held her breath underwater a bit too long in pursuit of actual style points and passed out, sinking to the bottom of the pool, a goner if not for the heroic actions of her coach, who'd rescued her once before for the same reason.

In the eyes of the average sports fan, the win-or-die-trying mentality that precipitates these crises seems kind of nuts. The athletes who possess this mentality think so too. "Every top athlete is a little crazy," wrote elite triathlete turned Oscar-nominated screenwriter Lesley Paterson in a 2012 op-ed for the *Guardian*.

If this is true, one has to wonder: Does an athlete *have* to be a little "crazy" to achieve greatness? The story of Callum Hawkins says maybe so. But the full story says even more, suggesting the possibility that being a little "crazy" is not merely essential to achieving athletic greatness but is perhaps even more important than speed or strength or stamina or any other physical trait for the athlete aspiring to greatness.

In his teens, Callum raced for the Kilbarchan Amateur Athletic Club, where he was overshadowed by older brother Derek. Nevertheless, he performed well enough to earn the chance to cross the pond and race at Butler University in Indiana, where he posted unremarkable times of 3:57 for 1500 meters and 14:11 for 5000 meters and qualified for a single NCAA championship, placing twenty-sixth. But whatever Callum lacked at this stage of his athletic development, he later made up for with something else—perhaps the very thing that nearly got him killed on a hot autumn morning on Australia's Gold Coast. While all but a handful of the twenty-five runners who beat him in his only NCAA Championship appearance faded into obscurity, Callum went on to make two Olympic teams and to finish as high as fourth at the world championships. Against all expectations, the kid who once wasn't even the fastest runner in his family became the fastest Scotsman ever, setting national records for the marathon (2:08:14) and half marathon (1:00:00).

What we have here is either an interesting anomaly or a tantalizing hint at the true secret to athletic greatness. And it's not an anomaly.

BLOOMERS AND FADERS

Each year in April the website MaxPreps releases a list of the top freshman high school basketball players in the United States. In 2010, for example, five boys were named first-team freshman All-Americans, five more earned second-team status, and another eighteen received honorable mentions. Of these twenty-eight young superstars, only five went on to play in the NBA, where they were joined by no fewer than seventeen players who'd also been high school freshmen in 2010 but failed to earn MaxPreps recognition.

There's nothing unusual about these numbers. I picked 2010 at random, but I could have picked any other year, and the data would have been comparable, with less than one in five of the most promising teen hoopsters going on to achieve professional success. And it's not just basketball that exhibits this pattern of early promise fading to disappointment. Take running. As I write this, not a single woman who holds an American record in a distance-running event previously held a junior record in a similar event. Which means, of course, that the runners who *did* set records at the junior level were subsequently surpassed by late bloomers.

I promise I'm not cherry-picking. Name a sport, any sport. Did I hear soccer? Excellent choice. No sport tries harder to identify future champions early, yet despite all of the resources that are poured into international soccer's talent development system, the same pattern holds. According to one report, 97 percent of youth players who earn selection to one of Great Britain's several elite soccer academies (which collectively represent the highest level of junior soccer in the UK) fail to advance to England's Premier League (the highest level of professional soccer in the UK).

Tennis, anyone? We think of tennis as a sport in which today's prodigies are tomorrow's champions. But the stats belie this perception. Only four male players ranked among the top ten juniors in the world in 2015 were ranked among the top *one hundred* professionals in the world in 2022, and just one held a top ten ranking.

While the average sports fan might be surprised by these figures, experts are not. It is common knowledge among authorities on elite athlete development that early success in a sport is a poor predictor of ultimate success. In the blunt words of one such authority, "The relationship between early performance and long-term success is not supported by available evidence."

At a population level, sure, athletes who are good at a particular sport in their early teens tend to still be good when they're all grown up. But at the apex of the performance pyramid, where we're no longer distinguishing between good and not so good but between elite and not quite elite, we see a high degree of flux. Simply put, the greatest youth athletes and the greatest adult athletes are not the same people.

Why not? Well, a lot can happen, good and bad, between the ages of fifteen and twenty-five: growth, development, learning, coaching, mentorship, relocation, injury, illness, competition, distractions, trauma—the list goes on. But these circumstantial factors, which are largely outside the athlete's control, tell only part of the story. Other, volitional factors are also at play. Regardless of where they sit in the pecking order as juniors (i.e., teens), the few, special athletes who achieve true greatness at the pro level work both harder and smarter than everyone else, their preparation ultimately exceeding that of other athletes in both quantity and quality.

It is customary to label the nonvolitional factors that allow inexperienced athletes to perform exceptionally in a sport "talent," and to attribute improvement over time to "practice." Conventional wisdom also holds that talent is innate, whereas practice is a choice. To be born with a natural gift for skiing or cricket or whatever is (in the mind of the average sports fan) a matter of luck. But to practice more and better than everyone else is something any athlete can choose to do.

Except it isn't. Think about it: By definition, only one athlete in a given group can be number one by any measure. If the measure is strength, only one can be the strongest. If the measure is speed, only one can be the swiftest, and so on. Likewise, only one athlete in a group of any size can work harder and smarter than the rest. If a thousand athletes are told that whoever among them works both harder and smarter than the other 999 will earn greatness and all that comes with it, only one of them actually will. Practice may look like a choice, and to a certain extent it is, but the fact of the matter is that not every athlete *has what it takes* to outhustle and outsmart every other athlete. And if that's the case, then the other major factor besides talent that contributes to athletic greatness isn't practice per se but what lies behind it, which is really just another form of talent: the ability to make the most of one's ability.

In his book *The Tyranny of Talent*, Joe Baker—the above-quoted authority on elite athlete development—uses the terms "early talent" and "later talent" to differentiate these two forms of athletic aptitude. The vagueness of the descriptors is deliberate—it's Baker's way of acknowledging that we don't fully understand what makes certain athletes successful in adolescence but less so as adults and certain others successful as adults despite being less so in adolescence. But we do know *some* things about early talent and later talent, including that early talent seems to be rooted in relatively stable physical traits like agility and dexterity, whereas later talent expresses more fluid, psychological characteristics, such as motivation and pain tolerance, which collectively are more impactful in the long run.

When we view talent through the lens of these concepts, the developmental process in sport looks like a large-scale team tryout with two rounds of cuts. The first cut eliminates all the athletes who lack the early (physical) talent to be elite in their chosen sport (regardless of their level of later talent). Genes aren't all that matter, but they matter first. The surviving athletes move on to face the second cut, which unfolds over many years, gradually culling the ones who, though they possess the physical requirements for greatness, lack the mental wherewithal to get the most out of their natural ability. Those left standing in the end are the true greats, the doubly blessed fraction of a percent who aren't necessarily the most physically gifted but who do possess the most combined early and later talent.

Which is rather curious. After all, we think of sports as physical pursuits, but the divergent paths of athletic development seen in the upper strata indicate that, contrary to our intuitions, the most successful sportspersons are more exceptional above the neck than below. I say "our" intuitions, but in truth I figured this shit out long ago, not because I'm clever but because, as an athlete myself, I struggled mentally in my formative years, confronted sooner than most with the cold, hard fact that physical talent in itself has limited value. Over time, what started as a grudging acknowledgment of a personal limiter matured into a deep admiration for those who possessed what I lacked and an abiding fascination with the role of the mind in athletic achievement, which led me to author a series of books exploring the mental side of sporting success, including *Brain Training for Runners, How Bad Do You Want It?,* and *The Comeback Quotient.*

A THEORY IS BORN

Another book in this series (I write a lot of books—it's a problem) is *Iron War,* a rivalry story in the tradition of the documentary film *Magic & Bird* that chronicles a decade-long struggle for triathlon supremacy between Ironman Hall-of-Famers Dave Scott and Mark Allen, whose epic final showdown at the 1989 Ironman World Championship is widely regarded as the single greatest race ever run. In hindsight, I recognize this clash of titans as an almost perfect case study of later talent, highlighting with almost clinical rigor what is truly essential to the full realization of athletic potential, and Exhibit A in what has become my very own theory of athletic greatness.

Both athletes fit the classic profile of the late bloomer, ascending from good to great between adolescence and manhood. They started out as swimmers, each dreaming of the Olympics, each falling well short in this ambition, topping out as second-tier collegiate racers. In achieving subsequent greatness in triathlon, Dave and Mark—like so many other sporting greats—surpassed athletes of superior early talent, competitive peers who kicked their respective asses as minors but whose names are now forgotten. At their peak, Dave and Mark weren't just better than everyone else but miles better, literally, with no equal but each other, accumulating six Ironman World Championship victories apiece over their fabled careers, a feat that no male triathlete has come close to matching since Mark (the younger of the two) retired in 1997. In their final face-off, a daylong battle of attrition that shattered existing notions of the possible and gave my book its title, the familiar foes finished *three miles* ahead of their closest chaser, lopping a gob-smacking nineteen minutes off Dave's course record.

Yet despite being exact equals in performance, Dave and Mark were about as different as two men could be psychologically. This is important, for if they'd had matching personalities as well as matching resumes, we'd have no way of knowing which of their shared mental traits contributed to their greatness and which did not. But Dave and Mark were in fact famously dissimilar in nature, and their many stark contrasts served to accentuate the few mental traits possessed by both, which logically *had to* account for their greatness.

Dave was an old-fashioned jock from the school of no pain, no gain. Nicknamed "The Man," he subscribed to a last-guy-standing ethos that, in a 1987 interview, he summarized in one simple sentence: "I had this idea that if I trained more than anyone else, I was bound to succeed." Dave cared little for elements of preparation extraneous to working out, scoffing at ancillary practices such as stretching, massage, heart monitoring, and visualization. All his eggs were placed in the single basket of a never-quit attitude, the results of which speak for themselves.

Mark was the yin to Dave's yang in more ways than one. He trained at low intensity most of the time and took a whole month off after Ironman each year to surf. Deeply spiritual, he dabbled in New Age practices for a while before plunging headlong into Huichol shamanism, going so far as to incorporate sweat lodges and vision quests into his Ironman buildup. Preferring traditional medicine to the Western kind, he was known to interrupt workouts on occasion to pick up a stray bird feather or an unusual stone. His nickname—one of them, anyway—was "Zen Master."

Fans and journalists delighted in the oil-and-water dynamic of Dave and Mark's agonistic pairing. But were they opposites on every level? They were not! As striking and manifold as their differences were, these contrasts disguised an underlying sameness—a core foundation of shared mental traits that were, I believe, the true secret to their success.

The first of these shared traits was the one Callum Hawkins demonstrated on the day he ran himself to death's door: a willingness to take bigger risks, make deeper sacrifices, and endure greater suffering in pursuit of victory than a "normal" person would. When we see a great athlete do something that we ourselves would never do, something that makes us say, "That's crazy," it is this unreasonable willingness we're referring to. Except it's not so much a willingness as a compulsion. All professional athletes want to win, but Dave and Mark *had* to win. For both men, the relentless pursuit of victory satisfied a deep psychological need that wasn't met in life outside of sport.

In Dave's case, the driving need was a sharklike impulse to keep moving and never stop—an exercise addiction to end all exercise addictions. "If I don't get it," he confessed to me in an interview, "it just makes me go haywire. I know I need to have that fairly high level of exercise on a daily basis. When I'm on, and I feel good about my exercise and I've been on a good wave, I feel invincible. I can handle any kind of hurdle and I can meet any kind of challenge head-on. And when I don't have it, when I don't have that morphine-like endorphin feeling that resonates throughout my body, it affects everything. It affects my personality, it affects my confidence, it affects my ability to interact with other people."

Mark's need was different—issuing from life experience rather than biological hardwiring—but no less powerful. In his case, athletic achievement started out as a means to win the love of a cold and distant father who, throughout Mark's childhood, expected perfection from his sons and penalized any and all imperfections. As time went by, however, success in sport came to mean something different for Mark, becoming less a vehicle for fatherly approval and more an avatar for the self-acceptance he truly needed. Understandably reluctant to share the specifics of his "rough and abusive" boyhood, as he's characterized it, Mark did on occasion crack open the lid of his psyche, granting brief glimpses into the void he sought to fill by winning. "If you dig deep enough into the life of any of the top athletes who are pushing their bodies to the absolute limits," he told one reporter, "you're going to find a story. You're going to find something that those athletes are trying to make up for that they didn't get when they were younger. Something that hurt them."

While working on *Iron War*, I talked to dozens of Dave's and Mark's friends, associates, family members, and fellow athletes, many of whom shared memories of abnormal behavior emblematic of one or the other's driving need. Craig Wilson, for example, who played water polo with Dave at UC Davis in the mid 1970s, recalled with special clarity a sweltering afternoon in late August when Dave invited Craig to join him for a weightlifting session at Hickey Gym, a glorified broom closet that lacked both windows and air-conditioning. Devoid of context, this seems only mildly "crazy." But here's the context: Dave and Craig had just completed the second of a pair of two-and-a-half-hour preseason pool workouts between which Dave, who captained the team and was in charge of its summer conditioning program, had forced his fellow players to run several miles in one-hundred-degree heat.

"You're completely psycho," Craig answered. By which, I suppose, he meant, "No thanks, I'll pass."

Mark's former training partners, meanwhile, told stories highlighting a singularity of focus that at times was almost frightening in its intensity. Paul Huddle, who not only trained with Mark but also lived with him in their respective bachelor days, completed countless bike rides in the Zen Master's slipstream, yet one ride in particular lingered indelibly in his memory. Paul was, as usual, hanging on to Mark's back wheel for dear life when suddenly—as though in answer to a prayer—he heard the unmistakable sound of a tire springing a leak. Expecting Mark to stop and fix the flat, Paul eased up, only to watch his friend disappear up the road, oblivious. It took Paul five miles to catch up to his cycling buddy, because that's how long it took for Mark to realize he was riding on a deflating rear tire.

In competition, Mark's laser focus enabled him to tunnel deeper into the proverbial pain cave than his opponents could ever hope to do. At the 1983 World Triathlon Championship in Nice, France, Mark pushed harder than he should have on the bike in an effort to bury Dave Scott and paid for it during the latter stages of a steamy afternoon run. Effectively cooking inside his own skin, he became first light-headed, then dizzy. His vision swam, blurring the road ahead to a soup of colors, light, and shadows. With three miles to go, Mark tilted his head back to take a swig of water and lost his equilibrium, toppling backward to the tarmac like a lightning-struck pine tree. But whereas a tree would have stayed down, Mark scraped himself off the road and, with the herky-jerky movements of the undead, resumed running, only to stagger into a parking meter. Spectators' cheers turned to gasps as the failing race leader staggered from one side of the Promenade des Anglais to the other, his eyes vacant and unseeing. Some were so moved by Mark's zombielike perseverance that they broke away from the curb and ran alongside him, urging him on as Dave stalked closer and closer from behind. By the time Mark reached the finish line, a crowd of hundreds surrounded him, urging him on. In his hotel room that night Mark sobbed uncontrollably, struggling to process what he'd done to himself. But hey, he'd won!

If Dave and Mark had shared nothing more than a loose screw—in other words, if their willingness to take bigger risks, make deeper sacrifices, and endure greater suffering than any "normal" person would do in the name of victory had not been complemented by a second key mental trait that balanced out the first—they would have self-destructed instead of winning consistently as they did. What kept them on the winning path was that, in addition to having a loose screw, Dave and Mark also had their shit together, which is to say both men exhibited a kind of disciplined, sensible steadiness, or prudence, that ensured their immoderate drivenness was (almost) always channeled productively.

Dave's discipline expressed itself in (where else?) his training. Almost single-handedly, Dave engineered the first scientific approach to training for long-distance triathlons, a type of competition that hadn't even existed before he started doing them in the late 1970s. It was important to Dave to know precisely how fit he was at all times, and his training regimen was designed to deliver this knowledge, right down to the tenth of a second. The crux of his method was mind-numbing repetition—a hamster wheel of endlessly recycled workouts that he used to predict his next Ironman result. By October 1989, when his climactic battle with Mark Allen took place, Dave had ridden his favorite cycling route, an out-and-back jaunt on Highway 31 through the hills east of his home in Davis, California, approximately three thousand times, and never faster than in the final weeks before the race.

"I think, on a good day, 8:09 is in sight in Hawaii," Dave declared at a press conference held on the eve of the competition. Pundits dismissed this number—an unthinkable nineteen-minute improvement on Dave's own course record—as bluster. But those same pundits were eating crow the following afternoon, when sure enough, the race was won in 8 hours, 9 minutes, and 14 seconds. The problem for Dave was that it was not he but Mark who broke the finishing tape, 58 seconds ahead of his archnemesis.

Mark's "shit together" side manifested as a kind of protean methodological adaptability. A lot of athletes stay within a comfort zone of familiar methods despite disappointing results, while others do the opposite, changing things up indiscriminately in search of a winning formula (or confidence). The few who have their shit together, however, maintain a pragmatic, "whatever works" mindset that enables them to avoid getting stuck in their ways or wasting energy chasing wild hares. And that was Mark.

Often injured in the early part of his career, Mark switched from the high-intensity approach favored by his training partners in San Diego to the low-intensity method touted by endurance guru Phil Maffetone and was rewarded with consistent health. Later on, frustrated by his inability to break through at Ironman, where he lost to Dave Scott in his first five attempts, Mark again tweaked his approach, increasing his weekly training hours to match Dave's, and he was rewarded with his first Ironman victory. Having finally broken through, Mark set a new goal: to top himself, repeatedly, until he'd elevated the art of Ironman racing as close to perfection as any mortal could. With each new season, Mark tried something different in the quest for the ultimate performance. One year he teamed up with bike wizard Steve Hed for wind-tunnel testing that yielded a more aerodynamic riding position on his bike. Another year he worked with strength and conditioning coach Diane Buchta to develop a weightlifting program that added several pounds of muscle to his lanky frame. His reward for these and other carefully selected and meticulously executed adaptations was a streak of six straight Ironman victories to match his rival's career total.

To summarize: Dave Scott and Mark Allen (1) stood head and shoulders above other triathletes of their day performancewise, (2) were late bloomers who demonstrated no greater early talent than their peers, and (3) were radically different from each other psychologically, except that (4) both had a "screw loose" and their "shit together." In isolation, these key elements of the Scott-Allen rivalry are intriguing. But a funny thing happened after I completed *Iron War* and moved on to other projects: I kept seeing the same two traits in other great athletes.

"I DID MY OWN RESEARCH"

Let's pause here to clarify who I'm talking about when I talk about "great athletes." If elite athletes are those who perform well enough in their sport to make a living at it, great athletes, by my definition, are the most successful elites—those who don't just make it to the pro level but kick ass, win championships, break records, and retire into the hall of fame. Scholars of sports performance call them "superelites." Frankly, though, there's not a lot of scholarship on the top 0.0001 percent, given the logistical difficulty of getting Serena Williams and Lionel Messi to show up at the same laboratory on the same day. I had to do my own research, therefore, in developing the theory of athletic greatness described in these pages, supplemented by studies on the less-rare category of elites, who, though not my subject, are relevant to it.

One thing my investigations taught me is that the traits constituting later talent have a fractal relationship to sports performance. What this means is that, within the total athlete population, the key traits are concentrated at the top, where the elites sit. And within the population of elite athletes, the same traits are again concentrated at the top, where the greats (aka superelites) sit. In other words, what's true of athletes in general is more true of elite athletes, and even more true of great athletes. But although my theory of athletic greatness, thus defined, has some bearing on others, including high performers outside of sports, it seeks only to explain what makes the Lindsey Vonns and Usain Bolts different from *everyone else.*

Science, I must confess, was never my strong suit in school. I just never had the mind for it. Joe Baker has written that "scientific perspectives should always have an element of 'fence-sitting,' not wanting to commit to a conclusion that might not bear the scrutiny of replication or the emergence of new data." He's quite right, of course, and frankly, I've never been the fence-sitting type. Like a lot of writers and most coaches, I'm more interested in impactful persuasion than in neutral truth seeking. What motivates me to go through the immense effort of writing a book is a sensed opportunity to say something that has never been said before and that has the potential to benefit athletes in a practical way. But I recognize that, in order to achieve this effect, I must convince athletes that the things I write are true, which in turn requires that, fence-sitter or not, I ground them in science.

The phrase "I did my own research" has been justly ridiculed as the slogan of tinfoil hat–wearing conspiracy mongers whose idea of doing research is listening to *The Joe Rogan Experience.* Still, it is possible for nonscientists like me to conduct a legitimate form of research. I did it in 2015 for a book called *The Endurance Diet,* which describes the eating habits of elite endurance athletes, a collection of core practices that I cataloged by traveling across the globe and breaking bread with world-class runners, cyclists, triathletes, and cross-country skiers. To supplement this shoe-leather research, I designed a formal dietary questionnaire that was distributed to and completed by athletes representing a total of thirty-two nations and eleven sport disciplines. Although my methodology lacked the rigor required for publication in peer-reviewed scientific journals, one of the world's leading sports nutrition researchers, Asker Jeukendrup, thought enough of it to contribute a foreword to the book, which, judging by sales data and reader feedback, has helped many thousands of athletes gain greater satisfaction and better outcomes from their diet. Not bad for a right-brainer.

Like the shared eating practices I noted in world-class athletes, the commonalities I observed in the mental makeup of all-time sporting greats, beginning with Dave Scott and Mark Allen, motivated me eventually to step outside my proper lane and undertake a para-scientific investigation. This time, however, I purposely cast a wider net, reasoning that, if all great athletes are alike on a deep level, their underlying sameness must cut across boundaries of sport, gender, time, and place, such that, the more diverse I could make my subject pool, the more conspicuous any shared mental traits would be. Dispensing with intercontinental travel and formal surveys, I brought the mountain to Muhammad instead, studying the champion athletes who comprised my subject pool simply by reading their biographies and memoirs, acquiring in the course of two years a small library that represented an array of sports, nationalities, and time periods, from boxing to golf, from Mexico to Ukraine, and from the Gilded Age to today. After all, what better way to get to know a large number of great athletes as human beings? Plus, I love to read!

In all honesty, I did not expect to love these particular books as much as I enjoy my normal pleasure reading, where I seldom stray outside the genre of literary fiction—a legacy of my days as a college English major. To my happy surprise, though, the jock-authored memoirs I consumed shared an unexpected virtue with the fancy novels I favor, which was their magnetic central characters. As I've said already, we tend to think of great athletes as being exceptional below the neck, whereas high achievers in other fields (science, culture, politics, industry) are regarded as having exceptional minds. But it's impossible to absorb the life stories of more than twenty great athletes, as I did, and come away seeing them as ordinary minds contained in extraordinary bodies, their achievements attributable to physical aptitude alone. You could swap out the athletic feats of these men and women for any other sort of accomplishment and the plot would still fit the character, so to speak. Universally, they come across as strong, complex, intelligent, and charismatic, just like the greats in other enterprises. "Character is fate," Heraclitus tells us, and in reading these narratives, I got a strong sense of fatedness, an inevitability of success that was determined less by physical endowment than by character.

I'm not suggesting that these heroes of sport are carbon copies of one another. To the contrary, each athlete I studied was unique in most respects, yet their differences accentuated the core sameness I sought to illuminate. Confirming my hypothesis, all of these people exhibited the same two-sided mental makeup I first identified in Dave Scott and Mark Allen, a productive melding of diametric qualities condensable to the four-word formula "screw loose, shit together."

Identifying the precise nature of the two-sided mental makeup that I kept seeing in great athletes became the second part of my research, a process that involved deep dives into various fields of psychology, from personality to addiction. With regard to the first part of this makeup, I came to understand that great athletes have a screw loose in the specific sense that they share an addiction-like compulsion to win at almost any cost, a genuine *need* to win that is a sublimation of some basic psychological need that has not been met by ordinary life. They're not "crazy" in the sense of lacking basic rationality, but they do things that the rest of us just wouldn't do—things that make us say, "Wow, that's crazy!"

As for the second part, I discovered that the popular notion of having your shit together corresponds to the psychological concept of self-regulation. Skilled self-regulators habitually make smart decisions in pursuit of their goals, as all great athletes do. They have a knack for figuring out how to get what they want and then getting it—against all resistance. In this way, great athletes, like other masters of self-regulation, are almost the opposite of "crazy"—sensible, methodical, meticulous, and careful.

Rarely are these two mental traits—each the apparent photo negative of the other—combined in a single individual. But it's easy to see how, when combined, they produce greatness in athletes blessed with a modicum of physical talent. Achieving greatness in sport is like striking the dead center of a tiny target from a vast distance, a task that requires both power and precision. Having a screw loose provides the power—the unbridled drive that propels the athlete's performance all the way to that far-off target. To work harder than everyone else, in other words. Having their shit together, meanwhile, provides the focus—the marksman's aim needed to keep all that energy from going to waste and ensure a reasonably straight path toward a perfect bull's-eye. To work smarter than everyone else.

The biggest surprise I encountered in my research was a slow-dawning realization that the "screw loose" and "shit together" mental traits I'd identified were not, in fact, the opposites they first seemed. When I embarked on the process, I couldn't wrap my head around how such contrary qualities could coexist so harmoniously in a single person. But my immersion in the science of mental health showed me there's a form of "craziness" that is fundamental to the human condition, stemming from unmet needs. Psychologist Abraham Maslow called it "the psychopathology of the average," which has a nice ring to it. Meanwhile, my exploration of the science of self-regulation taught me that, in essence, the ability to self-regulate is the ability to get one's needs met no matter how difficult. As we saw in the examples of Dave Scott and Mark Allen, great athletes are driven by an especially urgent unmet need, yet they are exceptionally good at fulfilling their needs by controlling their own actions, thoughts, and emotions. Seen this way, "screw loose" and "shit together" aren't so much opposites as complements.

We all know it takes a certain amount of early talent to become a truly great athlete. Yet, as a result of my research, I now believe that a "screw loose, shit together" mental makeup is also an absolute requirement for greatness in sport. This is my theory of athletic greatness, and if you're skeptical, that's okay. I've got nine more chapters to bring you around! For now, though, let me just say that my theory explains all kinds of things I've experienced over the years—including my own athletic journey and those of people close to me.

WE COULD HAVE BEEN CONTENDERS

If it's true that a "screw loose, shit together" mental makeup is an absolute requirement—alongside physical talent—for athletic greatness, it follows that some athletes will fall short of greatness for lack of one or the other of these key traits. In other words, if my theory of athletic greatness is correct, it will not only predict the greatness of the likes of Dave Scott and Mark Allen but will also make sense of the almosts— athletes who came close enough to true greatness to taste it but who, like the heroes of Greek tragedy, were held back in the end by a single missing ingredient.

One such athlete is my friend Cait Chock. Earlier in the chapter I mentioned that no woman who holds an American record in a distance-running event previously held a junior record in a similar event, which of course means that the girls who *were* setting records as juniors failed to do the same as adults. Cait puts a face on this unhappy statistic, plummeting like a modern-day Icarus from "next big thing" to "whatever happened to?" in the span of a few years.

Early talent wasn't her problem—that much is certain. From her very first stride, Cait was poetry in motion, just like her mother, Linda Chock, who qualified for the 1984 US Olympic Trials Marathon at age twenty-one. Unfortunately, Cait also inherited severe obsessive-compulsive tendencies from her biological father, who disappeared from her life *on her eighth birthday* but left behind a congenital legacy that proved combustive when sparked by Cait's exposure, in her early teens, to the sport she was born for.

Not right away, though. Cait's early talent rewarded her with a league championship title in cross country in her freshman year at Granite Bay High School in Roseville, California. The following season Cait ascended from league champion to state champion, but the match had been lit, and detonation was inevitable.

"Caitlin was the type who would fall over on the track from exhaustion if you let her train the way she wanted to," said her high school coach, Steve Barth, in a 2003 interview.

Strict measures were required to keep Cait from running herself into the ground. Among these was a form of athletic chaperoning provided by a concerned Linda Chock, who often ran with her fleet-footed daughter as a way to hold her back. But what got Cait in the end was not overtraining per se but anorexia, an all-too-common fate in young female athletes with OCD. Some cases are mild; Cait's was not, resulting a six-week involuntary psychiatric hospitalization at seventeen.

Remarkably, Cait recovered quickly enough to successfully defend her state cross-country title, and by the time she graduated from Granite Bay, she had broken the national high school record for 5000 meters and qualified for the World Junior Championships. On the strength of these performances, Cait was offered a contract to run professionally for Nike—straight out of high school!—and she lived happily ever after.

Well, not quite. A few short months into Cait's career as a sponsored athlete, her "life force" (her words) suddenly drained out of her body during a workout. That sounds rather vague, but no better diagnosis was ever found for her sudden and irreversible loss of mojo. All Nike's horses and all Nike's men couldn't put poor Cait back together again, so she quit competitive running and moved to Los Angeles to try her hand at standup comedy, as any twenty-year-old retired professional athlete with a lick of sense would do. To this day, it is still not entirely clear what's wrong with Cait's body, but my hunch is that she did some permanent damage during her teens that her brief comeback merely camouflaged.

The moral of the story is that Cait possessed only two of the three requirements for sustained athletic greatness. Early talent? Check. Screw loose? Double check. Before that awful day when the life force suddenly drained out of her, Cait shat herself in the middle of a high-altitude training session with her teammates. A "normal" person, safe to say, would have immediately quit the workout and scurried away to clean herself up. (Come to think of it, a "normal" person wouldn't have pushed so hard in a workout that she lost control of her bowels.) Cait, however, went ahead and completed the run in soiled drawers, mortified but resolute. What drove her to such extreme behaviors, I believe, was the pressing need she felt to give meaning to her compulsive nature. For those who experience it, OCD is more than just a condition—it is also *who they are*, and as such it needs to be expressed and not merely medicated.

There are many athletes with severe obsessive-compulsive tendencies who, unlike Cait Chock, have achieved lasting greatness. But these athletes—in addition to having a screw loose—also had their shit together, and Cait, I regret to say, did not. I'll get much deeper into the science of self-regulation in due time. For now, we can think of it as the capacity to avoid repeating mistakes. A loose screw can either power athletic achievement or cause an athlete to self-destruct. It all depends on whether the athlete's "craziness" is counterbalanced in such a way that "crazy" blunders don't often recur. Athletes who have a screw loose *and* their shit together are able to correct course in response to unwitting self-sabotage, but for Cait this was a struggle.

Mind you, I'm not talking behind Cait's back here. She knows better than anyone that she doesn't have her shit together, as evidenced by the title she picked for her erstwhile comedy podcast: *I'm a Disaster.* Nor do I fault Cait for not having her shit together. As we will see, the degree to which people get their shit together in life depends on factors that are largely beyond their control. It is possible, for example, that if Cait had been the youngest child in her family instead of the eldest, the familial dynamics of her upbringing would have differed in a way that saved her from implosion. But that's just speculation; we'll never know for sure what might have been.

Anyhow, that's what it looks like when an athlete has a screw loose but doesn't have their shit together. As for what it looks like when an athlete has their shit together but lacks a loose screw, I offer myself as an example.

Like Cait, I discovered a love of running at an early age, inspired by watching my dad run the 1983 Boston Marathon a few weeks shy of my twelfth birthday. Although I lacked Cait's superior early talent, I kept at it and enjoyed some success, earning all-state status in high school track and cross country.

Evidence that I had my shit together as a young runner can be found in the way I went about my college search. Recognizing the opportunity before me—four years of running, learning, and growing in the environment of my choice—I started the process at fifteen, long before most of my classmates were giving any thought to the matter, and by the time I made my final choice in the fall of my senior year, I had put more reflection and research into the decision than the procrastinators could possibly match. A major factor in my decision was college running's reputation as a meat grinder that systematically destroys promising athletes through over-racing and constant pressure to produce immediate results, a fate I hoped to avoid by settling on Haverford College, a Division III school with a well-regarded distance-running program headed by Coach Tom Donnelly, who had a strong record of developing second-tier talents like me into All-Americans through patient nurturing.

It was a wise move on my part. The only problem was that I quit running before I ever set foot on Haverford's charming arboreal campus (complete with duck pond). And the reason I quit—to oversimplify a bit—was that I didn't have a screw loose, or at least not the kind of loose screw that facilitates athletic achievement. In plain English, I hated the pain of racing, and I held back from hurting myself to the degree a runner must to discover their limit. Whereas Cait Chock regarded pain as a price worth paying for the reward of expressing her compulsive nature in a purposeful way, I lacked an equivalent motivator. Like her, I loved running. Unlike her, however, I got nothing from running that I needed so urgently I was willing to crap my pants midstride to become the very best runner I could be. In the words of Joe Baker, "the high-performance lifestyle, with all its costs and sacrifices, is not for everyone." Granted, my middling early talent would have kept me from becoming a truly great runner even if I'd had a loose screw. But I would at least have reached my full potential instead of flaming out at eighteen.

WHY I WROTE THIS BOOK

Thankfully, my athletic journey did not end with the apologetic letter I wrote to Tom Donnelly in May 1989, informing him that I would not be running for him after all. If it had, you wouldn't be reading this, and I'd probably be teaching creative writing somewhere (perhaps at Haverford, if I was lucky).

In my late twenties I returned to running, seduced by the endorphin-laced milieu in which I found myself after moving to California for no particular reason and taking a job at a newly launched endurance sports magazine (despite being sedentary at the time). Over the next quarter century—until post-acute COVID-19 syndrome forced me into permanent athletic retirement at age forty-nine—I metamorphized from a pain-averse underachiever to a bloodthirsty competitor who *craved* the pain of racing, not because I'd become some bug-eyed masochist but because *I'd gotten good at pain*, and I took pride in this aptitude, which enabled me to cross each and every finish line with the soul-deep satisfaction of knowing I had given everything I had.

And how did I get good at pain? In the only way possible: by discovering the loose screw I'd lacked as a younger athlete. In a later chapter I will explain more fully what it means to find your "crazy" in the sporting context, and how I did so. I mention myself here merely to make the point that it is possible for athletes who start life without one or the other of the mental traits required to reach their full potential to acquire it along the way.

I've written this book for two reasons. The first is that I find my theory of athletic greatness interesting, and I'm hopeful you will too. The second reason is that I believe the theory has practical value for all athletes, and for the coaches and parents who aid in their development, as well as for seekers of greatness in domains outside of sports. By no means does the "screw loose, shit together" hypothesis represent a blueprint for manufacturing great athletes, yet I am optimistic that it will help some athletes avoid the tragedy of failing to realize their full potential, as I did—until I didn't.

In the next chapter I will draw upon scientific, philosophical, and spiritual evidence to argue that, in a sense, we're all a little "crazy," yet only a few are "crazy" in the particular way that drives athletic achievement, exemplified by Jack Johnson (the boxing legend, not the singer-songwriter). Having elucidated the "screw loose" half of the mental formula for athletic greatness, I will do the same for the "shit together" half in Chapter 3, where we will explore the science of self-regulation as embodied in open-water swimmer Lynne Cox. We will then shift back to "screw loose" in Chapter 4, deploying new concepts in the neuro-psychology of habit formation and addiction to explain the nonrational risks and sacrifices that great athletes make in pursuit of victory, instantiating these concepts in the story of champion runner Frank Shorter.

In Chapter 5, we'll take a fresh look at the process of getting one's shit together through the science of emotional development, using tennis great Andre Agassi's maturation to demonstrate how personal growth drives athletic development. Chapter 6 attempts a kind of dialectical synthesis between the two key mental traits of great athletes through the science of personality and the example of Ukrainian pole vaulter Sergey Bubka.

From here the book takes a practical turn. Chapter 7 offers Canadian two-sport Olympian Clara Hughes as living proof that it is possible to get one's shit together later in life, and it also specifies the key elements in this process and how they benefit athletic performance. Similarly, Chapter 8 leverages the story of Welsh rugby player Gareth Thomas to open a discussion on ways to channel one's inner "crazy" into athletic achievement. The penultimate chapter explores the relevance of a "screw loose, shit together" mental makeup outside the sporting arena, using Drew Bledsoe's transition from NFL quarterback to winemaker to illustrate how even the less athletically inclined among us can use—and develop—these mental traits to reach our full potential in any area of life, be it entrepreneurship, teaching, or even parenting. Finally, we will glean lessons from my theory of athletic greatness for parents and coaches, grounding these learnings in the stories of Mexican golfer Lorena Ochoa and Russian-American wheelchair racer Tatyana McFadden.

I am keenly aware that some of the ideas put forward in this book are novel and challenging. You might not fully accept all of them. But I'm confident, at least, that my respect for the athletes profiled in these pages, and my overall appreciation for what it really takes to achieve greatness in sport, will not be obscured by my unvarnished approach to studying these rare individuals. If I succeed in nothing else, I want you to see what I see in the minds of the world's most brilliant athletic performers. The high-wire balancing act that occurs there is far more precarious, hence far more human, than the stolid pillar of action-hero confidence that is commonly imagined. It ain't always pretty, but to me it is beautiful.

CHAPTER TWO

We're All a Little "Crazy"

Brave, crazy, it's a fine line.
—HAL JORDAN (AKA GREEN LANTERN)

Some years ago, the online magazine *Cracked* ranked "The Most Badass (and Possibly Insane) Athletes of All Time." Number five on their list was John Arthur "Jack" Johnson, history's first Black heavyweight boxing champion and a terrific example of the athletic advantages of having a screw loose.

Jack was born in Galveston, Texas, in 1878, the third child of two former slaves. It was an inauspicious time and place to enter the world as a Black American, the Jim Crow era's brutal suppressions having recently shattered the brittle optimism of Reconstruction below the Mason-Dixon line. Most of white America, North and South, was united in an overt effort to quash African American progress in every domain of public life, including sports. In 1895, the year Johnson fought his first professional bout, *New York Sun* editor Charles A. Dana warned readers, "We are in the midst of a growing menace. The black man is rapidly forging to the front ranks in athletics, especially in the field of fisticuffs. We are in the midst of a black rise against white supremacy." Dana urged white athletes, teams, and sports leagues to uphold the policy of total refusal to compete against Black opponents that had been instituted by recently retired heavyweight boxing champion John L. Sullivan.

Jack Johnson didn't give a rat's ass about any of it. Not segregation. Not anti-miscegenation laws. Not "Yes sir, no ma'am." None of it. In one of his several autobiographies, he wrote, "I have found no better way of avoiding race prejudice than to act with people of other races as if prejudice did not exist." It was one thing for a Black man in Jim Crow America to express such bold sentiments on paper, quite another to live them, but Jack lived them, unwaveringly, at all costs, from the day he was born until the day he died. At a time when a Black man could be lynched for merely looking at a white woman, or for raising his hand against a white man in self-defense, or for dressing expensively, Jack did all of these things and more, to hell with the consequences.

In 1901, Jack's search for pugilistic opportunities took him to Stockton, California, where he impressed a white fight promoter, who agreed to take him on—until Jack ordered the man to fetch his luggage from the train depot, at which point he was shown the door. Unfazed, Jack found a more accommodating manager in Bakersfield, where he rented digs in the segregated city's white sector, laughing off the threats incited by his deliberate provocation.

Two years later, in Philadelphia, Jack fought an older Black heavy-weight named Joe Butler. In the dressing room before the bout, a white boxer, Harry Burke, told Jack to hand over his towel. Jack calmly refused, explaining to Burke that he saw no reason to do for a white man what a white man wouldn't do for him. At the end of the night, Burke snuck up behind Jack and smashed a bottle over his head.

No lesson was taught. Jack soon began to court white women pub-licly, not only in America but also in Australia—an equally bigoted coun-try that forbade immigration by nonwhite people—where Jack bedded a high-profile debutante who later sued the sports paper *The Referee* for reporting (truthfully) on the forbidden liaison. When Jack returned to the continent the following year to fight Tommy Burns for the heavy-weight title (having chased the Canadian literally around the world in an effort to secure the bout, succeeding only when a deep-pocketed promoter offered Burns the unheard-of sum of $30,000 to cross the so-called color line and take the fight), all of white Australia wanted to see the Black man take a whupping.

On December 26, 1908 (Boxing Day!), fifty thousand white men showed up at twenty-thousand-seat Sydney Stadium to see the chal-lenger get what was coming to him. Instead the hateful mob got what was coming to them. Jack landed the first punch, dropping Burns to his knees. He had no intention, however, of winning quickly. His plan was to prove beyond any possible gainsaying that he was the better fighter, to which end Jack dragged out the contest for fourteen long and one-sided rounds, taunting Burns relentlessly as he pummeled him into a state of purple disfigurement, more than once propping up his buckling opponent in order to prolong the beatdown.

White boxing fans all over the world lost their minds when they learned that a Black man now held the most coveted individual title in all of sports. Desperate to restore the natural order, as they perceived it, they turned their eyes to the mighty Jim Jeffries, who had retired from heavyweight boxing undefeated in 1905. Once again, money talked. Having held the color line throughout his career, Jeffries agreed to face Jack in Reno, Nevada, on July 4, 1910, in a showdown that was rightly billed as the Fight of the Century. Speaking at a Chicago church in the lead-up to the event, Jack expressed his outlook in brazen language that, even more than his greatness as a fighter, made him a hero to his oppressed people, telling the all-Black congregation, "I'll be surrounded by thirty thousand or forty thousand people on July 4, and some will holler 'good' and some will holler 'bad,' but most will holler 'bad,' and the more they holler 'bad,' the braver I'll be. That's Jack Johnson's motto."

On the eve of the contest, Jack stayed up well past midnight carousing with friends and hangers-on at the mansion he'd secured for use as his pre-fight headquarters, behaving as though he hadn't a care in the world. Hours later, he battered Jim Jeffries in the same lesson-teaching way he'd tamed Tommy Burns the year before, cheerfully stretching out the brutality to leave no question in anyone's mind who'd beaten whom. Jeffries had refused to fight Jack prior to his retirement, not because Jack wasn't qualified but because he was brown-skinned, and Jack hadn't forgotten. "How you like 'em, Jim?" he asked a hideously bloodied Jeffries between body blows in round fifteen. "Do they hurt?"

Moments later, Jeffries's cornermen stepped in to halt the travesty. Then all hell broke loose. Angry spectators flooded the ring, bent on dismembering the deserving winner, whose own cornermen hurried to form a protective shield around him, acting just in time to spare history's first Black heavyweight boxing champion from becoming history's shortest-reigning heavyweight boxing champion. White America's vengeance would have to wait—but not forever, given where the true power lay.

Payback began with a movement to block the film of the Johnson-Jeffries bout from being shown in theaters. Under the guise of moral outrage at boxing's glorification of violence, white evangelical racists largely succeeded in their true aim of preventing the world from seeing a Black man kick a white man's ass. A parallel crusade in England stopped Jack from defending his title there, but not before he embarrassed the solicitor general of the British government at a hearing held to determine the fate of a proposed match against the latest Great White Hope, Billy Wells, outwitting the more educated litigant—who was literally laughed out of court—in the same cheerful way he took apart his gloved opponents.

That was the thing about Jack Johnson: His mouthy swagger and flashy high living made him an object of white disdain, but his undeniable brilliance made it impossible to disdain him in good faith, confounding his enemies both inside and outside the boxing ring. All efforts to stereotype him as an empty-headed brute fell flat. Between the ropes, Jack won by outsmarting the other guy, becoming unhittable in round two by figuring him out in round one. Outside the ropes, he played the cello, knew more about Napoleon than most Napoleonic scholars, read and recited canonical poetry, cooked about as well as the professional chefs who worked for him, had a knack for mechanical tinkering that earned him two US patents for automobile-related inventions, held his own in conversation on topics ranging from astronomy to the plays of Alexandre Dumas, and had a rapier wit that could draw a laugh out of anyone except the hopelessly humorless. Asked by one reporter to share the secret to his success, Jack answered with mock solemnity, "Eat jellied eels, and think distant thoughts."

A white prizefighter possessing such qualities would have been hailed as a Renaissance man, but in Jack the same qualities were seen as a threat, heaping gas on the fire of white America's rush to eliminate him. In October 1911, Chicago authorities shut down Café de Champion, the popular "black and tan" (mixed-race nightclub) Jack had opened with his winnings from the Jim Jeffries fight. Less than a month later, a grand jury charged him with seven counts of violating the Mann Act, a federal law that had been passed for the express purpose of combatting so-called white slavery. Jack promptly fled the country, though he returned eventually to serve his one-year prison sentence. He died at age sixty-eight in a single-car accident after speeding away from a segregated North Carolina diner that refused to serve him.

FINE LINE OR NO LINE?

They say there's a fine line between brave and "crazy," and Jack Johnson is the kind of person they have in mind when they say it. Throughout his life, Jack took huge risks in pursuit of his desires. Some of these risks—such as his refusal to hand over his towel to a would-be bully—smack of bravery. You have to respect a man willing to have a bottle smashed over his head to preserve his dignity. Other risks—like his penchant for reckless driving, which got him killed in the end—seem just plain "crazy." The thing is, all of these risks—the brave, the "crazy," and the in-between—were taken by the same person, and what's more, they came from the same place within that person, as he himself recognized.

"One man falls out of bed and is killed," he told a reporter. "Another falls from a fifty-foot scaffold and lives. One man gets shot in the leg and is killed. Another gets a bullet in his brain and lives . . . I always take a chance on my pleasures."

Jack Johnson wanted what he wanted, he never questioned it, and he was willing to chance everything at all times to get it. Was he brave or "crazy"? To me this is a bit like asking if Vincent van Gogh was creative or tormented. Anyone familiar with the painter's biography can attest that he was both, and that his creativity was in fact inseparable from his inner torment, something he knew better than anyone. "I put my heart and soul into my work, and I have lost my mind in the process," he wrote. Similarly, Jack Johnson was not exclusively brave or completely "crazy" but "crazily" brave, or bravely "crazy."

I'll go one step further. There's a sense in which all humans are a little "crazy"—or, to put it somewhat differently, a sense in which "craziness" is woven into the human condition. As radical as this notion might seem to some, versions of it have existed since at least the fourth century BCE, when Siddhartha Gautama, aka Buddha, introduced his philosophy of the Middle Way. Comprising Four Noble Truths, it begins with a real zinger, commonly translated into English as "Life is suffering" but actually more nuanced in meaning. The Sanskrit word Buddha used was *dukkha*, which, in addition to "suffering," can mean "anxiety," "stress," and "dissatisfaction." Gautama identified three distinct categories of *dukkha*. The most basic is the kind we share with other animals—the pain and struggle of life, and the inescapable realities of conflict, hunger, sickness, aging, and death. The second category of *dukkha* relates to the inexhaustible nature of desire—our inability to stay satisfied for very long, a bottomless psychic hunger that exists for reasons both ontological (you can't eat your cake and still have it) and constitutional (by nature we always want more cake, or if not more cake then something else after cake). Finally, the third category of *dukkha*, unique to humans, is a gnawing existential disappointment, a despairing sense of meaninglessness rooted in our peculiar awareness that we are born to die. (German speakers have their own word for this phenomenon: *Sehnsucht*, which translates as "inexpressible longing.") Gautama perceived a void in the souls of all intelligent beings, an emptiness we spend our whole lives trying to fill in mostly inept ways, and though he himself did not describe this characteristically human way of being as "crazy," I think it's fair to do so. If there's a better definition of "crazy" than having needs that cannot be satisfied, I'd like to see it!

Granted, Buddha was just one dude. And like any dude, he might have been a fool, his head full of silly ideas lacking any correspondence to the reality they purported to describe. But if this were so, modern science would have debunked Gautama's ideas, and it hasn't. Quite the opposite, in fact. Since the mid-twentieth century, the concept of *needs*, which carries echoes of *dukkha*, has been central to psychologists' understanding of mental health. In 1943, Abraham Maslow introduced a theory of motivation whose centerpiece was his now-famous hierarchy of human needs. Maslow argued that humans have distinct categories of needs that exist in a clear order of relative priority. Of these, physiological needs rank first, followed by safety needs, love needs, esteem needs, and self-actualization needs. "What this means specifically," Maslow wrote, "is that, in the human being who is missing everything in life in an extreme fashion, it is most likely that the major motivation would be the physiological needs rather than any others. A person who is lacking food, safety, love, and esteem would most probably hunger for food more strongly than for anything else."

No sooner is this first need satisfied, however, than safety becomes a person's main focus. And no sooner has the need for "a safe, orderly, predictable, organized world which [one] can count on and in which unexpected, unmanageable, or other dangerous things do not happen" been satisfied than the need for love comes to the fore, and so on. Critics of Maslow have taken issue with his choice of categories, their ordering, and other aspects of his theory. In Chapter 6, I will introduce a newer and more empirically grounded set of basic psychological needs that goes further in explaining athletic greatness. What remains valid, though, is a certain implied postulate of Maslow's theory, which is that *humans always need something.*

Buddhism isn't the only religion that's wise to this element of human psychology. Take Judaism. Why did Eve defy God's admonition and taste the forbidden fruit? Because Eden wasn't enough! But don't blame Eve. Adam was no different, nor was anyone who came after him. If you're going to blame anyone, blame God himself, or Mother Nature, or whoever it was that designed us to exist in a state of perpetual need that survives the satisfaction of any particular need. It can almost be said that humans have *a need to need,* and are therefore doomed to experience what Buddha called *sankhara-dukkha,* a kind of buyer's remorse, where the thing we bought was life.

"Hold on a second," you say. "Isn't it true that most people rate themselves as happy in surveys?" Yes, and most people also rate themselves as excellent drivers in surveys. Jokes aside, it's possible to be desperate and happy at the same time. In fact, that's just it: For us humans, happiness is hard-won and tenuous, challenged from all sides by substandard parenting, ruthless school social dynamics, the soul-sucking trap of social media participation, body loathing, the rat race, consumerism, romantic disappointment, money worries, loss and grief, biological decline, war, pandemics, politics, climate change—I could go on and on. Sustaining some measure of happiness in the face of this onslaught requires nothing short of desperate measures.

Psychologists have a special term for the desperate measures we take to get by in life, one I've alluded to already: "coping." The American Psychological Association defines "coping" as "the use of cognitive and behavioral strategies to manage the demands of a situation when these are appraised as taxing or exceeding one's resources or to reduce the negative emotions and conflict caused by stress." To the extent that life in general is taxing and stressful and finite, coping is all we do in our earthly existence. Psychologist Jeff Greenberg, inspired by this insight, developed *terror management theory* in the 1980s, proposing that most of the ways people create and find meaning in life are rooted in existential fears. What we call "personality," others argue, is really just the sum of the coping strategies each person learns in order to get by (an idea I'll expand upon in Chapter 6). Or, as Stuart Ross, MD, puts it in his book *We're All a Little Bit Crazy*, "personality . . . can be viewed as a collection of reactions during emotional development, each deriving its characteristic features as an adaptation within the developmental environment."

Life is like a bottomless pool of water that each of us gets tossed into at birth, not knowing how to swim. To attain happiness, we must find a way to stay afloat. What works for one person doesn't necessarily work for another. There are different ways to keep one's head above water: eggbeater kicks, sculling with the arms, doggy paddling, dead man's float. These various anti-drowning measures represent the disparate personalities we cobble together to fend against *dukkha*. Given the stakes—"to be or not to be"—there's always something frenzied, unbalanced, or extreme in the particular coping formula that a person comes up with, which is a way of saying we're all a little "crazy."

Consider the people you know best and how distinctive their individual ways of being are. Now picture a drowning person reaching for a life preserver. They're one and the same! What we regard as "Ralph being Ralph" or "Veronica being Veronica" is each person's unique way of coping with a fraught and fleeting existence, a method of getting by that is "crazed" in much the same way that the behavior of a creature fighting for its life is "crazed." For one person the winning formula for well-being might be extreme religiousness, for another rampant hedonism, and for still another unchecked workaholism, or a bottomless desire to nurture, or an all-consuming need to be liked, but it's always *something*.

In Jack Johnson's case, that something was personal autonomy. From cradle to grave, Jack was driven by a burning need to assert his independence, act freely, and have his way. In the last interview he gave before his death, Jack told his profiler, "Just remember that, whatever you write, I was a man." But wait: Isn't every man a man? Not as Jack Johnson saw it.

Boxing is essentially one man's effort to dominate another man, and as such it was the perfect sport for Jack Johnson—the perfect way to express his need to become and remain a freestanding soul. This explains why, at the age of sixteen, Jack stowed away on a cotton steamer bound for New York City, and from there made his way to Boston, intent on meeting Joe Walcott, a West Indian welterweight Jack idolized—the first of many "crazy" things he did in his quest to become the world heavyweight boxing champion, things almost no one else would have done, even with Jack's gifts.

Henry Olusegun Olumide Adeola Samuel (better known as the musical artist Seal) had it right: *"We're never gonna survive unless we get a little crazy."* Getting a little "crazy," in other words, *is how we survive.* Great athletes are neither more nor less "crazy" than the rest of us. What's unique about Jack Johnson and his ilk is that their particular brand of "crazy" serves them well in competition, and it does so in part because, beyond having a screw loose, these people also have their shit together and are able to keep their "craziness" between guardrails. More on that later. For now, though, let's continue to talk about humans in general.

According to Stuart Ross, who spent his entire career in a mental hospital (as a doctor, I should say, not as a patient), one out of every fifty adults has "optimal psychological health." That's 2 percent! In the aforementioned book, Ross explains that the dominant force in shaping the strategies people use to stay afloat in the bottomless pool of life is parental behavior during childhood, early childhood especially. At the facility where he worked, the vast majority of patients, whose diagnoses ranged from anorexia to schizophrenia, were victims of severe abuse or neglect of one kind or another during childhood, and almost always the chief perpetrators were their own mothers and fathers. But other, more common parental failings also left a mark, according to Ross: "Overprotecting, smothering, excusing, blaming, putdown messages, misdirected anger, unfairness, broken promises, lies, favoritism," he writes—"when you consider all of the forms of painful, hurtful and harmful types of negative experiences that occur during these significantly influential years of our lives, it's no wonder that we are all just a little bit crazy."

To be clear, Ross isn't saying all parents are terrible and that's why everyone's insane. He's saying all parents are imperfect, and that's the main reason all children grow into adults who cling desperately to their individual coping styles, evincing what Buddhist teacher Chögyam Trungpa poetically labeled "medium madness." My own form of medium madness is a sort of achievement complex rooted in brotherly competition for my father's inconstant approval—a relentless compulsion to seek recognition of my abilities (such as they are). This penchant I have for ruthlessly subordinating all competing priorities to the quest for distinction has rewarded me with a fulfilling career—that I can't deny—but it has done so at no small cost, to my relationships especially. When I was a teenager, my brother Josh gave me a half-admiring, half-mocking, wholly fitting nickname: Project Matt. Decades later, I'm still Project Matt, as my long-suffering wife will attest.

This book isn't about me, but I've made it about me briefly to drive home the point that when I say we're all a little "crazy," I mean we're *all* a little "crazy." Indeed, while society might consider bipolar Nataki the "crazy" one and me the well-adjusted high achiever, my own opinion is that we're both about equally nuts. The only difference is that my kind of "crazy" is fairly lucrative. Stuart Ross backs me up here, writing that "there are very common and socially welcomed psychological 'disorders,' such as people-pleasers (typically females) and workaholics (typically male)."

Which brings us back to great athletes. As I stated above, the difference between great athletes and others is not that the former are "crazier" but that they are "crazy" in a way that aids athletic performance. In their struggle to keep their heads above water in the bottomless pool of life, they grab hold of a life preserver that, to the rest of the world, looks like natural talent for a particular sport. And having done so, they cling to it as desperately as drug addicts seek their substance of choice.

POSITIVE ADDICTION

Alcoholism and drug dependency are widely regarded by today's scientists, doctors, and rehabilitation specialists as a brain disease. But not all experts buy into the addiction model. In *The Biology of Desire: Why Addiction Is Not a Disease*, neuroscientist and former addict Marc Lewis argues persuasively that addiction is a learned habit like any other, albeit more extreme and damaging. The disease theory of addiction, Lewis explains, is based almost entirely on research showing lasting changes in the brains of addicts. Yet there is nothing even remotely special about this rewiring, which is a universal signature of desire-based habit formation. "The kind of brain changes seen in addiction also show up in people *who become absorbed in a sport*, join a political movement, or become obsessed with their sweetheart or their kids," he writes (emphasis added).

What *is* different about alcohol and psychoactive drugs is that their effects are experienced as intensely pleasurable by some, and as we know, pleasure breeds desire, which breeds repetition, which breeds habit. Not everyone is equally susceptible to forming a habit around alcohol or drug use, however. Individuals who experienced major trauma during childhood or who are depressed or under severe stress, or suffer from chronic pain, tend to find the greatest relief in intoxication, and thus they crave it more strongly. There isn't anything broken or abnormal about the brains of these individuals, typically; they just get more out of being drunk or high than others do.

In 1976, psychiatrist William Glasser coined the term "positive addiction" to denote compulsive habits that resemble alcohol and drug addiction in many respects but are, on balance, beneficial rather than harmful to the addict's well-being. The two examples Glasser examines in his book on the phenomenon are meditation and running. The latter, of course, is a sport, and it's hardly unique among sports in its capacity to hook certain people. Great athletes are people who find in sports what others find in intoxicants. Like alcohol and drugs, sports are something that most people are exposed to at some point in their lives, yet only a fraction of those who try them end up pursuing them compulsively in the way great athletes do.

What is it that causes a certain fraction of athletes to react to sports exposure by saying, in effect, "Wow! Gimme more!"? Two things. The first is early talent. With all skills, not just sports, there is a strong correlation between ability and enjoyment. The better we are at something, the more we like doing it. But being great at Wordle is one thing, while being great at baseball is quite another. Because our society places high social value on success in sports, being gifted athletically enables a person to meet a variety of needs, ranging from the physiological (sports achievement as an escape route from poverty) to self-actualization (sports achievement as fulfillment of personal purpose).

Even among the most talented, though, only a small minority are willing to do the work, make the sacrifices, and take the risks that are required to achieve greatness. What's different about these athletes is that they benefit more from their sport psychologically than others do. For one reason or another—and the reason is different for each—they have an inordinate need for something their sport gives them, so they cling to the pursuit of athletic greatness in the way a drowning person clings to a life preserver, and as others do alcohol or drugs.

I won't say Jack Johnson was addicted to boxing, but I will say that he kept boxing until age sixty-seven, and he might have gone longer if he hadn't died at sixty-eight. Granted, he needed the money, having lost everything after losing his heavyweight title. But there was a need beyond money in his unyielding embrace of the sport that defined him, one deeply connected to his driving need to assert personal autonomy. In the late 1930s, a fifty-something Jack Johnson walked unannounced into a nondescript Black boxing gym in Los Angeles, dressed as nattily as ever despite his comedown. All sound and movement ceased, for although Joe Louis now held the heavyweight title, Johnson remained a godlike figure among African Americans. Like a stickup artist executing a well-rehearsed plan, he buttonholed the gym owner and made a demand: "Give me the fastest guy you got." Without so much as removing his topcoat, he stuffed his hands into a pair of boxing gloves and stepped into the ring, where he dodged every punch the fastest guy threw at him until the young man was exhausted, at which point he turned to address the mesmerized onlookers.

"You've just seen something that a lot of people didn't want to see," he said before vanishing as abruptly as he appeared. "I was a brunette in a blond town. But gentlemen, I did not stop stepping."

Again, I won't say Johnson was addicted to boxing, or that any other great athlete is addicted to their sport. But I will say that great athletes have an addiction-like attachment to their sport that is easily explained by current psychology and neuroscience. "The brain is certainly built to make any action, repeated enough times, into a compulsion," Marc Lewis writes. Addicts will do anything—risk anything, sacrifice anything, endure anything—for a fix, and great athletes will do the same to win.

MOSTLY BOTH

The question we have not yet answered is where this compulsion comes from. What's obvious to anyone who studies as many great athletes as I have is that, as I've intimated already, the driving force is different for each. Some are born "crazy," or seem so, exhibiting that special drive from day one. In others, the drive appears to be more of a reaction to life events. It's the old nature/nurture dichotomy, a time-tested if oversimplified explanatory construct that will come up again, more than once, in the chapters ahead.

In Jack Johnson's case, the balance tips in the direction of nature. Those who knew him best certainly saw him that way. His friend Ada Smith, who sang and danced at Café de Champion during its brief and meteoric existence, said of him, "His behavior only made stronger my belief that you're either born with it, or you're not. [His] greatness comes from knowing who he is, being satisfied with nothing but the best, but still behaving like a warm, gracious human being."

To be sure, early life experience played a big role in shaping Jack's life trajectory. Galveston's Twelfth Ward, where he grew up, was among the least segregated parts of the South in the late nineteenth century. As a young scrapper, Jack had about as many white friends as Black friends and thought nothing of it. "No one ever taught me that white men were superior to me," he later wrote. Discovering in adolescence that most white men (and women) did in fact regard themselves as superior gave him quite a shock. All of a sudden, the equal treatment Jack had always taken for granted was ripped away from him—or would have been, had he allowed it. But Jack didn't allow it. *Because it wasn't in his nature.*

In the interest of self-preservation, most of Jack's Black peers submitted to the second-class status thrust upon them by the American Way, just as most whites would have done had the roles been reversed. Jack, however, went out of his way to provoke his would-be superiors. When, for example, American authorities convinced the Mexican government to hand the fugitive Jack Johnson over to them within thirty days, he stayed forty-five days, explaining to a journalist, "Well, word was passed out that I had to leave Mexico by July 5 and I want to show them all that I don't have to leave until I get ready." Clearly, self-preservation was not as high on Jack's priority list as it is on most people's, regardless of where, when, or how they grew up. Nobody taught Jack to "take a chance on [his] pleasures," to repeat a phrase that bears repeating. To the contrary, plenty of people tried to teach him not to. But he did it anyway, for more or less the same reason bees make honey: instinct. And need.

At his graveside in Chicago, moments after Jack Johnson's casket was lowered into the ground beside that of his first (white) wife, Etta, a reporter asked his third and last wife (also white), Irene, what she loved about him.

"I loved him because of his courage," she answered. "He faced the world unafraid. There wasn't anybody or anything he feared."

Had she known him as a boy, Irene Johnson would have said the same thing. "He saw himself as someone special from the very first," writes biographer Geoffrey C. Ward in *Unforgivable Blackness: The Rise and Fall of Jack Johnson*, "someone set apart, not subject to the limitations holding others back." Among the first schoolbooks young Jack read was a history of "great men" of Texas—all of them white, of course. Jack's takeaway? That one name was missing from the tome—his—and he aimed to fix it.

Whether we call him brave, as his third wife did, or "crazy," as Jack's many enemies did, or mostly both, as I do, what's certain is that nobody made him so. He came that way.

THE OTHER JACK JOHNSON

It's easy to understand how Jack Johnson's courage served him as a boxer. Fear is paralyzing, physically and mentally, and a paralyzed boxer is a sitting duck. Jack's fearlessness kept him loose and in control in the ring, always looser and more in control than his frightened opponents. But if that's all he'd had going for him as a boxer—"crazy" bravery—he would not be rated as one of the greatest heavyweights of all time. For all the risks Jack took outside the ropes, he took virtually none between them. Most heavyweights before him were maulers— bear-pawed brutes who went for the knockout—but Jack patented a uniquely patient, defensive style, winning less by punishing opponents than by avoiding punishment. Watching his old fight films (the white evangelical racists couldn't keep them hidden forever), you see not the slightest hint of the unbridled wildness that characterized his behavior outside the ring, an inconsistency that Jack appreciated better than anyone, writing in one of his memoirs, "I made a lot of mistakes out of the ring, but I never made any in it."

In short, what made Jack such a great fighter was that not only did he have a screw loose, as evidenced by his fearlessness in competition, but he also had his shit together, as evidenced by his patient, cautious, methodical, and opportunistic style of combat, which he borrowed from no one and passed on to many subsequent champions. But what does it really mean, scientifically, to have one's shit together as an athlete? Having used the example of Jack Johnson to elucidate the scientific meaning of having a screw loose, let's now try to answer this next question.

CHAPTER THREE

White Whales and Whatever Works

The intelligent desire self-control; children want candy.
—RUMI

The story of Lynne Cox—as she tells it—begins at sea, specifically the Bering Sea, halfway between Alaska's Little Diomede Island and the Soviet Union's Big Diomede. Wearing only a swimsuit, goggles, and a neoprene cap, Lynne has been swimming in thirty-eight-degree water for about an hour, and her body has begun to rebel. Her mind, however, continues to click.

"Systematically I check my body," she writes on page one of her memoir, *Swimming to Antarctica*. "My lips feel pickled; my throat is parched and raw from the briny water. I want to stop to drink some fresh water [supplied by her support crew] and catch my breath. But the water is too cold to allow me to pause for even a moment. If I do, more heat will be drained from my body, heat that I will never again regain."

So she presses on, plunging headlong into ever deepening discomfort and anxiety. In an effort to combat these feelings, Lynne gives herself a silent pep talk, remembering why she's doing what she's doing, which is to ease tensions between the USA and the USSR. *Swim faster!* she thinks. *Don't focus on the cold or the pain. Don't give any energy to it. Focus on the finish."*

HAVING YOUR SHIT TOGETHER AS SELF-REGULATION

Lynne Cox is (to the best of my knowledge) not an expert on the science of self-regulation, yet the opening passages of her autobiography read as if she wrote them with the conscious intent of showing us all what virtuosic self-regulation looks like. In a paper published in the 2021 *Annual Review of Psychology*, researchers at the University of Toronto and the University of Illinois described self-regulation as "a broad term that refers to the dynamic process of determining a desired end state (i.e., a goal) and then taking action to move toward it while monitoring progress along the way." Like any other mental process, self-regulation can be done with varying degrees of skillfulness, and in the crisis moments of her solo crossing of the Bering Strait in 1987, Lynne self-regulated like a champ, systematically scanning her body, overriding the impulse to pause her forward progress, reconnecting with her purpose for doing what she was doing, and engaging in positive self-talk. In circumstances that would have caused just about anyone else to lose their shit, Lynne kept her shit together masterfully.

Psychologists who study self-regulation pay a lot of attention to athletes, and with good reason. Sports have a way of boiling life down to its competitive essence. Strict scorekeeping and unrelenting time pressure make the athletic arena an ideal laboratory for studying self-regulation. You couldn't ask for a purer test of self-regulatory ability than a race, match, or other sporting contest. The better an athlete self-regulates, the better they perform, the more they improve, and the likelier it is that they will eventually reach the pinnacle of their sport.

Everything we do in life is goal centered in one way or another, which perhaps explains why we're so sports obsessed as a species. Doing well in school, achieving distinction at work, marrying Mr. or Ms. Right—these are just a few examples of commonly pursued life goals that require self-regulatory ability to achieve. "People high in self-control and low in impulsivity live the good life," state the authors of the review paper I mentioned. "They are healthier, happier, wealthier, and more law abiding than their less controlled, more impulsive peers."

When we observe a person who sets big goals; pursues them with outstanding control of their actions, thoughts, and emotions; and is rewarded with good health, happiness, wealth, and respect, we are inclined to say of that person, "Dang, they've really got their shit together!" To be an exceptional self-regulator, then, is to have one's shit together, and vice versa. At the close of the preceding chapter, I posed a question: What does it really mean, scientifically, to have one's shit together as an athlete? Well, there's your answer!

The science of self-regulation helps us answer another question, which was raised in Chapter 1: Why are the best youth athletes and the best adult athletes generally not the same people? Lynne Cox was not a great youth swimmer, but she became the greatest open-water swimmer the world had ever seen *because she had her shit together,* scientifically speaking. Whatever talent Lynne had for the natatory arts came from her maternal grandfather, Arthur Daviau, who in his prime spent his summers splashing across the lakes of central Maine—up to three miles at a go—and achieved local fame by rescuing a group of college students whose canoe had capsized on the Hudson River. Born in Manchester, New Hampshire, Lynne followed her older brother, David, into competitive pool swimming as a youngster, but it was obvious from the beginning that she was better suited to a different kind of swimming—namely, her grandpa's kind. A natural endomorph, Lynne couldn't match the speed of the top performers on the Manchester Swim Team, but she thrived in cold water and harsh conditions. One summer morning a storm blew through town in the middle of practice. While the rest of the team—coaches included—fled indoors, Lynne swam through the tempest, enjoying herself more than she ever had before. She was eight years old.

In 1969, the Cox family moved to Long Beach, California, affording Lynne the opportunity to train under Don Gambril, an icon of the sport who coached the US Olympic team. Lynne dreamed of becoming an Olympian herself, but after two years with Gambril's elite Phillips 66 club (named after its oil-company sponsor), she remained among its slowest members. What she lacked in zip, however, she more than made up for in stamina. Gambril noticed that, unlike his other swimmers, who tended to fade in long workouts, Lynne kept chugging along at the same barge-like tempo regardless of whether she'd covered five hundred yards or five thousand. One day he pulled Lynne aside and suggested she participate in the Seal Beach Rough Water Swim, an event that played to her strengths, as he perceived them. Three options were available: one mile, two miles, and three miles. Lynne swam all of them, winning two.

Had a surprise fourth race been announced, Lynne would have done that one as well. Instead she heard Coach Ron Blackledge announce that he was currently training a group of teenage members of the Seal Beach Swim Team to swim from Catalina Island to Long Beach—a distance of twenty-one miles—and he welcomed anyone interested in joining to do so. No force in the universe could have stopped Lynne from signing up on the spot, and after a few short weeks of practice in the chilly Pacific, she completed the challenge, narrowly missing the record for the fastest crossing of the Catalina Channel by any swimmer—female, male, child, or adult—a record she would have broken if she hadn't stopped several times to wait for her slower peers to catch up.

The following week, Lynne asked her parents for permission to swim the English Channel. Classic adolescent impulse, right? But no, the roots of this ambition went back several years, to that wild July morning in southern New Hampshire when Lynne thrashed her way through a sudden squall that drove everyone else indoors. Turns out this early demonstration of a loose screw did not go unwitnessed but was seen by the mother of a teammate of Lynne's, who sat in the comfort of her parked car and marveled at the girl-versus-nature battle unfolding before her. Afterward, the woman pulled Lynne aside and prophesied, "You're going to swim the English Channel one day!" That day came sooner than anyone, Lynne included, could have imagined—on July 20, 1972, to be precise—when Lynne crawled ashore at Cape Gris-Nez, France, nine hours and fifty-seven minutes after wading into the British sea at Shakespeare Beach, England, in the shadow of the majestic white cliffs of Dover, establishing a new world record. She was fifteen.

The following summer, another American—who happened to be male, and a full decade older than Lynne—beat her time by thirteen minutes. The next chance she got, Lynne returned to England and snatched the record back.

She seemed unstoppable. But there isn't an athlete on Earth who wins every time, and Lynne's next two swims ended disastrously. In Egypt, she was pulled from the Nile River five miles from the finish of a twenty-mile race she'd led most of the way, sick with dysentery. Months later, she got separated from her guide boat in a blinding fog off the coast of Southern California and was forced to abandon an attempt to claim the world record she deserved for the Catalina Channel swim crossing.

Skillful self-regulators do not fail less often than other athletes—they just learn more from their failures. And Lynne Cox learned from hers. Two weeks after her failed attempt to cross the Catalina Channel, she tried again and succeeded, nipping two minutes off the record. From there she went on to become the first woman to swim across Cook Strait between New Zealand's North and South Islands, as well as the first human to swim across the Strait of Magellan at the southern tip of South America, and around the Cape of Good Hope at the southern tip of Africa, and across the Bering Strait between Alaska and Russia, and yes, to Antarctica (from a boat floating a mile offshore in the frigid Southern Ocean)—all without a wet suit.

Physiological testing done while Lynne was a student at the University of California, Santa Barbara, revealed that her core body temperature *increased* slightly when she swam in water that was equal in temperature to the English Channel, an astonishing feat of physiological self-regulation that researchers had never observed in any other subject. But if this had been the extent of Lynne's self-regulatory abilities, she would not have achieved a fraction of what she did. Having her shit together meant that Lynne was able to control her thoughts and emotions as expertly as she controlled her body, and that's what really made her great, and what makes all great athletes great—provided they're also "crazy."

THE PRINCIPLES OF SELF-REGULATION

In the 2021 book *Social Psychology: Handbook of Basic Principles*, Dutch psychologist Nico Van Yperen of the University of Groningen identifies ten evidence-based principles of self-regulation that sports coaches should adhere to in working with athletes. While not the final word on the topic, these principles help us understand the greatness of athletes like Lynne Cox and may be useful to athletes (and others—for there is no human pursuit that lies outside self-regulation's sphere of relevance) aspiring to their own version of greatness. Let's have a look at them.

Principle One: "Enhance performance and self-regulation through goal-setting."

There has been an unfortunate tendency among scientists who study self-regulation to take goals for granted, assuming that what distinguishes the best self-regulators from others is how they pursue goals, not the goals themselves. In recent years, however, psychologists have gained a better appreciation for the role that goal setting plays in positioning a person for self-regulatory success. Among the more consistent (and counterintuitive) findings in this area of research is that, although skillful self-regulators have a high capacity for controlling their actions, thoughts, and feelings, they exercise *less* self-control than others during goal pursuit. The reason, it appears, is that these individuals frame their goals in a way that forestalls future wavering, when the going gets tough. In particular, they set what *Built to Last* authors Jame Collins and Jerry Porras termed BHAGs—Big, Hairy, Ambitious

Goals—whose all-consuming nature leaves no room for distractions, reducing the amount of active willpower needed to stay on track as they proceed toward the goal's fulfillment.

"Intruding thoughts" is the term psychologists use to denote the distractive doubts and waverings that arise at key points of goal pursuit—those gut-check moments when we ask ourselves, "Is this really worth it?" Such thoughts arise less often and are more easily dealt with when the goal in question has supreme value in the mind of the athlete. My own term for these big hairy ambitions is "white-whale goals," a nod, of course, to *Moby-Dick*, Herman Melville's novel about a giant sperm whale that bites off the leg of Captain Ahab at the knee, provoking the maimed sailor to devote the rest of his life to a single purpose—revenge—which he pursues with monomaniacal dedication.

Great athletes set white-whale goals. They do this first by selecting goals that have high intrinsic value (such as qualifying for the Olympics, an achievement that absolutely everyone regards as a very big deal) and then fixating on these goals as though the fate of the universe depended on their success. Former Liverpool FC manager Bill Shankly once told reporters, "Some people believe football is a matter of life or death. I am very disappointed in that attitude. I can assure you it is much, much more important than that." Shankly was playing for laughs, of course, but a kernel of truth lies hidden in the droll hyperbole.

Lynne Cox, too, set white-whale goals. On her first day with the Phillips 66 swim club, Coach Gambril led the twelve-year-old newbie through a brisk orientation, explaining the strict hierarchy by which practices were organized, with the slowest swimmers in lane one (where Lynne would start), the next slowest group in lane two, and so on. When they reached lane eight, Lynne was introduced to the group's alpha dogs, a strapping pair of European men who would go on to win medals at the 1972 Munich Olympics. Though duly awed, Lynne—who was often told she didn't look like a swimmer—immediately put the fast guys on notice, albeit politely, telling them, "Someday I hope I will be able to swim in your lane."

Like other great athletes, Lynne not only aimed high in her athletic aspirations but also attached life-or-death importance to them. "I wanted to do it more than anything I had ever done before," she writes of one early goal. And when the next goal came along, and the next, she wanted to do *that* more than anything—*anything*—she had ever done before.

You may have noticed that, with respect to white-whale goals, having one's shit together looks a lot like having a screw loose. Such goals are brazen, often risky, and sometimes just plain unrealistic. Lynne never even came close to earning a spot in lane eight with the strapping Europeans. And yet, as we've seen, setting and pursuing outlandish goals with the monomaniacal devotion of a Captain Ahab is also *reasonable* in that it facilitates self-regulation by tamping down intruding thoughts during goal pursuit. Hence, even when they are unrealistic, white-whale goals lead to better performance than lesser goals, which is the whole point. Whatever intrinsic value these goals have is far exceeded by their use value as vehicles to stretch athletes beyond present limits. This is why achieving them offers such fleeting satisfaction, as Lynne discovered after setting her second English Channel record and deciding to move on to other challenges, noting in her memoir: "For me, I think it was that I needed another goal, something to focus my energy."

So, which is it? Do white-whale goals come from the "screw loose" side or the "shit together" side of a great athlete's mind? The answer, I believe, is both. There's no law that says two mental traits can't overlap. A behavior can be sane and "crazy" at the same time, rational in the sense that it demands discipline and achieves a practical end, yet irrational in the sense that only a person with a screw loose would engage in that behavior. An example from outside the realm of sports is Malcolm Little's conduct before the US military draft board in 1943, where the eighteen-year-old zoot-suited hustler later known as Malcolm X escaped serving in World War II by pretending he was a homicidal maniac keen on stealing guns and "killing up a whole bunch of crackers," a performance that did not necessarily fool the psychiatrist responsible for judging the future civil rights icon's fitness to serve but achieved the same effect by convincing the good doctor that the army didn't want him either way. No "normal" person would have acted as Malcolm did to get what he wanted, yet the thing he wanted was quite sensible, and that was to not die fighting on behalf of a country that treated his people like dirt. And he got what he wanted, achieving a sane outcome by "crazy" means. White-whale goals serve great athletes in a similar way, lending a method to their madness.

Principle Two: "Structure the multifaceted nature of achievement goal pursuit into a hierarchical goal system."

The second of Van Yperen's ten principles of self-regulation in sport distinguishes three types of achievement goals. At the top of the hierarchy are outcome goals, where success is measured against external references. Defeating the opponent is the obvious outcome goal in team sports and match competitions. Next come performance goals, which measure success against empirical targets derived from assessments of current capacity. Endurance athletes, for example, often chase the performance goal of achieving a personal best time at a particular race distance. And then come process goals, which define the *how* of success as opposed to the *what*, encoding the key measures an athlete or team must take to achieve their outcome and performance goals. A basketball team might pursue the outcome goal of winning a particular game by playing to its strengths with a process goal of keeping the tempo high through fast-break offense and pressure defense.

Athletes tend to focus too much on outcome goals, which are inherently fraught, their attainment hinging on factors beyond the athlete's control (such as how other athletes perform). At the same time, athletes tend to focus too little on process goals, which are the only type of achievement goal an athlete controls entirely, as even performance goals are contingent on things like weather and menstrual cycles. In other words, most athletes approach goal achievement as a form of wish fulfillment. They want things to go their way without necessarily *making* them go their way. Like the children in Rumi's epigram, they want candy (successful outcomes) and are less interested in self-control (mastery of the process).

Great athletes do just the opposite. It's not that they don't have outcome goals—of course they do—they just don't fixate on them. Major League Baseball manager Joe Maddon said it well: "You're not trying to beat the Yankees or the Red Sox or the Blue Jays. You're trying to beat the game of baseball through execution." Lynne Cox's game wasn't baseball, but she brought the same mindset to swimming. A case in point is the lengthy process she undertook to prepare to swim the Bering Strait. Like most of her goals, this one was based on outcome by its very nature—either Lynne succeeded in reaching her destination or she failed by quitting (or dying). But instead of wishing for success, she spent years making sure she succeeded, taking on a series of preparatory swims in progressively colder bodies of water, so that by the time she got to the Bering Strait, luck had been removed from the equation.

It would be difficult to overstate how rare and special this mindset is. You really have to have your shit together to keep your white-whale goals in perspective, judging your progress mainly by factors you control. After failing in his own bid to break the English Channel swim record, Lynne's brother, David, dismissed the entire undertaking as a waste. "I thought this was sad," Lynne reflects in *Swimming to Antarctica*. "It seemed so much out of perspective to train so hard, to have such a high goal, and then discount it all because you didn't break the record. There was still a great challenge in just completing the swim." Few athletes will deny the wisdom of this sentiment, but fewer still have the wherewithal to heed it.

Principles Three through Five: "Differentiate achievement goals on the basis of evaluative standard and valence. Set approach goals rather than avoidance goals. Develop interventions that focus on self-based and task-based approach goals."

Van Yperen makes a further distinction between approach goals and avoidance goals, either of which may be other-based, self-based, or task-based. The resulting matrix consists of six achievement-goal subtypes: other-based approach goals (beating an opponent), other-based avoidance goals (not losing to an opponent), self-based approach goals (doing better than before), self-based avoidance goals (not doing worse than before), task-based approach goals (executing correctly), and task-based avoidance goals (not screwing up).

On the basis of research both within sports and in other domains, Van Yperen advises coaches to encourage athletes to eschew avoidance goals and other-based goals, both of which are driven by fear and tend to generate lots of intruding thoughts that negatively impact self-efficacy and performance. A prime example of the consequences of pursuing avoidance goals is the 2017 Super Bowl, where the Atlanta Falcons blew a 28–3 lead against the New England Patriots and lost in overtime, a historic collapse that was widely blamed on bad decisions by the Falcons' coaches reflecting an implicit strategy of playing not to lose instead of playing to win.

As for other-based goals and their consequences, the example that comes to mind is the 2008 Olympic Women's Marathon, won unexpectedly by thirty-eight-year-old Constantina Diță-Tomescu of Romania. Her decisive move came halfway through the race, when the favorites were so preoccupied with one another that some didn't even realize they'd been left behind by a competitor they'd discounted. Among them was *the* favorite, reigning world champion Catherine Ndereba of Kenya, who confessed after finishing second, "She just disappeared from us." Now, it's possible Constantina was the strongest woman that day, but it's also possible she won because the strongest woman was too focused on certain others than on running her own best race.

Van Yperen stops short of prescribing a blanket prohibition on avoidance and other-based goals, noting that such goals may be helpful for some athletes in particular situations. It's sound advice, but not advice that Lynne Cox needed to hear, having discovered it by instinct. For the most part, Lynne leaned on approach goals, self-based goals, and task-based goals to get where she wanted to go as an athlete, but when the situation demanded it, she didn't hesitate to improvise an appropriate other-based avoidance goal.

A prime example is her crossing of Cook Strait on the Tasman Sea, where she found herself trapped between a typhoon to the north and an Antarctic storm to the south, swimming through eight-foot waves and vicious crosscurrents, which at times dragged her farther from her destination despite her best efforts to keep moving forward. Even Lynne Cox has her limits, but when she threatened to quit, a quick-thinking friend jumped out of the guide boat and swam beside her for a while, knowing Lynne wouldn't abandon a teammate. And she was right. It was the friend who abandoned Lynne, reaching her own limit within minutes of exposing herself to the hell that Lynne had endured for hours.

Alone again, Lynne went right back to threatening to quit. What kept her from doing so, ultimately, was the fact that the entire nation of New Zealand was tracking her progress and rooting for her, and Lynne knew it, because her crew made sure she knew it. Kiwis all over the North and South Islands sat glued to their radios, listening for live updates. Dozens called in to wish her well, including the prime minister. A ferry boat pilot broke away from his route to pass within sight of her, hoisting an American flag in her honor. An airplane circling above dipped its wing in salute. Lynne Cox completed that swim because she couldn't bear to let all these people down—an other-based avoidance goal that worked.

Principle Six: "Delineate athletes' idiosyncratic developmental trajectories to better understand the process of goal attainment and self-regulation."

Self-regulation operates on multiple timescales. The first is moment to moment—the fluid self-regulation that unfolds within workouts, practices, and competitions. A second timescale encompasses the process of preparing to achieve longer-term goals such as completing an open-water swim. And the broadest span is the one Van Yperen refers to in his sixth principle, which is developmental, straddling the athlete's entire sporting career. At this level, self-regulation consists of learning to self-regulate more effectively over time.

Research has revealed that athletes who self-regulate well from moment to moment also self-regulate more effectively on broader timescales. For example, novice runners who do a pretty good job of pacing themselves in their first race are likely to improve more as they gain experience than runners who botch their debut. As Van Yperen's use of the word "idiosyncratic" suggests, each athlete has their own unique self-regulatory style, and for this reason, the long-term process of learning to self-regulate is largely a process of discovering one's optimal style. In all cases, however, the key to maximizing progress in this journey is openness to learning.

Throughout *Swimming to Antarctica*, we see Lynne Cox exhibiting and benefiting from such openness. Consider the following description of her first big open-water swim workout with the Seal Beach Swim Team: "I kept working hard, enjoying it, drawing from every experience, learning how to feel the rhythm of the ocean, hear the tempo of the waves, and dance with the water using my balance, my strength, and all my senses . . . I improvised, adjusting the pitch of my hand, changed the rate of my strokes, and pressed my head deeper into the water so I could move through the waves instead of using more energy to bounce up and over them." While her companions were focused on getting from point A to point B, Lynne was *learning*, not just in this one swim but in every swim, and as the days became weeks, weeks months, and months years, her learning compounded, which explains why she kept topping herself with her swimming feats.

Principle Seven: "Work on strengths and weaknesses simultaneously."

All athletes have strengths and weaknesses in relation to others in their sport. A triathlete, for example, might lose time to their competitors in the swimming and cycling portions of races but reclaim it in the running portion. Studies indicate that athletes tend to try harder, gain more confidence, and enjoy themselves to a greater degree when practicing their strengths than they do when working on their weaknesses. For these reasons, most athletes spend the majority of their time working on their strengths, which is not the most effective way to improve overall performance.

One of the key things that distinguishes exceptional self-regulators from other athletes is a "whatever works" mindset toward improvement, which I first mentioned in Chapter 1 in describing Mark Allen. "Many are stubborn in pursuit of the path they've chosen," wrote Friedrich Nietzsche. "Few in pursuit of the goal." Whereas the typical athlete is biased toward certain pathways to improvement and against others, athletes like Mark Allen and Lynne Cox are not. If they believe that working as hard on their weaknesses as they do on their strengths is necessary to maximize their overall improvement, they won't hesitate, despite enjoying it less and perhaps not gaining as much confidence from it. Amateur golfers are famously obsessed with increasing the length of their drives. Why? Because they are biased toward this means of improving—they *want* length off the tee to be the key to a lower handicap. Meanwhile, the pros spend far more time learning to finesse their wedge shots, which aren't as sexy but confer a bigger competitive advantage if mastered.

Lynne's greatest natural strength was her tolerance for cold water, yet she worked relentlessly to bolster this strength, and she succeeded in measurable ways. Her most stubborn weakness, perhaps, was speed, and she worked on that too. Upon returning to Long Beach from her triumphal first crossing of the English Channel, Lynne rejoined the Phillips 66 team for a celebratory workout, having not swum with them in two years. Although she remained much slower than the two Olympians in lane eight, Coach Gambril did her the honor of allowing her to share their coveted space, fulfilling the wish she had voiced three years before. Lynne did not treat the experience as a mere honor, however. Instead, she seized the opportunity to study the technique of the speedier swimmers from up close and to ask them to analyze her stroke and offer pointers, which they gladly did.

Principle Eight: "Distinguish between high-pressure situations and athletes' psychological reactions to pressure."

Pressure has been defined as "the psychological stress associated with expectations to perform well in a situation," and as such it is intrinsic to sports competition. We experience pressure as a state of heightened arousal, or alertness, that arises from the perceived importance of a desired outcome, the indeterminacy of that outcome, the strain of exerting maximal effort in pursuit of it, and the need to react and make decisions quickly. Pressure can either facilitate or sabotage performance depending on how the athlete interprets it. As Van Yperen explains, "Performers' appraisal of their increased arousal level will be determined, among other things, by their perceived abilities to cope effectively with the pressure situation. When they feel they have the requisite physical, technical, tactical, and mental resources, they are likely to interpret their increased arousal level as a functional coping resource that aids rather than harms performance."

Pressure accentuates differences between skillful and unskillful self-regulators. Studies have shown that when an element of pressure is added to a situation through time constraints or heightened stakes, small disparities in individual performance become big ones. This is why great athletes want the ball when the game is on the line. They crave pressure because it gives them a competitive advantage over those who crumble under pressure and presents them with opportunities to really test their capacity to self-regulate.

Of the many intense situations Lynne Cox put herself in during her career, none was more pressurized than her swim across Alaska's Glacier Bay. It took place in thirty-eight-degree water jammed with icebergs and so-called pan ice—invisible sheets that Lynne had to break up by whacking at them with her forearms while she swam. Completing the swim as quickly as possible was of paramount importance, not only for the obvious reason that she risked becoming hypothermic if she took too long but also because the sun was sinking and the air temperature dropping, and if Lynne and her support crew didn't get out of the area soon, their boat would become trapped in ice. "The intensity of this swim was like nothing I had ever experienced," she writes. "There was so much to be aware of, and yet, throughout it all, I had to stay absolutely focused on how my body was responding."

This divided attentional focus—one eye on the icebergs and pan ice that threatened to cut Lynne up or imprison her entire crew, the other on her sinking core body temperature—would be the very first thing to go in a lesser self-regulator in a similar situation. Either the external threat or the internal crisis would trigger a panic state and absorb the athlete's full attention, like a chef allowing a kitchen fire to rage while attending to a scalded hand. Not Lynne. Far from panicking, she broke out laughing, enjoying the absurdity of her predicament (picture her shouting "Hi-yah!" as she karate chops a pane of frozen water midstroke) even as she put everything she had into the serious task of getting out of it alive.

Principle Nine: "Accept fluctuating internal states and focus on goal-relevant cues and contingencies."

In the pursuit of athletic goals, only one thing remains fixed: the goal itself.* Everything else—thoughts, emotions, perceptions, sensations— is in flux. Staying on track toward a goal requires continuous, active management of these internal states. No single psychological tool has the power to successfully corral every internal state that threatens to derail an athlete's progress toward their goal. An athlete must have a variety of self-regulatory tools at their disposal and know which one to use in a given situation.

There are moments when athletes need to be hard on themselves, calling upon their inner drill sergeant to deliver an old-school berating. But there are other moments when athletes need to be gentle with themselves, calling upon their inner Mister Rogers for a timely dose of unconditional love. Most athletes are better at one or the other— the stick or the carrot—but great athletes are good at both. Lynne Cox knew instinctively when to administer the stick and when to apply the carrot in her swims. During her first English Channel crossing, a violent shift in Lynne's internal state occurred when strong currents dragged her past the original landing site, requiring that the fifteen-year-old greenhorn find an alternative finish in literal midstream with nothing less than a world record at stake. Her spirit deflated at the prospect, a sinking feeling perilously close to actual sinking. Having never before found herself in such a pickle, Lynne needed to conjure a novel solution.

---

* And even the goal isn't always fixed. A 2023 study by University of Lincoln sport psychologist Patricia Jackman and colleagues found that high-performing runners tended to adjust their goals during race execution to ensure they met the underlying goal of achieving the best possible result, all things considered.

And she did. Obeying a sudden impulse, she put her head in the water and sprinted, refusing to look up and check her progress until she'd counted out a thousand strokes. It worked, and the thousand-strokes trick became a staple in her self-regulatory toolkit, one she pulled out whenever the proverbial stick was needed.

Which wasn't always. In December 1976, two weeks before a planned attempt to swim the Strait of Magellan, Lynne arrived in southern Chile knowing she would have to spend at least an hour in forty-two-degree water to achieve her goal. Imagine her dismay when, on her first day of acclimatization, she was only able to wade knee-deep into the gelid Atlantic, lasting a measly twenty minutes before retreating to the beach. *How in the world am I ever going to make this swim?* she thought. Any other athlete in Lynne's place would have felt the same. But unlike those other athletes, Lynne didn't allow herself to get stuck on this thought. Instead, she pulled a carrot out of her self-regulatory toolbox, not because she preferred Pollyanna denial to facing the difficult reality before her but because she understood that if she had any chance of achieving her goal, this particular tool would be needed. "I had just traveled to the other half of the Americas," Lynne reasoned. "[I was] tired and jet-lagged, and I told myself to take that into consideration, to give myself a break."

There's something almost ruthless in the way great athletes select whichever tool is best suited to keep them on track toward their goal in the face of a negative turn in their internal state. In fact, you can delete the "almost." A 2017 study by British scientists found that, within a group of fifty-four high-performing athletes, two key traits were found to distinguish the "super champions" from the mere "champions" and the "almost champions." One was selfishness. The other, ruthlessness. Negative connotations notwithstanding, these traits—ruthlessness in particular—amount to little more in the self-regulatory context than a single-minded attachment to one thing—the goal—and a cold-blooded nonattachment to any particular means of achieving it. Great athletes, as supreme self-regulators, have no loyalty to any particular tool. Carrot, stick, balloon, who cares? Whatever works.

Principle Ten: "Control the controllables."

From a certain distance, expert self-regulators look a lot like control freaks. In the athletic environment, both types leave no stone unturned in the effort to maximize performance. But when we zoom in, a clear difference between control freaks and expert self-regulators becomes evident. Great athletes focus exclusively on controlling performance-relevant factors *that are actually within their control.* Control freaks, meanwhile, also try to control (or worry about their inability to control) other factors, such as the weather.

What expert self-regulators have that others lack is an internal locus of control, or a belief that their own chosen actions are the primary determinants of the outcomes of their athletic endeavors. Control freaks, lacking this sense of agency, seek it externally, trying anxiously to eliminate all uncertainty from their situation by controlling absolutely everything.

Shortly after Lynne Cox landed in England in anticipation of her first English Channel crossing, she and her mother met with Reg Brickell, a fishing pilot who held a sideline as a guide for English Channel swimmers. Decades older, he was taken aback when the teenage American peppered him with astute questions about his boat, the channel itself, and other pertinent matters. A control freak might have done the same thing, yet Lynne was no control freak. When factors outside her control impacted her swims, she showed a remarkable ability to accept them and move on.

Case in point: While practicing for her crossing of Iceland's Lake Myvatn, Lynne broke out in mysterious hives all over her body. A local woman explained to her that the rashes were caused by bites from the larvae of an indigenous fly species.

"Is there anything I can do to stop the itching?" Lynne asked.

The woman shook her head.

"That's okay," Lynne said. "It will just be part of my story about swimming Lake Myvatn."

And so it is.

GETTING IT TOGETHER

I'm confident I've successfully demonstrated that Lynne Cox possesses an extraordinary capacity to self-regulate. But what I haven't done is explain the origin of this capacity. Where does self-regulatory genius come from? How does one get their shit together to such a high degree? What does it take to become a setter of white-whale goals and possessor of a "whatever works" mentality? We'll begin to answer these questions in Chapter 5. But before we do that, we must first delve deeper into the "screw-loose" part of the mental formula for athletic greatness.

CHAPTER FOUR

What Doesn't Kill Us

**Problems are not the problem;
coping is the problem.**
—VIRGINIA SATIR

Frank Shorter is running. He is three years old, and he is fleeing barefoot across hot asphalt, having just soiled his diaper, an offense for which he's been punished with a sound thrashing that will recommence the moment daddy catches him—*if* he catches him.

Years later, Frank will become famous for running, and he will still be fleeing his father, though no longer literally, and he will still be in pain, albeit pain of a less tangible variety. But the key difference is that he will run by choice, and he will control his pain, and his unique capacity to do so will make him the finest marathoner in the world for a time.

All great athletes have a screw loose. Some are born this way, or at least appear to be, entering the world preloaded with an addiction-like hunger for something more than they get from mere *life*. We've seen examples of this type already in Dave Scott and Jack Johnson. To become great, such individuals must discover a sport in which pursuing greatness fulfills the hardwired personal need (for Dave, a need to move and never stop; for Jack, a need for absolute personal sovereignty) that defines their special flavor of "crazy." Others have a screw loosened by life experience, and become great by discovering a sport in which pursuing victory satisfies a need generated by that experience. Dave Scott's nemesis, Mark Allen, belongs to this type, and so does Frank Shorter. It's no coincidence that both of these men had terrible fathers. If the twenty-plus biographies I read in researching this book taught me anything, it's that fatherly abuse and neglect are among the most common sources of unmet needs in the lives of great athletes. I wish it were otherwise, but there you have it.

It's tempting to condemn abusive parents as monsters. The trouble with this way of thinking is that most abusers were themselves abused as children. Hurt people hurt people, as the saying goes. Frank's father, Sam Shorter (or Dr. Sam, as he's called throughout Frank's memoir, *My Marathon*—a sardonic nod to his daytime guise as a respected family physician), was typical in this regard, having been abused by his own father while growing up. Frank remembers the elder Shorter as "a hard, dour man who never showed any affection for his grandchildren." Dr. Sam liked to tell the childhood story of a summer road trip his family took from upstate New York to Missouri, Mom and Dad up front, Sam and his siblings in back. You can only drive so far with three young kids and open windows before someone loses something, and in this case it was a teddy bear that went sailing out the rear hatch, incensing Sam's father. Not knowing who the culprit was, he reached back and raked his hand across all three faces, punishing two innocents to ensure he got his intended target—a sadist's logic.

It's likely that Dr. Sam's father did worse things to his kids. What is certain is that Dr. Sam did worse things to *his* kids, of whom Frank arrived second of eleven. Most of the beatings occurred at night, after Dr. Sam returned from his rounds. From his upstairs bedroom, Frank heard his father grilling his mother in the kitchen below, intent on prying out of her a reluctant word or two about some peccadillo committed in his absence, a pretense for his daily fix of corporal punishment.

The girls had it especially bad. Dr. Sam raped at least one of his daughters, and Frank suspects he sexually abused all of them. Frank himself escaped the most unthinkable of his father's atrocities, but that's not saying much. Imagine being subjected to frequent naked belt whippings as a child and counting yourself lucky. Dr. Sam would lash Frank's bare bottom until he was exhausted, grunting like a weight lifter with every stroke. But as much as Frank disliked being beaten, bearing witness to his brothers' and sisters' beatings hurt far more. As the oldest functional male of the household (Frank's older brother Sam Jr. was also abusive), Frank felt responsible for protecting his younger siblings, yet powerless to do so.

No less damaging than the physical abuse Frank endured was the psychological cruelty—and the neglect. Not once in Frank's entire childhood did his father make an appearance at a practice, game, recital, or parent-teacher meeting. Oftentimes he forced Frank to ride along with him on his rounds, captive experiences that functioned mainly as opportunities for Dr. Sam to pit Frank against his brothers and sisters— or try anyway. One time he dragged Frank into the local emergency room, where he was met with the horrific spectacle of a man who'd just had his head split open in a bar fight. God knows what lesson Dr. Sam hoped to teach, but it involved brandishing a loose piece of the fully conscious patient's brain tissue in the traumatized boy's face.

Not all children cope with the trauma of abuse the same way, but they all cope one way or another. They have no choice. Frank realized early on that physical activity helped him "stay even." Through normal childhood exposure to various forms of purposeful exertion—tearing around the playground with his classmates during school recess, swimming at the local YMCA, skiing with his family, Little League baseball—he discovered that his heart and mind steadied when his muscles were working. But it was his initial encounter with long-distance running at age eleven that unlocked the door to a deeper and more abiding way of coping with the trauma he experienced at home.

It started, ironically, with skiing—Dr. Sam's great passion. While watching a downhill competition on television one day, Frank got the notion that he would become a champion ski racer. Not long afterward, he learned from a ski magazine his father subscribed to that elite French downhillers kept in shape over the summer by running. So Frank started jogging, wanting nothing more from the activity than fitness he could transfer to the slopes. But it soon became an end in itself, the most potent vehicle for "staying even" he'd ever experienced. Yet the thought of running competitively did not occur to him until he finished a surprising seventh in a compulsory 4.3-mile race held during his freshman year of boarding school in western Massachusetts, bested only by the varsity members of the school's league champion cross-country team. Intrigued by the fleet-footed newcomer, their coach invited Frank to join, and he accepted.

Despite his obvious potential, Frank did not immediately set the world on fire in the maroon-and-blue uniform of Mount Hermon Academy. What he did instead was improve, clawing his way up the New

England prep school ranks until, in his final year, he dominated. The same pattern was repeated at Yale University, where Frank rose from Ivy League also-ran as a freshman to NCAA champion at six miles as a senior. Along the way, he patented his own signature racing style, a strategy of sadomasochistic aggression that ensured every contest became a test of pain tolerance—a test Frank couldn't lose.

"I had the ability to run fast when I was tired," Frank writes of his self-discovered tactical advantage. "That was my only physical talent, the one thing that set me apart. I could stand at a distance from my pain, draw a sort of energy from it. Partly this was due to the diligence of my training, partly it was due to my efficient stride . . . and partly it was due to the savage boyhood beatings I'd received from my father: I had already learned to ride my pain."

A runner whose only talent is the ability to ride their pain and run fast when tired is bound to gravitate to the marathon, and Frank did so. On August 18, 1968, not yet twenty years old and having never run farther than twelve miles, he jumped into the US Olympic Trials Marathon on a lark, wearing borrowed shoes a size and a half too small. Unsurprisingly, his cramped feet blistered badly, forcing him to drop out before the finish, but by then he'd glimpsed his future.

In his second marathon, a qualifier for the 1971 Pan American Games, Frank finished second, and in the Pan Am Games marathon itself he took gold. Already he'd nearly perfected a new approach to marathon racing that was based on his special gift, a strategy he further refined in Fukuoka, the Japanese city that in those days hosted the world's most competitive marathon outside of the Olympics, attracting even more international talent than the older, more celebrated Boston Marathon. Step one of the Shorter Plan was to "yahoo the start," or go straight to the front and establish an honest early pace, a trick he'd learned from an older teammate at Mount Hermon.

Step two was to surge abruptly around a third of the way through the race, accelerating to a pace that was unsustainable for everyone, himself included—an almost unheard-of tactic in those days, when the marathon was fought as a war of attrition. Step three came another two to four miles down the road, depending on the circumstances. When Frank felt he'd put enough distance between himself and his demoralized chasers, he slowed down fractionally, aiming to preserve the gap he'd suffered so dearly to create. And from there he rode his pain to the finish line.

If Frank Shorter had a tattoo, it would probably be that: *Ride the pain.* And it would be on his heart.

In December 1971, on the streets of Fukuoka, Frank's gutsy new approach to marathon racing worked beautifully. Having scouted the course the day before, he launched a surprise attack at the ideal spot, a hairpin turn at seven miles that bottlenecked the lead group, allowing the American upstart to separate himself from the pack. He ran the next two miles in the low 4:40s, a pace the others either could not or dared not match, before downshifting to a more sustainable tempo and cementing his victory by doing what he knew how to do better than any other marathoner: hurt.

To fortify the Shorter Plan, Frank developed his own method of training that leveraged his "only physical talent." Like other elite marathoners of his day, he logged 120 or more miles per week, including 20 miles on Sunday. Unlike other elite marathoners, he hit the track twice a week, subjecting himself to searing high-intensity interval workouts of the kind that were typically done by 5000-meter specialists like Steve Prefontaine, a frequent training partner of Frank's. The objective of these workouts was as much psychological as it was physical, a means of boosting Frank's already exceptional capacity to suffer without cracking. "The goal," he writes in *My Marathon*, "was to learn to moderate and manage my pain over precise, predictable distances and to mimic the pattern of pacing I'd employ during the marathon race."

If you know just one fact about Frank Shorter, it's probably that he won the 1972 Olympic marathon in Munich. Originally scheduled for September 9, the race was pushed back a day after terrorists infiltrated the Olympic Village and abducted eleven Israeli athletes, who were later killed in a botched rescue attempt. Now, a last-minute race postponement is likely to rattle any runner, especially if the reason for the delay isn't thunderstorms or bridge repairs but mass homicide. But Frank wasn't any runner. After the schedule change was announced, he ate lunch in the athlete dining hall with Ron Hill of Great Britain, who complained bitterly about the decision. Having recorded the fastest marathon time in the world that year, Hill posed a serious threat to Frank's hopes of winning, but Frank now wrote him off, knowing he'd lost the mental focus required to compete at the highest level in such an unforgiving event. And he was right—come race day, the United Kingdom's great hope for gold finished a disappointing sixth.

Ron Hill was not the only Olympian who, understandably, found himself unable to block out the surrounding horror and perform at peak capacity. Frank, however, though he was no less horrified than his fellow athletes, had little trouble staying focused, for reasons he wouldn't fully comprehend until long afterward, when he sat down to write his story. "Unconsciously, perhaps," he reflects, "I was echoing the behavior of my childhood. [My father] had wanted to stomp around inside my head, dominate my every moment, and I responded by denying him that power, putting the man out of mind."

The race that made Frank Shorter famous started just twenty-four hours after he and his fellow athletes attended a memorial service for the victims of the attack, with the possibility of a second attack—this one on the runners themselves, who would be easy targets on the streets of

Munich—hanging over them. Frank understood that by surging ahead of the pack at nine miles, as he intended to do, and thereafter running alone with the letters *U-S-A* emblazoned on his singlet, he would make an especially soft and juicy target of himself. But he did it anyway, without a hint of misgiving, and the Shorter Plan worked to perfection once again. Frank won in a personal-best time of 2:12:19, beating the silver medalist by more than two minutes.

Frank finished the year as the number-one-ranked marathoner in the world. The following year, he did it again, cementing his claim to the top spot with his fourth consecutive victory at Fukuoka. By January 1975 Frank was at the height of his powers, just a few short months away from setting a personal-best time at 10,000 meters that fell just short of breaking Steve Prefontaine's American record. That's when he received an invitation from Dr. Kenneth Cooper—father of the aerobics movement—to undergo physiological testing at the Cooper Institute in Dallas, Texas. Nineteen other elite distance runners accepted the same invitation, including Prefontaine himself. Among the various tests the athletes completed was a VO_2 max test, which measures an athlete's capacity to consume oxygen during exercise, the sine qua non of long-distance running ability. As expected, all of the subjects performed well, though results varied by individual, ranging from 71.3 milliliters of oxygen per kilogram of body weight per minute at the low end to 84.4 ml/kg/min at the high end. The highest score was achieved by none other than Steve Prefontaine. The lowest—lower than those of Jim Crawford, Nick Rose, and a bunch of other guys you've probably never heard of—belonged to . . . can you guess? That's right: Frank Shorter.

Frank was right. He was not more gifted than other runners of his era. He was just better able to run fast when tired, because he was able to ride his pain, because he'd been abused as a child.

TALENT NEEDS TRAUMA

Stories like Frank's—which is to say, stories of great athletes who endured major trauma during their formative years—are surprisingly common. The great gymnast Simone Biles spent time in the foster care system as a child. Four-time Olympic gold medalist Mo Farah was the victim of child trafficking before he became a runner. Tennis champion Andy Murray survived a school massacre at age eight. Such experiences are all too frequent in the general population, but there's evidence that a disproportionately large number of people who experience major trauma while growing up go on to become great athletes.

Some of this evidence can be found in a study described in the 2017 book *Sport and the Brain: The Science of Preparing, Enduring and Winning*. A team of British scientists interviewed thirty-two former athletes, their coaches, and their parents about various aspects of their personal and athletic development. Half of the athletes were classified as "elites" on the basis of having qualified for and competed in major championships, the other half as "superelites" on the basis of having each won multiple medals at major championships. All sixteen super-elites were found to have experienced traumas such as physical abuse or parental death during childhood. Only four of the sixteen non–medal winners reported similar experiences.

Findings of this kind (and there are others) have prompted some sports psychologists, including Mustafa Sarkar of Nottingham Trent University, to propose that trauma—or at the very least adversity— is *essential* to athletic greatness, no less indispensable than physical ability. Sarkar himself conducted a study quite similar to the one just mentioned and got comparable results, prompting him to coin the provocative phrase "talent needs trauma." In his view, traumatic experience functions as water, soil, and sunlight to the seed of genetic potential, at least for those athletes who reach the top. But why? And how? We think of trauma as a bad thing, and in isolation it unquestionably is. What, then, is the mechanism by which traumatic experiences nurture talent in athletes like Frank Shorter?

The obvious answer is the right one: Adversity is an unavoidable part of the athletic experience. To excel in any sport, an athlete must be good at coping with adversity. And one way to get better at coping with adversity is to face adversity. Individuals who experience trauma in their formative years gain valuable early practice in facing adversity. Many of these individuals develop overall coping styles that don't serve them particularly well in life. Childhood trauma strongly predicts future mental illness, addiction, and incarceration. But when the right kind of trauma meets the right person at the right time, one possible outcome is an exceptional capacity for coping with adversity in sports. This is not to say these individuals escape their traumas unharmed. Childhood trauma also predicts marital disharmony, and Frank Shorter is twice divorced. Would a happier childhood have made him a more successful husband and a less successful runner? It's possible.

HUNGRY GHOSTS

In Buddhist lore, Earth is haunted by hungry ghosts. These supernatural beings originated in stories of greedy or stingy mortals who, after death, returned as demons tormented by an insatiable hunger. Like most of Buddhist mythology, hungry ghosts are grounded in solid realities of human psychology. We all know people—flesh-and-blood human beings, not ravenous zombies—who yearn in vain to satisfy some glaring emotional want, to quiet a screaming void inside them that nothing ever satisfies. Indeed, more than a few psychologists today classify survivors of childhood trauma, particularly those who cope with addiction, as "hungry ghosts." None has taken this conceit further than Gabor Maté, a Hungarian Canadian addiction expert and author of *In the Realm of Hungry Ghosts: Close Encounters with Addiction*, a book whose message is tidily summarized in these two sentences: "Not all addictions are rooted in abuse or trauma, but . . . they can all be traced back to painful experience. A hurt is at the center of *all* addictive behaviors."

Those last three words are crucial. Like Stuart Ross, who believes we're all a little bit "crazy," Maté refutes the notion of a binary distinction between addict and nonaddict, displacing it with a catchall category of "addictive behaviors" that encompasses everything from socially sanctioned compulsions such as workaholism to purely destructive habits like opioid dependency. The realm of hungry ghosts, in Maté's reckoning, is inhabited by all who "seek something outside ourselves to curb an insatiable yearning for relief or fulfillment," a yearning that, more often than not, issues from traumatic life experience.

In the preceding chapter we talked about self-regulation, or the psychology of goal pursuit. We can all agree that the ultimate goal of every human—the overarching aim of our self-regulatory efforts—is to feel happy most of the time. As Maté sees it, addiction results when a person is unable to achieve happiness through internal resources (self-esteem, self-love) and turns to external resources to fill the gap. "People are susceptible to the addiction process if they have a constant need to fill their minds or bodies with external sources of comfort, whether physical or emotional," he writes. "That need expresses a failure of self-regulation—an inability to maintain a reasonably stable internal emotional atmosphere."

As much as I admire Maté's work, I'm not sure I agree with this last point. And I'm not sure that psychologists who specialize in the study of self-regulation would agree either. Maté seems to suggest that successful self-regulation takes place entirely inside our heads, and that outward behaviors lack the power to help us "maintain a reasonably stable internal emotional atmosphere." But that's not entirely accurate. External actions have as much power to satisfy our overarching self-regulatory goal of feeling happy most of the time as internal thoughts and emotions. Getting drunk or high every day happens to be an ineffective method of behavioral self-regulation, granting moments of bliss at the cost of misery in between. However, there are lots of other behaviors that do a very fine job of fulfilling our self-regulatory ends. Discovering things we love to do, for example, and working to master them, has tremendous proven efficacy in making us feel good, not in the meretricious way that alcohol and drugs do but in a healthier, steadier way. This is precisely what running did for Frank Shorter. Long before he discovered he had a knack for running and could fashion a fulfilling life around it, he discovered that it gave him relief from the way his father made him feel.

Some might argue that in becoming a runner Frank was literally running away from his problems—that the relief the sport gave him and the glory it brought him merely distracted him from the damage his father's abuse had wrought on his psyche yet did nothing to heal it. If we accept this argument, then Frank's running was little different from an addiction to alcohol or drugs—an *expression* of psychic damage rather than a remedy for it. But does anyone ever truly erase the damage of severe childhood trauma, whether through therapy or mindfulness meditation or Olympic running or anything else? Probably not. In which case, an effective distraction from the immutable pain inside just might be the next best thing.

There's no law stating that an outwardly directed behavior can't be two things: *both* an expression of emotional damage resulting from life trauma (evidence of a loose screw) *and* a healthy self-regulatory response to trauma (a way of keeping one's shit together). And in my view, Frank's running was indeed both. Throughout his competitive career, Frank routinely subjected himself to intensities of pain that few others could bear, not just in races but also in training. "At the end of [a] workout," he writes, "had someone held a gun to my head and ordered me to run one more interval . . . I would have said go ahead and shoot because it would hurt less." Taken by itself, this confession sounds perilously akin to the self-harming behaviors that certain survivors of abuse engage in. But the same guy who makes this confession, in the same book, also says this: "Discovering that I love to run literally saved me from my childhood and put me on a life path that still continues."

Psychiatrist Thomas Szasz famously proclaimed that insanity is the only sane response to an insane society. What he meant, I think, is that sanity may look a lot like insanity in those who have been forced to cope with insane circumstances. Or, if you prefer: having your shit together can look a lot like having a screw loose in the aftermath of screw-loosening life events.

The word "coping" has come up before in this book, and I mention it again with intent. For it is within the coping process that the seeming polarities of "screw loose" and "shit together" intersect and conjoin. Let's now have a look at the science of coping.

SELF-REGULATION UNDER STRESS

In the preceding chapter we defined self-regulation as "the dynamic process of determining a desired end state (i.e., a goal) and then taking action to move toward it while monitoring progress along the way." Coping is exactly the same thing, but in special circumstances—namely, bad circumstances. Psychologist Ellen Skinner defines coping as "self-regulation under stress." Setting and pursuing a goal of losing ten pounds to fit into a wedding tuxedo is an example of a self-regulatory challenge not initiated in response to extreme negative stress, hence not an example of coping. Setting and pursuing a goal of not becoming like your father, as Frank Shorter did "very early on" in life in response to the extreme negative stress of Dr. Sam's abuse, *is* an example of coping.

Psychologists interested in self-regulation have tended to focus their attention on children, while those interested specifically in coping have focused on adults. It makes sense. Self-regulation is learned in childhood, after all, whereas coping happens mostly in adulthood, that crisis-ridden phase of life throughout which we do the best we can with the self-regulatory skills we developed while growing up. Extreme negative stress is not the exclusive province of maturity, however. Too often, children are forced to cope with major adversities when their self-regulatory skills are not yet fully formed, a cruelty that in many cases damages self-regulatory development, resulting in ineffective coping later in life.

Here's the kicker: Research shows that nothing matters more with respect to the development of self-regulatory skills than "secure attachments" to adults during early childhood. Those of us who have been blessed with loving, dependable caregivers during this critical period tend to become skillful self-regulators, and those who lack them don't. Which means that the most damaging kind of trauma a person can experience in their early years is parental abuse or neglect, an experience that creates a dire need for coping tools that it simultaneously denies.

Worst of all, because the brain itself is still developing in early childhood, the damage caused by abusive parents or guardians is very difficult to undo. Animal studies have shown that brain regions involved in generating impulsive actions—including the amygdala, which also plays a key role in threat perception—are overdeveloped in offspring deprived of secure parental attachments in early life, while regions involved in impulse inhibition are underdeveloped. This is why, as Frank Shorter succinctly puts it, "When you learn to be afraid at an early age, the fear never dies."

Again, though, not all victims of severe childhood trauma are affected equally. Consider these lines from Stuart Ross's book, *We're All a Little Bit Crazy*: "When a child is emotionally neglected, made to feel unwanted, living without love, told blatantly that they are bad, sexually or physically abused, they can only come to one conclusion— that they are bad and unlovable. To think otherwise is impossible—that their 'caregivers' are wrong or crazy or abusive." Now consider these lines from Frank Shorter's memoir: "During my boyhood beatings, as Dr. Sam snorted and heaved and Felix the Cat winked obscenely at me from my father's tattoo, I realized that I was innocent—the darkness had nothing to do with me."

The irreconcilableness of these two passages could not be starker. Ross tells us it is impossible for a child to blame an abusive parent for their abuse. Yet Frank recalls doing precisely this in his memoir. Perhaps what Ross should have said was that he had never personally encountered a child who rejected blame in such circumstances, for it only takes one exception to prove something's possible. But what made it possible in Frank's case? It's worth mentioning that he had not yet discovered running at the time of his naked belt whippings, so it wasn't running's transformative effects on body, mind, and spirit that enabled him to defend his mind and spirit, if not his body, against his father's lashes. Perhaps, then, there was something in Frank that preceded all of it, a resilience that enabled him first to preserve his sense of innocence in the face of the ultimate betrayal and later to use running as a means to lay claim to a life path that far exceeded mere survival.

Lending credence to these speculations is the fact that, according to research, extraordinary resilience in the face of severe childhood trauma is not unheard of. In 1989, for example, psychologist Emmy Werner published the results of an ambitious study that tracked nearly seven hundred people for the first thirty-two years of their lives, one-third of whom experienced significant trauma during childhood. Of these individuals, Werner reported, another third went on to become "competent, confident, and caring young adults," while the rest struggled with issues ranging from depression to delinquency. These findings help explain why we seldom encounter someone who has *both* a screw loose *and* their shit together. One-third of one-third is one-ninth.

A number of factors distinguished the thrivers from the strugglers in Werner's study. Some of these were environmental. Most notably, thrivers tended to have at least one secure attachment with an adult while growing up. Even among those who lacked such advantages, though, some thrived by virtue of possessing certain key psychological qualities—namely, independence, autonomy, and (as Werner phrases it) a tendency "to meet the world on their own terms"—that contribute to effective coping. In idiomatic terms, these individuals kept their shit together as adults despite having had a screw loosened by early-life experiences because they had their shit together naturally in the first place.

Scientists have identified a number of genes that influence a person's capacity to self-regulate. In 2021, Richard Karlsson Linnér of Leiden University and colleagues created a scoring system made up of hundreds of genes with known connections to self-regulation, hypothesizing that those with higher scores would in fact be better at regulating their behavior in the big, bad world. Linnér's team then ran the genomes of 1.5 million people through this scoring system and looked for associations between individual scores and various behavioral outcomes. Sure enough, they found that the more favorable a person's genetic makeup was for self-regulation, the less likely that person was to experience addiction, unemployment, criminal conviction, venereal disease, and suicide—all of which can happen to anyone but are more likely to happen (according to prior research) to those who aren't good at self-regulating, no matter how they grew up.

Frank Shorter says he can't explain why he survived his childhood "relatively intact," but it seems probable that, if he'd taken part in Linnér's study, his genome would have indicated a strong innate capacity to self-regulate. What is certain is that Frank possessed all of the attributes Emmy Werner found to be common in those who cope as well as humanly possible with childhood trauma, beginning with independence. We see this in the private vow he made as a young boy to define himself in opposition to his father, a mission he pursued through a combination of escape and self-discovery, using running as his primary vehicle. It's telling that Frank was self-coached throughout his entire elite running career, starting before he even left college. No male authority figure was going to tell Frank how to run.

An incident that occurred at Frank's second Olympics—the 1976 Games in Montreal—displays at full maturity the coping style that emerged from the intersection of his innate resilience and his childhood trauma. Less than thirty minutes before the start of the marathon event, while he was warming up on the infield of the Olympic Stadium, Frank's right shoe spontaneously fell apart—an absurdly ill-timed stroke of bad luck, like something out of an anxiety dream. Frank did have another pair of shoes with him, but they were heavy trainers. He also had a second pair of racing flats, but they were back at the hotel. This was quite a pickle. How would he cope?

I know how Elena Libin would answer. Libin is a clinical and research psychologist best known for developing *coping intelligence,* an instrument for assessing individual coping ability. There are lots of other coping models out there, but I like Libin's best because coping ability really does strike me as a kind of intelligence. As complex beings in a complex world, we humans have a lot of options for responding to stressful situations, and choosing the best response takes a good deal of mental wherewithal. In the coping intelligence model, coping occurs along three axes: cognitive, emotional, and behavioral. The specific coping choices we make on each axis are either efficient, meaning they achieve desired outcomes, or inefficient, meaning they fail to make the best of the situation. In a 2017 validation study of the instrument, Libin offers the following examples:

Inefficient cognitive coping: get caught up in thinking about insignificant details

Inefficient emotional coping: feel that I will never get over it

Inefficient behavioral coping: do anything but the task at hand

Efficient cognitive coping: break up the problem into simple, manageable components

Efficient emotional coping: use my desires and interests [to direct] where I want to go in solving the difficulty

Efficient behavioral coping: work through the difficulties until the situation is completely resolved

Frank's cognitive, emotional, and behavioral responses to his footwear crisis before the 1976 Olympic Marathon were worthy of a gold medal in coping efficiency. "Instead of feeling panic," Frank recalls in *My Marathon*, "I immediately thought of what my options might be." That's a two for one: efficient emotional coping in remaining calm and efficient cognitive coping in pivoting immediately from problem recognition to problem-solving. After dismissing the idea of sprinting back to the hotel to retrieve his backup racing flats himself, he scanned the grandstands in search of a familiar face. Recognizing US race-walking coach Bruce McDonald, Frank called out to him, explaining his conundrum and requesting a favor. While Bruce dashed away on the errand, Frank's efficient coping continued. "Instead of cursing my bad luck," he writes, "I reverted to my default mode of dealing with stress: movement. I jogged back and forth in my training shoes . . . I felt confident this would all work out." And it did, thanks in no small part to this masterpiece of self-regulation (and the just-in-time arrival of his backup racing flats): Frank took the silver medal this time, beaten only by a little-known East German later outed for blood doping.

THE "CURSE" OF THE CHARMED LIFE

It's impossible to know if Frank Shorter would have become a great athlete if he hadn't endured a traumatic childhood. What we do know is that no one's opinion on this matter carries more weight than Frank's own, and he believes he probably would not have become the world's number one marathoner with a better father, writing that "my private pain and guilt . . . formed the source—at least one source—of my gift for the marathon." For the sake of argument, let's assume (and it's a very safe assumption) Frank is right. And while we're at it, let's pretend for a moment that you are a gifted young athlete who dreams of future greatness. Taking Frank's example to heart, you might find yourself in the odd position of wishing trauma upon yourself for the purpose of escaping the "curse" of the charmed life.

In reality, thankfully, there's no need for such perverse wishes. For every great athlete who believes they wouldn't have gotten where they are without childhood trauma, there are several more who had no such experience while growing up. Proof of this comes from the British study I described in the preceding chapter, which found that, within a group of fifty-four high-performing athletes, those classified as "super champions" on the basis of their achievements had no more trauma in their personal histories than (mere) "champions" or "almost champions." But this isn't to say that all three groups were the same. What distinguished one from the next, according to the study's authors, was not the *amount* of trauma they'd experienced but how successful they were in coping with it, leading the authors to conclude that, although no athlete achieves greatness without facing challenges, what matters is not the challenges themselves "but what performers *bring* to the challenges," as we've seen in Frank Shorter's case.

Furthermore, who says that the challenges serving to cultivate athletes' coping skills must occur outside of sports? While it is true to an extent that athletes who experience little adversity in their lives must go looking for adversity to become great, they do precisely this in pursuing athletic greatness. An athlete can get only so far in their climb toward the proverbial mountaintop before they're knocked down by defeat, injury, or some other setback that's tough to cope with. Indeed, a second study by the researchers just mentioned found that, in a group of twenty elite athletes, most of the past experiences regarded as traumatic had occurred within the sporting context.

Look at Tom Brady, the legendary American football quarterback. Tom grew up happy and privileged in a stable family. Nothing really went wrong in his life until the 2000 NFL draft, when he was chosen by the New England Patriots in the sixth round, behind 198 other players. Having expected to hear his number called much earlier, Tom felt disrespected. Of course, no rational person would compare the trauma of being hired by a major professional sports team to the trauma of parental abuse, but keep in mind, trauma is an effect, not a cause, and judging by how he talks about it, Tom's draft disappointment traumatized him, and like the extra-athletic traumas others experience, it served as a "motivational trigger" (to borrow a term used by sports psychologist Karen Howells) that drove Tom to become a far better professional football quarterback than he was a college quarterback.

Point being, an athlete can achieve greatness without being born with a screw loose, like Jack Johnson, or suffering a traumatic childhood, like Frank Shorter. The addiction-like drive to win at all costs, which is an unquestionable requirement for athletic greatness, can be acquired through other "screw-loosening" life experiences. I'll have much more to say on the subject of "finding your crazy" in Chapter 8.

CHAPTER FIVE

Know Your Butterflies

**I don't want to be at the mercy of my emotions.
I want to use them, to enjoy them,
and to dominate them.
—OSCAR WILDE, *THE PICTURE OF DORIAN GRAY***

It really is quite amazing how many great athletes have terrible fathers. When you read a bunch of athlete biographies, as I did in researching this book, you just can't escape them—they're everywhere! We've met two already (Mark Allen's cold and exacting dad, Frank Shorter's bullying and sadistic sire), and you'll meet another in the next chapter, and the next, and I'm afraid I have to mention one here, too.

I assure you I had no intention of stuffing these pages with loathsome male parents. It just happened. The present chapter is a case in point. It addresses the topic of emotional self-regulation, and my search for an individual whose story illustrates how great athletes transform the "screw loose" side of their mental makeup from a liability into an asset by getting their shit together emotionally led me to Andre Agassi, the tennis legend. Only when I read his critically acclaimed 2009 memoir *Open* did I discover that Andre had a terrible father. I swear!

Not all terrible fathers beat the crap out of their kids. Some engage in subtler forms of ill-use like treating their children as their own second chances at life, pawns in an egomaniacal quest to avenge past failures through a vessel that carries their name and DNA. That's the kind of terrible father Andre had. Born and raised in Iran, Emmanuel "Mike" Agassi competed in the 1948 and 1952 Olympics as a boxer, losing in the first round on both occasions. He then immigrated to the United States, where he somehow got the notion that playing tennis was the surest path to abundance and subsequently forced the game on all four of his children, of whom Andre, born in 1970, was the youngest. When Andre was a baby, his father created a hanging mobile out of tennis balls and positioned it directly above Andre's crib, ensuring those fuzzy green orbs were the first things he saw when he woke up in the morning and the last things he saw before he closed his eyes at night. Later, he taped a ping-pong paddle to Andre's wrist and taught him to swat the balls. Mike Agassi had a plan for his son, and it was only just beginning.

By the time Andre was seven, his father was forcing him to hit 2,500 tennis balls a day—balls shot his way at 115 mph out of a specially modified pitching machine that young Andre nicknamed "the Dragon" because it terrified him. The poor child *hated* tennis, and he used what little power he possessed to escape it—exaggerating small injuries, for example, or sending the occasional ball sailing far beyond the confines of the hand-built tennis court that filled the backyard of the Agassi family's otherwise unremarkable home in Las Vegas, knowing the penny-pinching taskmaster would fetch it, granting Andre a few minutes' reprieve from the Dragon.

"Hold on a second," you say. "How does a kid who hates tennis go on to make fifteen Grand Slam finals, winning eight of them?" The answer is that Andre's aversion for tennis was counterbalanced by a prodigious talent for the game. Mike Agassi wanted nothing less than perfection from his children, something the first three couldn't deliver. But Andre sometimes could, and as he explains in *Open*: "When I do something perfect, I enjoy a split second of sanity and calm." Additionally, Mike's merciless chastisement conditioned Andre over time to hate losing even more than he hated tennis, and if he couldn't escape tennis, he could at least escape losing by mastering tennis. And with mastery came opportunity. As Andre grew older, he awakened to the possibility that the sport his father wouldn't allow him to escape might ultimately enable him to escape his father.

At thirteen, Andre left Las Vegas to hone his skills at the Nick Bollettieri Tennis Academy in Bradenton, Florida. Three years later—on his sixteenth birthday—he turned pro. Then Nike came calling, lured by Andre's early success on the ATP Tour, hooking Andre to the sport he hated with yet another attachment: money. But his trajectory soon changed, and not for the better, transitioning from the steady upward vector of the Man of Destiny to the chaotic seismograph of a Boy Who Doesn't Have His Shit Together. In 1988, Andre made the semifinals of two Grand Slam tournaments, which was good. But he also skipped Wimbledon (having lost in the first round the year before) and failed to advance out of his bracket at the ATP Masters Cup, which was not so good.

Erratic performance has a well-established link to erratic emotions. The first major study to demonstrate this link was conducted by kinesiologist Elizabeth Brown around the time Andre was battling the Dragon seven days a week. One hundred and twenty female college students completed a standard test of emotional stability and then performed a motor-skill test that involved using a wand-like instrument to trace the movement of a small white disk as it rotated around a kind of turntable. In the control condition, the students completed the task in silence, but in the experimental condition, they faced added pressure in the form of intrusive prerecorded noises. Shaw found that students with less emotional stability were more rattled by this external pressure than students with greater emotional stability. Everyone performed worse with noise, but the gap was larger for those with less control of their emotions.

A hard-fought tennis match is an emotional roller coaster for any player. Think about it: Matches are made up of multiple sets, which are made up of multiple games, which are made up of multiple points, and each point is won by one player and lost by the other. That's a lot of winning and losing! In most sports, winning and losing happen only at the final buzzer, but tennis players ricochet between winning and losing the whole way through every match. And every win is felt, as well as every loss—you see it in the fist pumps and muttered expletives. But champions do a better job of containing these emotional swings, at least on the inside, compared to lesser players.

Andre Agassi exhibited poor emotional stability in the early part of his professional tennis career. In 1990, for example, he faked a muscle pull to get out of playing a match he didn't want to play, a reprise of a phantom soccer injury he'd once used as a kid to get out of facing the Dragon. The following year, after a stunning loss in the first round of the US Open, Andre told reporters, "I'm starting to view competition as a challenge now, as opposed to an inconvenience or something." These are not words we expect to hear from a grown man in his fifth year of professional tennis.

Let us not be too quick to judge, however. In hindsight, it's clear that Andre was doing the best he could, and about as well as anyone could have done with a father like Mike Agassi. A part of Andre—a big part—still wanted nothing to do with tennis, yet walking away from the sport did not seem like a viable option, so he found other ways to express his discontent. The rebellion started at Bollettieri, where he took to wearing his hair in a pink mohawk and once showed up to a tournament final (which he won) festooned in dungarees and punk makeup.

Imagine yourself in his position. You are, perhaps, the most gifted male tennis player on Earth, yet you hate tennis. You carry a lot of emotional baggage from an unhappy childhood, but underneath that baggage is an intelligent, complex, sensitive, earnestly striving person. If you are this person, how might you harness your emotions to achieve greatness on the tennis court? One possibility would be to direct your rage and bitterness at your opponents. And that's precisely what Andre did in 1995, in what he dubbed "the Summer of Revenge."

The target of this campaign was German star Boris Becker, who made some disparaging comments about Andre to reporters after beating him at Wimbledon. It is possible to enjoy being angry—we've all done it—and Andre enjoyed the anger stoked by Becker's slight. "I want to feel rage," he writes of this episode. "Endless, all-consuming rage." He won his next four tournaments, snatching the number one world ranking in the process. But he craved Becker, whose loose lips had turned him into the unwitting projection of Andre's loathing of the game that imprisoned him. The two met again in the semifinal of the US Open, where the mulleted avenger vanquished the smack-talking Teuton in four sets. Trouble was, revenge did nothing to salve the pain that festered behind the fury Andre had unleashed on Becker. After losing to Pete Sampras in the final, Andre fell into a depression that quickly morphed into something approaching a total personal implosion.

An ill-timed recurrence of an old wrist injury didn't help, sidelining Andre from competition and leaving him with too much time to brood. And if he needed something to brood on, he got it when the daughter of Andre's personal trainer and substitute father, Gil Reyes, broke her neck in a snow sledding accident. By this time Andre was engaged to model-actress Brooke Shields, a loveless romance that closely mirrored his relationship with tennis—a matter of doing what he felt was expected of him rather than what he truly wanted—further intensifying his feelings of emptiness and isolation. One night, after squabbling with Brooke over the telephone, Andre smashed all of his tennis trophies in a fit of jealousy, an act whose symbolism wasn't lost on him.

Days later, Andre's personal assistant, a ne'er-do-well former schoolmate he'd hired out of compassion, asked his boss if he'd like to get high. Having never tried any drug stronger than alcohol prior to that day, Andre said yes to crystal meth. And he liked it. Liked it so much, in fact, that it became a habit, as chemical highs so easily do for people who, as a result of childhood trauma, struggle to achieve natural highs through emotional self-regulation.

Andre skipped the first two majors of 1997—the Australian Open and the French Open—but somehow managed to make his way to England for Wimbledon, his least-favorite major on account of its stuffy all-white dress code. Days before the tournament began, however, he abruptly withdrew, citing "vapor lock."

"What the hell does 'vapor lock' mean?" asked his coach of three years, Brad Gilbert.

"I've played this game for a lot of reasons," Andre explained, "and it just seems like none of them has ever been my own."

Now twenty-seven years old, a three-time Grand Slam winner and recently the number one ranked player in the world, Andre should have been hitting his peak, but instead he was in free fall. Trapped between a desire to quit, which he lacked the backbone to act upon, and a manifold obligation to continue, which he resented right down to the marrow of that same spine, he pulled himself together just enough to return to the court, but only to lose, and lose again, exiting four of his next five tournaments in the first round.

After the last of these defeats, Andre received a call from an unknown number. Against his better judgment (he was doing a lot of things against his better judgment in those days), he answered. The caller identified himself as a doctor employed by the Association of Tennis Professionals, whose unpleasant duty it was to inform Andre that trace amounts of methamphetamine had been found in a urine sample he'd given recently as part of the ATP's drug-testing program. Lucky for Andre, the ATP didn't want a scandal any more than he did, and by submitting a half-truthful written confession to his offense, he got off easy, with a three-month suspension and no public exposure. But he paid a heavy price privately, in the dreadful emotional currency of shame. The shame of admitting his drug use to his coach, his trainer, and his wife (yes, he'd gone ahead and married Brooke Shields—against his better judgment). But most of all, the shame of admitting to himself what he'd become.

"Time to change, Andre," he told the man in the mirror, not once but repeatedly, like a sutra. But *could* he change?

FROM INTEROCEPTION TO TRANSCENDENCE

Emotions exist for a reason. They play a critical role in self-regulation, helping us define and prioritize the goals we pursue to fulfill our needs. Emotions tell us how we're doing, what is good and what isn't, and what to move toward and away from. And because we always need to know how we're doing, emotions are omnipresent in human consciousness.

Everything we experience—and I mean everything—is tinged with emotion, including things we tend to think of as purely rational, like solving math problems. If you didn't feel a pinch of frustration while struggling with a differential equation or experience a frisson of elation when at last you solved it, you'd be even worse at math than you actually are.

According to psychologist Lisa Feldman Barrett, who wrote the book on how emotions are made (literally—it's titled *How Emotions Are Made*), emotions start with interoception, or awareness of what's happening in your body. Feeling cold when you step inside a walk-in freezer, feeling wet when you swim, and feeling hungry when your stomach is empty are examples of interoception.

Except not quite. Cold, wet, and hungry are concepts—not raw interoceptive perceptions but categorical summaries thereof. To understand the distinction, ask yourself if you were born knowing the words "cold," "wet," and "hungry." The answer is no. Now ask yourself (or your parents, who will remember better) if you were born with the capacity to feel the sensations these words refer to—if you cried when you felt uncomfortably cold, wet, or hungry. The answer (as your parents will affirm) is yes. We begin life knowing nothing about what we feel, and because of this our feelings are undifferentiated, occupying four basic buckets: good, bad, calm, and aroused. Research shows, for example, that toddlers can't distinguish between sadness and anger. This doesn't mean they feel exactly the same way in both conditions. On a purely interoceptive level, a sad child might experience a sagging of the body, while an angry child might experience a corporeal clenching. On a conceptual level, however, the child feels bad and aroused (uncalm) in both instances because they haven't yet learned the concepts "sad" and "angry."

The scientific word for the proto-emotions that humans share with other animals is "affect." Nonhuman animals never progress beyond affect—feeling either good or bad, aroused or calm. But most humans do, thanks to language. Experiments conducted by Lisa Feldman Barrett and others have demonstrated that children are taught to apply certain emotion concepts to their interoceptive experiences by their parents, teachers, and other adults. Emotions are inseparable from the words we give to them, which is why our emotional repertoire expands as we mature and why not all emotions exist in all cultures.

Emotions are also predictive in nature. In fact, consciousness in general is predictive in nature, beginning with our perceptions. We see and hear not what is really there but what we *expect* to see and hear based on prior conditioning. Only when our expectations are thwarted through brain tricks—such as neuroscientist Edward Adelson's famous checkerboard shadow illusion (examples of which you can find via internet search)—do we recognize that the reality we perceive is largely constructed by our minds.

What's true of our perceptions is also true of our emotions. When a particular experience triggers a certain set of interoceptive changes in a person, the brain's so-called control network quickly sifts through similar past experiences and selects the most appropriate emotion concept. We tend to think that the interoceptive changes we perceive *are* the emotion, but that's not the case. One person might interpret a given set of feelings as contempt, while another person who experiences precisely the same feelings but doesn't know what contempt is interprets them as anger, and a third person who experiences the same feelings and *does* know what contempt is but doesn't identify with this emotion interprets them as resentment.

I started this discussion on emotions by stating that they help us identify and prioritize goals. This is not how the average person thinks about emotions, but from a self-regulatory perspective, it's the whole story: emotions would not exist without goals—nor goals without emotions. We've talked a lot about goals in this book. That's because self-regulation (i.e., having your shit together) is central to athletic achievement, and goals are central to self-regulation. Emotions are one of three basic means by which humans self-regulate (the other two being thoughts and actions). When our brains construct emotions, they do so for the sake of first selecting and then facilitating a goal for a given situation. Returning to the previous example, a person's brain might construct an instance of contempt to facilitate the goal of retaliating against the person whose behavior triggered this emotion, or the goal of disassociating from this person, or the goal of not making the same mistake twice by getting entangled with a similar type of person in the future. But while the specific goal of the emotion may vary by circumstance, the underlying function doesn't.

Psychologists today use the term "emotional intelligence" to designate the ability to deploy emotion skillfully toward the purpose of defining and pursuing goals. In the past, the same ability was more often labeled "emotional maturity." Frankly, I prefer the older term because it better captures the developmental nature of emotional self-regulation. Intelligence is an attribute, maturation a process. You can't fix stupid, but we all grow emotionally as we move through life. Well, most of us. From here on, if you please, think "emotional maturity" when you read "emotional intelligence."

THE NINE STAGES OF EMOTIONAL DEVELOPMENT

In a 2018 paper published in *Behavioral Science*, psychologists Athanasios Drigas and Chara Papoutsi presented "A New Layered Model of Emotional Intelligence" that outlines the normal course of emotional development. The model comprises nine sequential stages stacked hierarchically in the form of a pyramid. Each of us starts at the base of the pyramid, and we must master each stage of development before ascending to the next. None of us, in other words, is born with a high capacity for emotional self-regulation. Some of us, however, begin life with strong *potential* in this area, ascending more quickly through the various stages of emotional development. But even those with the greatest potential need time to grow into full self-regulatory maturity.

For athletes, there are clear benefits associated with rising toward the apex of Drigas and Papoutsi's pyramid, and there are decided disadvantages in being stuck at lower levels of development as Andre Agassi was in the first half of his professional tennis career. One of Andre's favorite films is *Shadowlands*, a biographical drama about the writer C. S. Lewis, who once wrote, "God doesn't want us to suffer, he wants us to grow up." The movie resonated with Andre because it made him realize that what he wanted for himself more than anything was just that—to grow up. Was this recognition an early sign of his potential for emotional self-regulation? Likely so, and to the extent that Andre did earnestly desire to grow up, it was inevitable that he would, eventually. Let's have a look at the nine stages of emotional development and see how Andre benefited, athletically and otherwise, from his arduous ascent of the pyramid.

Stage One: "Emotional Stimuli"

As we've seen already, emotions begin with interoception, which supplies the stimuli for constructing emotions. You might assume that all of us are equally good at feeling what's going on in our bodies, but if you do, you're wrong! There is in fact a high degree of individual variation in interoceptive sensitivity, and elite athletes happen to be really good at feeling what's going on in their bodies—or more accurately, at learning to feel what's going on in their bodies in ways that facilitate performance in their chosen sport—which indeed is one of the reasons they're elite athletes.

Andre Agassi was no exception, as we see in the rationale he gives for using a custom racket grip made and remade to his precise specifications. "My grip is as personal as my thumbprint," he explains in his memoir, "a byproduct not just of my hand shape and finger length but the size of my calluses and the force of my squeeze . . . A millimeter difference, near the end of a four-hour match, can feel as irritating and distracting as a pebble in my shoe." A millimeter difference! You can't get more sensitive than that.

Stage Two: "Emotional Recognition, Perception/Expression of Emotions"

It's one thing to be attuned to your body, another thing be able to interpret and express what you feel in goal-serving ways. People whose capacity for recognizing emotions is poorly developed experience them in black-and-white terms. They're either sad or happy or mad or scared, and that's about all. Contrast this to the kaleidoscope of complex and nuanced emotions experienced by those with a highly developed capacity for emotion recognition. Lisa Feldman Barrett refers to this phenomenon as "emotional granularity," a cognitive capability that gives those favored with it "many more options for predicting, categorizing and perceiving emotion, providing [them] with the tools for more flexible and functional responses."

Throughout his autobiography, Andre Agassi demonstrates an exceptional degree of emotional granularity. Here's how he describes his emotional state after winning his first Grand Slam, the 1992 Wimbledon Championship: "I'm unnerved by how giddy I feel. It shouldn't matter this much. It shouldn't feel this good. Waves of emotion continue to wash over me, relief and elation and even a kind of hysterical serenity, because I've finally earned a brief respite from the critics, especially the internal ones." In much the same way that a master sommelier can identify eight distinct flavors in a sip of wine, Andre is able to perceive multiple layers of emotion in moments of intense experience. Though his worst days lay ahead of him, we see in this episode Andre's potential to harness his emotions in the service of his best interests, both on and off the court.

Stage Three: "Self-Awareness"

At lower levels of emotional maturity, we live inside our emotions. Our gladness is all around us, like a sunny day, our sadness inescapable, like a rainstorm. But when we reach stage three in the process of emotional maturation, we gain the cognitive ability to step outside our emotions—to observe ourselves experiencing gladness or sadness or whatever. When we experience emotions from the inside, they control us, like the weather. But when we're able to gain distance on our emotions, we have more options for how to behave. We still feel the emotion, of course, but objectifying it allows us to consider a variety of ways to react and to select the option that moves us furthest toward our goal.

Andre Agassi did not lack for self-awareness, even before he hit rock bottom. If anything, he was *too* self-aware, as his coach recognized. "Stop thinking about yourself and your own game," Gilbert told him, "and remember that the guy on the other side of the net has weaknesses. You don't have to be the best in the world every time you go out there. You just have to be better than one guy."

It was here that Andre got stuck in his emotional development, hence also in his development as a tennis player. Years and years of relentless criticism from Mike Agassi had trained Andre to turn his attention inward, to seek and destroy his own errors and faults in emulation of his father. Research has shown that the well-known sports phenomenon of choking, or underperforming under pressure, is caused by hyper-self-consciousness. Failed parenting rendered Andre hyper self-conscious on the tennis court, and it cost him. Notably, he lost his first three Grand Slam semifinals, his first three Grand Slam finals, and his first four five-set matches—numbers that defy the odds, and not in a good way. Numbers that signal a choker.

Andre is able to pinpoint the precise moment he became a choker. He was eight years old and already getting a bit cocky, having cruised through his first seven tournaments with an unblemished record despite facing mostly older opponents. But in his eighth junior competition he tasted defeat for the first time, and its bitterness remained on his tongue long afterward—far longer than it should have. "After years of hearing my father rant at my flaws," he writes, "one loss has caused me to take up his rant. I've internalized my father—his perfectionism, his rage—until his voice doesn't just feel like my own, it is my own. From this day on, I don't need my father to torture me. I can do it all by myself." To grow as a person and as a tennis player, Andre needed to get out of his own head, and to do that he needed to get Mike Agassi out of his head.

Stage Four: "Emotional Management"

To take full advantage of the freedom afforded by self-awareness (as distinct from hyper self-consciousness), a person must be skilled in managing emotions. As Drigas and Papoutsi explain, "Self-management allows you to control your reactions so that you are not driven by impulsive behaviors and feelings." Before he bottomed out, Andre Agassi struggled mightily in this area, most especially with the rage he internalized from his dad. "I can't let go of my sudden anger," he recalls of a match against Daniel Nestor in 1997, when his downward spiral was approaching terminal velocity. Giving in to the emotion, Andre intentionally whacked a ball clear out of the stadium, reverting to the tactics he'd used as a lad to protest his father's endless Dragon sessions. But Mike Agassi was elsewhere, and in his place sat the chair umpire, who issued a warning. Andre dropped an f-bomb in retort and was promptly disqualified.

This regrettable incident had no precedent in Andre's career, nor was it repeated. But on countless other occasions, his inability to manage his emotions cost him points, sets, matches, and tournaments. As previously noted, studies have established a strong link between emotional stability and athletic achievement. Andre was never going to realize his full potential as a tennis player unless he matured in this area.

Stages Five and Six: "Social Awareness, Empathy, Discrimination of Emotions/Social Skills, Expertise in Emotions"

Once we've learned how to manage our own emotions, we are ready to learn how to read (step five in the process of emotional maturation) and influence (step six) others' emotions. Useful in any social context, these advanced emotional skills are as advantageous to the tennis player as a 140 mph serve. Ask any master of the game and they will tell you that getting inside your opponent's head is half the battle. Andre's father used to call this "putting a blister on the other guy's brain," which I must admit is a nice turn of phrase.

Perceptive by nature, Andre showed tremendous promise in the area of psychological warfare. Like a veteran poker player, he could easily identify other players' tells. For example, he always knew where Boris Becker's next serve was going based on which way his exposed tongue pointed during his windup. But as Brad Gilbert noted, Andre's ability to get inside opponents' heads was hampered by his being too much inside his own head. To fully command the art of putting blisters on other players' brains, Andre needed to heal the blisters on his own brain.

Stage Seven: "Universality of Emotions, Self-Actualization"

The self-actualization stage of emotional development, according to Drigas and Papoutsi, is reached by those who discover who they truly are emotionally, and who feel empowered by this realization to move toward becoming their true selves. Andre Agassi views his entire life as a quest to discover and become who he really is. The story he tells in *Open* is fundamentally that of a man boy who does not know who he is, wants desperately to solve the mystery of himself, and suffers immensely in his long quest to self-actualize. It begins at the end, so to speak, on the morning of Andre's last victory before retiring, with the tone-setting words, "I open my eyes and don't know where I am or who I am. Not that unusual—I've spent half my life not knowing."

There's a difference between not knowing who you are and not caring, however, and only in his darkest hour did Andre stop caring, an hour of which he writes, "I've given up on understanding myself." Thankfully, Andre had what it took to move past this instant of apathetic surrender and continue the journey toward finding himself.

Stages Eight and Nine: "Transcendence and Emotional Unity"

Drigas and Papoutsi describe these last two stages of emotional development in distinctly spiritual terms. The person who reaches the transcendence stage "helps others to self-actualize, find self-fulfillment, and realize their potential." Sounds wonderful, doesn't it? But it gets better. The lucky soul who takes the ninth and final step to emotional unity, they propose, "feels intense joy, peace, prosperity, and a consciousness of ultimate truth and the unity of all things."

It can be no accident that Andre got his first taste of transcendence at his lowest point, when he was ranked 141st in the world and facing a drug suspension from the ATP. It happened in a hospital room, where Gil Reyes's daughter, Kacey, was recovering from a second neck surgery, the first one having been botched. Moved by compassion, Andre raced out to a nearby toy store and bought an inflatable inner tube that he used to reposition Kacey's head, reducing her suffering a mite. "A look of pure relief, and gratitude, and joy, washes over her face," he recalls, "and in this look, in this courageous little girl, I find the thing I've been seeking, the philosopher's stone that unites all the experiences, good and bad, of the last few years . . . How many times must I be shown? This is why we're here. To fight through the pain and, when possible, to relieve the pain of others. So simple. So hard to see."

Having seen it, Andre could never go back, nor did he want to. Within weeks of this epiphany, he'd set up a charitable foundation centered on a charter school for at-risk youth. This is how one of the greatest comebacks in sports history began—with a giving gesture that had nothing to do with athletics. *God wants us to grow up.*

KNOW YOUR BUTTERFLIES

Throughout his comeback, Andre Agassi focused his attention almost exclusively on emotional self-regulation, trusting that as his mental state improved, his performance on the tennis court would follow. On Gilbert's recommendation, he started at the very bottom, gorging himself on humble pie by playing in so-called challenger tournaments, the lowest level of professional tennis, where players have to fetch their own balls. Right away, Andre noticed a difference. Motivated now by something bigger than himself—his desire to bring attention to his new charter school—he shifted from playing not to lose to playing to win, a reversal of his prior incentive structure. He competed with a sense of gratitude but also a sense of mission, the combination of which kept him calm and focused.

At the 1998 Wimbledon Championship, Andre was robbed of a critical point by a linesman's error. Instead of arguing, he laughed it off. Andre's media critics—of which there were many—couldn't believe what they were seeing. *Who is this bald-headed nice guy,* they wondered, *and what has he done with the mulleted brat we knew and hated?* One month later, at the du Maurier Open in Toronto, Andre blew a comfortable lead to Richard Krajicek and lost the match. Instead of brooding on the defeat for weeks afterward, as the pre-implosion Andre would have done, he said to his coach, "That's tennis, right?"

I'd be overstating things a bit if I told you Andre emerged from his darkest hour as a fully transcendent emotional finished product. Growth is a process, after all, not a miracle drug that instantly induces eternal bliss. In fact, eternal bliss isn't even the goal of emotional maturation, as Andre's close friend and spiritual advisor John Parenti—a one-time Christian pastor who left the pulpit to become a Hollywood music producer—explained to him during one of their many late-night tête-à-têtes. Having described to Parenti his newfound confidence on the court, a serene self-assurance rooted in his fresh sense of purpose, Andre asked him, "So, how come I still feel all this fear? Doesn't the fear ever go away?" To which Parenti answered, "I hope not. Fear is your fire, Andre. I wouldn't want to see you if it ever completely went out."

This was good advice, and Andre got similar counsel from Gil Reyes, who often urged Andre to "seek the pain, woo the pain, recognize that pain is life." An athlete cannot achieve greatness without experiencing negative emotions such as fear, anger, and disappointment. What separates the greats from the almosts is not how often these emotions are felt but how they are managed. As Drigas and Papoutsi caution in their discussion of the self-management stage of emotional development: "This does not mean that you must crush your negative emotions, but if you [recognize] them, you can amend your behavior and make small or big changes to the way you react and manage your feelings even if the latter is negative."

Perhaps the earliest sign that Andre had what it took to achieve champion-level emotional maturity was his recognition of emotional maturity in others. Long before he became the person he wanted to be, he caught glimpses of that person in folks he came across in his life as a professional tennis player, and when he did, he latched on to them. Gil Reyes, John Parenti, Brad Gilbert, and eventually Steffi Graf, the German tennis star who became his second wife in 2001—showed him the way to his true self, which was also the way to total fulfillment of his potential as an athlete.

In 1999, Andre made the final of the French Open, his first Grand Slam final appearance in four years. Facing Ukraine's Andrei Medvedev, he lost the first set six games to one and the second set six games to two, and in the third set he found himself just five points away from defeat after missing five consecutive serves. It was another classic Andre Agassi emotional implosion.

Except it wasn't. At a moment when Andre once would have lost control, he took control, rallying to win the set, the match, and the tournament, becoming only the fifth male tennis player to win all four Grand Slam events, as well as the first (and still the only) athlete to win these tournaments plus the ATP Year-End Championship and an Olympic gold medal. He went on to compete in seven more Grand Slam finals, winning four of them. And despite all his ups and downs, to this day no tennis player has equaled Andre's consistency at the US Open, his first and last Grand Slam, where he played twenty-one years in a row.

In the second round of his twenty-first and last US Open, Andre faced Marcos Baghdatis of Cyprus. His account of the match, which bookends his memoir, shows just how far he has come in his emotional growth. Before the match, Andre observed Baghdatis loosening up in the changing room and thought, *"He's doing too much. He's antsy."* Later, Andre exploited this piece of emotional intel by slightly delaying his entry to center court, creating separation between the crowd's polite cheers for Baghdatis and its raucous welcome of Andre, once the most reviled tennis player in the world and now the most beloved, owing to his maturation. "Without hitting a single ball I've caused a major swing in his sense of well-being," he notes.

Andre himself had a tummy full of butterflies, but this wasn't a problem. "Butterflies are funny," he writes. "Some days they make you run to the toilet. Other days they make you horny. Other days they make you laugh, and long for the fight. Deciding which type of butterflies you've got . . . is the first order of business when you're driving to the arena. Figuring out your butterflies, deciphering what they say about the status of your mind and body, is the first step to making them work for you."

You can't ask for a clearer demonstration of what emotional intelligence looks like in a great athlete. But you *can* ask how personality influences the "screw loose" and "shit together" components of later talent, and the answer's coming at you like an Andre Agassi overhand smash.

(He beat Baghdatis in five sets, by the way.)

CHAPTER SIX

The Right Stuff

**A multiple personality is in a
certain sense normal.**
—GEORGE HERBERT MEAD

Sergey Bubka was born under the zodiac sign of Sagittarius, on the eighth day of December in 1963. In Western astrology, this particular sign is represented by the centaur, a hybrid of two very different beings: man and horse. Astrology is bullshit, of course, yet throughout his life, Sergey—who set an astonishing thirty-five world records in the pole vault between 1984 and 1994—has seemed centaur-like to those who know him, two disparate natures inhabiting a single body.

"What makes Sergey so extraordinary is the two opposite traits he has," said his longtime sport psychologist Boris Tulchinsky in a 1988 interview. "It is strange to see in one man so strong a nature with so subtle a soul. He feels small nuances deeply."

Had you encountered Sergey during his athletic prime, you would have been struck at first by his feral intensity, a caged-beast quality that expressed itself through ceaseless fidgeting, pacing, and darting of the eyes. Conscious of his restiveness but powerless to contain it, he joked that he felt sorry for anyone unlucky enough to sit behind him in a movie theater. It's hard to imagine a personality less suited to the pole vault, an event that, at championship-level track-and-field meets, often takes several hours to complete and consists almost entirely of sitting around and waiting for your next turn to jump. But when it came time to compete, Sergey suddenly transformed into something far more resembling a lamb on quaaludes than a feral beast. Whereas most elite pole vaulters of his day tried to stay loose between attempts to clear the bar, stretching and twitching and whatnot, Sergey did the exact opposite, shutting down almost to the point of inertness. To the bafflement of his competitors, he would lie completely still, often *facedown* on the grass infield, corpse-like, until his turn came, and then he would streak down the runway and catapult over some great height like a force of nature, beautiful and terrifying and utterly unstoppable.

Sergey's two-sided nature came from his parents, most likely. His mother, Valentia, worked as a nurse in Voroshilovgrad, the sooty mining town in eastern Ukraine where Sergey was raised. Described in one magazine article as "kind and generous, easily moved to tears," she was as different from her husband, Nazar Bubka, as a man is from a horse. Surly, brooding, and infectiously unhappy, Comrade Bubka served as a corporal in the Red Army, and his life's purpose, it seemed to Sergey, was to ensure that his wife and children experienced as little joy as he did. Picture him in the family's drab, government-issued apartment, chain-smoking cheap Russian cigarettes in unbroken silence, except when moved to bark a command or to reprimand the perpetrator of some small breach of the barracks-level order he imposed at home. Nothing Sergey ever did was good enough for Papa—not his chores, nor his school performance, nor even his athletic achievements. At night in bed he often heard his father shouting, his mother weeping, pleading.

Sergey was fifteen years old when his parents split. By then he'd already discovered the pole vault, having developed a fascination for track and field's weirdest event (believed to have originated in the practice of using long sticks to leap across Dutch canals) six years earlier when a schoolmate described to him its basic elements: the stiff-armed runway dash, the perilous bowing of the stick, the acrobatic flight. In Sergey's impressionable young mind there formed a vision of vertical escape, a vision so irresistible that he immediately tracked down the local pole vault coach, Vitaly Petrov, and convinced him to waive a state-mandated minimum-age requirement and teach him to soar.

The boy's aptitude for the discipline he would come to personify revealed itself almost immediately. The pole vault requires a sprinter's fleetness, and Sergey had it, once clocking 10.2 seconds for 100 meters. It also demands a gymnast's strength, and Sergey had that as well, launching a sixteen-pound shot forty-four feet before dropping other field events to focus on his specialty. Intelligence, too, is rewarded in the pole vault. It's pure physics, after all, and Sergey approached his craft like a physicist, engineering techniques—such as a higher hand placement on the pole, which afforded better leverage—that remain in use today. But what set him apart most of all was the depth of his *need* to vault. As he explained it to one interviewer, "I pole vault from the bottom of my heart."

The 1983 IAAF World Outdoor Championships were held in Helsinki, Finland. Sergey arrived as a complete unknown and left as the world champion, aged nineteen. The following January, in Vilnius, Lithuania, he set his first world record, vaulting 5.81 meters (19 feet, ¾ inch) indoors. Four months later, at a meet in Bratislava, Czechoslovakia, he set his first outdoor world record—and he was just getting started. Over the next eleven years, Sergey would set sixteen more world records outdoors and another seventeen indoors.

HOW TO EAT AN ELEPHANT

How does a man set thirty-five world records in the pole vault? The same way he eats an elephant, according to a familiar expression: one bite at a time. Or, in this case, one centimeter at a time. Sometimes two. But never more than six.

In any sport, setting records has measurable value. Athletes who go faster, farther, or higher than anyone else has ever done are rewarded not just reputationally but also financially. In the rigidly egalitarian socioeconomic system in which Sergey Bubka operated, where wealth was distributed evenly across the population (at least in theory), world-record bonuses were the athlete's most reliable means of getting ahead. Each new mark Sergey set earned him the 1980s ruble equivalent of $385—a pittance by capitalist standards but sufficient on his side of the iron curtain to raise his standard of living meaningfully. Then came the fall of the Soviet empire, ushering in a new era of opportunity for the world's second most recognizable track athlete (after Carl Lewis), one Sergey didn't waste, jilting longtime sponsor Adidas in 1992 for free-spending Nike, who'd promised him vastly larger sums for record-setting vaults—up to $100,000, according to some reports. The last six of Sergey's three dozen world bests were set under this new contract, which explains why he drove a better car than most Ukrainians in those days.

By raising the bar (literally) in such tiny increments, Sergey Bubka displayed impressive shrewdness, milking his talent for all it was worth monetarily. But it took more than shrewdness to slow-walk his ascent to 6.15 meters. When Sergey said he pole vaulted from the heart, he meant it, and his heart's desire was to go full gas in pursuit of his ultimate limit. Financial self-interest alone could not have made him throttle back. Also needed was the basic psychological wherewithal to act against his heart's desire, whether it was for the sake of money or any other reward that he valued highly, but not as much as he valued his life's calling.

No athlete reaches the level of greatness Sergey did without a burning desire to reach the absolute zenith of their potential. In his case, this meant finding out just how high he could vault. But in choosing to eat the proverbial elephant one bite at a time, he deliberately held back from flying as high as he could on any given day. If you look at video footage of Sergey's record-setting vaults—including his last, an outdoor leap of 6.14 meters (20 feet, 1¾ inches) in Sestriere, Italy, in July 1994, which would remain unsurpassed for nearly a quarter century—you will see that in many cases he clears the bar with plenty of room to spare. IAAF rules allow vaulters to keep trying until they fail three times at a given height, even when the athlete has already won the competition. But Sergey often quit before he failed, saving something for the next meet. Tellingly, the title of his 1987 biography translates from Russian to English as *An Attempt in Reserve*. Bowing out with something left in reserve—not once but repeatedly—must have required a tremendous effort of will from a man who once said of his profession,

"I want to be an artist of the pole vault. I want to create something new and unusual. I want to break barriers."

Rarely is such restraint seen in a person as intensely competitive as Sergey Bubka. Among great athletes, however, Sergey's mix of fiery competitiveness and cool discipline is downright commonplace. Like other great athletes raised in a toxic home environment, Sergey survived and overcame the challenges he faced by cultivating an insatiable hunger to prove his worth, and the pole vault became his preferred vehicle for doing so. "I love it because the results are immediate and the strongest is the winner," he told *Sports Illustrated* writer Gary Smith. "In everyday life that is difficult to prove."

Warm and well-mannered in most contexts, Sergey turned downright ornery on the rare occasion when his dominance was threatened by a competitor, and not just ornery but vicious on the even rarer occasion when he was beaten, as he was by Billy Olson at the 1986 Millrose Games. "He's never won a major competition, an Olympic Games, or a world championship," Bubka said of the victorious American at a post-meet press conference. "He hasn't even made the Olympic national team. If he was in a major competition, he wouldn't know which way to go on the runway." Having enjoyed cordial relations with Sergey prior to this outburst, Olson felt blindsided by the Ukrainian's sudden animus. But Sergey's coach—the same Vitaly Petrov he'd been working with since he was ten—understood. "He *has* to be first in everything," Petrov said years after this unisolated incident.

By an odd twist of fate, Sergey became a passive witness to his own final defeat in the discipline he personified. After leaving the sport at age thirty-seven, he founded an event called Pole Vault Stars that he hosted each year in the city of Donetsk, where in 1978 he had moved alone as a teenager to chase a dream, and where, five years later, his triumphal return by rail from the world championship was greeted by cheering throngs bearing roses, the city's symbol, and where, in 2001, he had celebrated the completion of his unparalleled career. And it was there, too, that, on the night of February 15, 2014, Frenchman Renaud Lavillenie cleared a height of 6.16 meters, eclipsing Sergey's outdoor world record by two centimeters and his lifetime best (set indoors) by one centimeter. The TV broadcast of the event cut quickly from Lavillenie standing on the crash mat with hands clasping his head in joyous disbelief to Sergey rising from his seat and applauding, his lips stretched in a smile that, frankly, appeared more than a little strained.

Back in 1984, at a meet in Rome, another Frenchman, Thierry Vigneron, broke Sergey's outdoor record when it stood much lower. On that occasion, however, Sergey was not only present but also competing.

"One minute," he said to American pole vaulter Larry Jessee in unfazed English as Vigneron celebrated. "It will be okay."

And he was right. Technically, though, it took Sergey ten minutes—not one—to get the record back.

"Without a rival to equal me, I will never show my potential completely," he told one reporter. "Sometimes it appears other vaulters' results are near to mine, but in reality they are not near at all. Often I jump only what I need to jump to win. If the world record were 6.20 right now, I'd jump 6.30. That is simply the way I am."

Renaud Lavillenie hadn't quite jumped 6.20, but he had moved Sergey to number two on the all-time list as the retired legend watched helplessly from above. At fifty, with thinning hair and crow's feet, he seemed otherwise very much the same man who simply could not tolerate second place, wanting nothing more than to grab a pole and show that gloating parvenu who was truly best. Perhaps the only thing that stopped him was the expensive suit he wore.

FROM NEEDS TO GOALS AND REPRESENTATIONS

To be fair, astrology does have some basis in reality. In its recognition of personality as something that is conferred rather than chosen, its identification of distinct personality types, and its acknowledgment that seemingly contradictory traits may coexist within a personality like Sergey Bubka's, horoscopic psychology has been validated to some degree by modern empirical psychology. But the idea that our personalities derive from planetary alignments has not been validated by science, and the twelve signs of the zodiac do nothing to explain the minds of great athletes, or anyone else, for that matter. Science, however, does.

Vestiges of astrological thinking persist in the layperson's understanding of personality, despite all we've learned. There's a tendency still to think of personality as being distinct from our animal nature, expressing a person's unique, intangible soul rather than our common, creaturely needs. In fact, though, personality is nothing more than a sophisticated, language-enhanced version of animal behavior. Or so say the experts.

We've caught glimpses of the scientific perspective on personality already in this book. In Chapter 2, Stuart Ross informed us that "personality . . . can be viewed as a collection of reactions during emotional development, each deriving its characteristic features as an adaptation within the developmental environment." And remember Marc Lewis, the neuroscientist and former drug addict who believes that addiction is a normal manifestation of the mind's propensity to form habits? In *The Biology of Desire*, Lewis points to personality as another manifestation of this same propensity, writing, "I could summarize who you are, in the simplest terms, by listing your most distinct habits . . . And one way to capture those habits is with the word 'personality' . . . Isn't that what we do when someone asks us, 'What's he or she like?'"

Neither Ross nor Lewis would call himself an expert on the subject of personality. But Stanford psychologist Carol Dweck certainly is. Her seminal 2017 paper "From Needs to Goals and Representations: Foundations for a Unified Theory of Motivation, Personality, and Development" leaves plenty of unanswered questions on the topic, as Dweck herself acknowledges, but the ideas it presents are highly useful in fleshing out my theory of athletic greatness. In line with mainstream thinking in her field, Dweck believes that personality is rooted in basic psychological needs. Although it is impossible to cleanly disentangle biological needs from psychological needs (you may recall that Abraham Maslow's hierarchy of human needs encompasses both), Dweck argues that certain needs are primarily psychological in nature and are the main drivers of personality.

Of these needs, exactly three meet Dweck's definition of "basic," meaning they are present from birth; they cannot be reduced to other, even more basic needs; and they *must* be satisfied to ensure well-being and optimal development. Only the need for predictability, the need for competence, and the need for acceptance, according to Dweck, possess all of these characteristics. "Why might these particular needs be built in?" she asks. Here's her answer:

> Infants must know how their world works (prediction) and they must learn how to act on the world (competence). This learning will lead to effective functioning over time. But there is a long period during which infants, while surprisingly smart, are largely incompetent when it comes to many behaviors necessary for their survival and well-being, such as coordinated goal-oriented actions and self-regulation. Other people must help them perform these functions. Thus, part of the world— other people—is separated from the rest of the world as a special

case. Infants must know whether people will be responsive to them when they are needy or in distress, and how they can best make this happen (acceptance).

There's plenty of evidence that humans come factory equipped with needs for predictability, competence, and acceptance. Clues to a hardwired need for predictability are found in studies showing that newborn babies are able to identify and adapt to linked events—learning, for example, to close their eyes in response to hearing a certain tone after having received a puff of air to the face each time they heard it previously. Other experiments have found that babies prefer learning new tasks to repeating easier tasks they've already mastered, which wouldn't happen if the need for competence wasn't innate (and explains why athletes tend to settle on the sport in which they improve quickest even if it's not their favorite). Something else that babies show a strong preference for is human contact, attending to faces and voices above all other environmental stimuli—indications of an instinctive need for acceptance.

What makes a need a need, naturally, is that our well-being depends on it, and the leading psychology journals are filled with proof that our well-being suffers when our needs for predictability, competence, and acceptance are thwarted. One example of the harm caused by a lack of acceptance, cited in Dweck's paper, is a 2007 meta-analysis conducted by Bryce McLeod and colleagues at Virginia Commonwealth University, which reported that various forms of parental rejection in early childhood increased the risk of developing anxiety disorders later in life.

Other psychological needs emerge from the admixture of the three basic needs, Dweck suggests. The need for predictability and the need for competence combine to produce a need for control. The need for predictability and the need for acceptance come together to generate a need for trust. And the need for competence and the need for acceptance merge to produce needs for self-esteem and status. Finally, the confluence of all these psychological needs yields a need for self-coherence, as Dweck calls it—a meta-need that we experience as a desire for personal identity and a hunger for meaning.

While not basic in the sense of being present from birth, these other needs are no less needful, causing equal damage to our well-being when unfulfilled. They differ from the basic needs only in that they are more sophisticated and require a certain amount of prior development before they kick in. For example, the need for self-esteem or status presupposes a sense of self and the ability to compare oneself to others, faculties that don't appear in humans until around the second year of life.

Dweck's theory of personality postulates that the seven psychological needs we've just identified—predictability, competence, acceptance, trust, control, self-esteem/status, and self-coherence—exist in every person who develops beyond the infant stage of intellect. Yet we don't all have the same personality. How is it that these universal psychological needs give rise to diverse personalities? Dweck proposes that two factors—first, our individual temperaments (irrespective of shared needs, some babies are naturally fussy while others are mellow, some sociable and others reserved, some as timid as others are intrepid), and second, our unique life experiences—comingle in unique ways in each individual, causing us to place more or less value on particular needs, to set different kinds of goals to satisfy our needs, and to pursue these goals in different ways and with diverse styles.

Dweck's theory goes on to specify two distinct components of personality. The first consists of "patterns of thoughts, feelings, and behaviors that accompany need-fulfilling goal pursuit." That's the part that others see and upon which we base our assessments of other people's personalities. The second component sits behind these visible expressions of personality and is made up of mental representations of three types: beliefs, emotions, and action tendencies (or "BEATs," collectively). Conditioned by past experiences, these mental representations constitute a kind of personal tool kit that people pull from in evaluating needs and setting and pursuing goals.

An example from Dweck's prior work on mindsets is the belief that talent is either fixed at birth ("fixed mindset") or can be cultivated through hard work ("growth mindset"). In a series of experiments, Dweck and her collaborators were able to show that these beliefs affect how individuals try to satisfy their need for competence. Specifically, those who believe their talents are fixed tend to shy away from challenges and give up quickly in the face of obstacles and setbacks, whereas those who believe their talents can increase do the opposite. Sergey Bubka clearly had a growth mindset, believing the sky was the limit (literally) for his vaulting.

Dweck's theory of personality allows us to effectively deconstruct the various personality traits we observe in one other. Take neuroticism, for example. This personality trait expresses itself through anxiety, hypervigilance, self-soothing, and avoidant coping. Dweck proposes that neurotic behaviors are how people try to satisfy their need for control when they believe the world is dangerous and largely beyond their control—a belief that is almost always animated by adverse childhood experiences.

The thing I like especially about Dweck's theory of personality is that it makes sense of how a single person can possess seemingly contradictory personality traits, including Sergey's yin/yang combination of fiery competitiveness and cool restraint. If it's true that personality traits form around basic psychological needs, which are highly disparate, then it's not surprising to see highly disparate traits jumbled together in a cohesive self. As Dweck herself explains it, seemingly contradictory traits like competitiveness and restraint "are not incompatible because different traits can arise within different need domains (e.g., conscientiousness arises within the competence and control needs, whereas extraversion arises within social needs) and because BEATs and traits can be context-specific such that a person might be passively agreeable in some social settings and assertively extroverted in others."

TRAITS OF THE GREATS

All of this is quite interesting. But what you and I really want to know is which constellations of personality traits appear uniquely in great athletes, and whether these traits match up with the "screw loose" and "shit together" traits I've claimed are essential to athletic greatness. Thus far, we have studied the psychology of great athletes largely through the lens of self-regulation. What's nice about Dweck's theory of personality is that it looks at personality through the same lens. Self-regulation, you will recall, is defined as "the dynamic process of determining a desired end state (i.e., a goal) and then taking action to move toward it while monitoring progress along the way." Goals are equally central to Dweck's theory of personality, which proposes that "as individuals experience needs and pursue need-fulfilling goals, they form representations of their experiences. These representations then serve as guides on how to fulfill the needs of the individual as they navigate life. As such, they help turn latent needs into active goals and thus are at the heart of motivation (and personality)." Personality, then, is a person's individual style of self-regulating.

Hence, it should be possible to recast the two defining mental traits of great athletes—"screw loose" and "shit together," which are also need based and goal directed—as personality traits. Our efforts in this direction are aided by a bountiful scientific literature on personality in elite athletes. The first thing that jumps out at us when we delve into this research is the consistent finding that elite athletes are different from other athletes (and even more different from nonathletes) in terms of personality. As the researchers themselves put it, *personality is strongly predictive of athletic achievement.*

It's not easy to design and execute a study that reliably answers the question of whether (and how) personality contributes to athletic achievement. It requires that groups of athletes be monitored over the course of many years, and that other factors that contribute to performance—in particular physical ability (aka early talent)—be controlled for. The most enlightening studies of this kind recruit elite junior athletes as subjects and track them as they strive toward the professional level, then sift the data for correlations between specific personality traits and fulfillment of promise.

One such study followed thirty-two members of a junior championship–winning Australian rules football team over a period of seven years. At the outset of the experiment, a standard personality inventory was used to measure sixteen different components of each athlete's personality, and coach assessments were used to rate their physical ability and potential. Seven years later, the study's author, Eugene Aidman of the University of Sydney, sought out his now-adult subjects to see how they were faring. Two distinct metrics were used to evaluate relative progress, one of them objective (specifically, whether or not the athlete had successfully ascended to the senior league), the other subjective (an evaluation provided by the athlete's former junior coach).

Seven years is a long time to wait for the other shoe to drop, but Aidman's wait turned out to be worthwhile. Of the thirty-two athletes included in the study, thirteen made it to the senior AFL (Australian Football League), achieving varying degrees of success at the professional level. A statistical analysis revealed that coach assessments of physical ability and potential were 59.4 percent accurate in predicting matriculation to the senior league. "This accuracy is not much better than random prediction obtainable by flipping a coin," Aidman noted.

Personality was another story. As a group, the thirty-two footballers differed from their peers in the general population in a number of dimensions of personality. That alone is quite remarkable. But even more striking is the fact that, within this group of elite athletes, the thirteen players who made it to the senior AFL also differed from the nineteen who didn't make the cut in a few key ways. Most notably, the footballers who were able to take that final step exhibited higher levels of conscientiousness, a trait the American Psychological Association has defined as "the propensity to follow socially prescribed norms for impulse control, to be goal directed, to plan, and to be able to delay gratification." In combination, this key difference in personality between the two groups, and a couple others we'll get to presently, predicted successful matriculation to the senior AFL with 84.4 percent accuracy.

Similar findings were obtained by Pamela Karp in a study of elite ice hockey players. The same personality inventory was used to measure the traits of 126 athletes drafted into the National Hockey League between 1987 and 1994. Additionally, Karp talked to team scouts and collected their assessments of each player's physical ability, then waited five years to see which was the better predictor of a player's success in the NHL: personality or physical ability. The results aligned perfectly with those Eugene Aidman later obtained in a different sport on a distant continent. According to Karp, "Analyses revealed that personality . . . significantly discriminated among players who have achieved or underachieved based upon draft expectations," whereas "physical ability ratings did not significantly contribute to the prediction of professional hockey achievement." Among the strongest predictors of success were the personality traits of boldness (a composite of fearlessness, confidence, and self-assuredness) and competitiveness.

Already we are beginning to see the contours of a signature personality in great athletes—a combination of traits that constitute "the right stuff" for high achievement in sports. In study after study of personality in elite athletes representing a wide range of sports, the same few traits stand out. Adding to this portrait of later talent are the results of a 2021 study published in the *International Journal of Environmental Research and Public Health*. Polish researchers recruited 1,260 athletes as subjects, of whom 118 were classified as "champions." As in the studies already described, a personality assessment was administered to all of the participants. The researchers then looked for statistical differences between the champions and the rest with respect to particular traits. The most striking difference concerned neuroticism. In the blunt words of authors Pawel and Zbigniew Piepiora, "the lower the level of neuroticism, the greater the probability of an athlete being classified as a champion."

Neurotics are known to have a hard time self-regulating. When confronted with challenging or stressful situations, they tend to fixate on their emotional state instead of taking active steps to bring about a desired outcome. They are also more impulsive and less resilient than those who are less neurotic. For these reasons, it's easy to see why neuroticism is a barrier to athletic greatness. To underscore this point, a 2019 study led by Guodong Zhang of China's Southwest University found that, within a group of 210 boxers, higher levels of self-control (a component of self-regulation) were associated with greater competitive success, and the most self-controlled and successful boxers were the least neurotic.

It's obvious that self-regulatory ability cannot issue entirely from an *absence* in one's personality (specifically a lack of neurotic

tendencies). Something else must also be present, and that thing—
one of them, anyway—is conscientiousness. If you know someone you
would describe as really having their shit together, it is likely this person would land above the 80th percentile for conscientiousness in a
standard personality inventory, as do most champion athletes. We've
seen this already in Eugene Aidman's study of Australian rules footballers, and we see it again in the boxing study I just described, which,
in addition to finding negative correlations between neuroticism, self-
control, and competitive performance, identified equally strong positive correlations between conscientiousness and achievement. Experts
on personality in elite athletes were hardly surprised by this particular finding, the *Journal of Sports Sciences* having printed the following
remarks two years before:

> Individuals with high levels of conscientiousness are described
> as orderly, industrious, and disciplined. On the other hand,
> individuals with low levels of conscientiousness are described
> as undisciplined, lacking attention to detail, and unreliable. This
> trait has been positively associated with many types of perfor-
> mance including occupational performance, academic perfor-
> mance, and athletic performance. Conscientiousness is related
> to higher levels of sport achievement, better training and
> preparation, and greater levels of athletic success. Specifically,
> research demonstrates that elite athletes have higher levels of
> conscientiousness when compared to non-professional athletes.
> Additionally, conscientiousness positively predicts quality of
> preparation and increases the likelihood of successful perfor-
> mances. Finally, Piedmont et al. tested the direct relationship
> between conscientiousness and athletic performance in soccer
> players. Results indicated that when combined with neuroticism,

this variable accounted for 23% of the variance in coach ratings of performance. Furthermore, conscientiousness independently predicted 8% of the variance in actual game statistics.

In 2022, I got the opportunity to make my own contribution to this field of knowledge, teaming up with my friend Jake Tuber, an organizational psychologist and host of adult running camps, and Hogan Assessments, a private company created by husband-and-wife psychologists Robert Hogan and Joyce Hogan, to conduct a scientific survey of elite distance runners. A total of twenty-five current professionals, including a pair of national record holders, agreed to complete the Hogan Personality Inventory, arguably the most comprehensive personality testing instrument. Hogan's chief science officer, Ryne Sherman, analyzed the data and presented a detailed report to Jake and me.

The standout number was an average competitiveness score that ranked these athletes in the 94th percentile against the general population, meaning they were more competitive *than just about everyone*. "Crazy competitive," you might say. They were also well above average (70th percentile) in boldness. These findings mirror the results of Pamela Karp's study of personality in professional hockey players, as well as those of a recent Hogan-led study of NFL draft prospects, who landed in the 78th percentile for competitiveness and in the 84th percentile for boldness.

When you put these two traits together—a fiery will to win and exceptional risk tolerance—you get a person who will never blink first in a game of chicken. If two cars are speeding toward a head-on collision, and you're in one car, and a person who sits at the 84th percentile for boldness and competitiveness is in the other car, and whoever swerves first loses, *you will lose*, because your competitor ain't swerving. Which is kind of nuts!

Pole vaulting is much like a game of chicken. By far the most dangerous track-and-field event, it selects for boldness. What's more, the way the winner is determined is completely different from any other event save the high jump. Three misses at a given height, and you're out. As the competition unfolds, participants drop off one by one until two remain, either of whom will inevitably accrue two misses as the bar is raised. All eyes are on them as they make their third attempt, a gold medal on the line. "Normal" people feel intense anxiety at this pressure-filled juncture and are prone to choke, forgetting everything they know about pole vaulting and missing badly. Not Sergey Bubka. "Under stress I feel alive," he said in a 1997 address delivered at a conference in Budapest, Hungary. "I love to make a third attempt at a height that can win a competition or leave me in a bad place if I miss." That's bold!

Evidence suggests that boldness is largely inborn—a matter of temperament, as Carol Dweck would say. Longitudinal studies have shown that infants who neither cry nor show other signs of distress in response to exposure to novelty or falling tend to be uninhibited and risk-seeking (i.e., bold) at later stages of development. Competitiveness is different, at least in its most extreme manifestations. Psychologists define hyper-competitiveness as "an indiscriminate need to compete and win (and to avoid losing) at all costs," a need that appears to arise as a reaction to certain childhood experiences. For example, a 2021 survey of more than 2,500 adults by Kevin Shafer of Brigham Young University found that those who reported having been raised by "highly withdrawn" fathers were more likely to be hypercompetitive.

Let's see, have we encountered anyone recently who was raised by a highly withdrawn father? Oh, yes: Sergey Bubka! And is he hypercompetitive? You bet he is! "I would run like crazy because I just had to win," he recalled once of his days as a youth soccer player. "I could really run until I was dead on the sports field because I had to win."

Dweck's theory of personality makes it easy to understand how a father such as Nazar Bubka could produce a son like Sergey, willing to "die" to win. You will recall that among the basic psychological needs Dweck identifies is a need for acceptance, which later gives rise to a need for self-esteem. If these needs are thwarted by bad parenting, and if the person in whom they are thwarted is endowed with a high degree of temperamental boldness, it should surprise no one that the person learns to meet these needs by risking all for victory.

Sergey's self-described rationale for dedicating himself to the pole vault bears repeating in the present context: "I love it because the results are immediate and the strongest is the winner. In everyday life that is difficult to prove." Translation: *I love it because it makes me feel like a person of value. At home I was made to feel like a person of no value.*

On the "shit together" side of things, Jake Tuber's and my study of personality in elite runners revealed a strong "mastery orientation" (77th percentile). When I asked Ryne Sherman via email to explain what this meant, he supplied the following answer: "Mastery has to do with wanting to be precise and perfectly achieved (e.g., 'I strive for perfection in everything I do')." Nowadays, perfectionism is widely perceived as unhealthy, but there are different kinds of perfectionism, and one of them—mastery orientation—is desidedly healthy, associated with effective self-regulation and athletic achievement. According to research conducted by Joachim Stoeber at the University of Kent, athletes with "perfectionist concerns" are motivated by fear of imperfection, the ironic consequence of which is a tendency to set avoidance goals (as described in Chapter 3) that cause the athlete to underperform. Athletes with "perfectionistic strivings," meanwhile, focus less on outcomes and more on the approach goal of mastering their sport, a mindset that is proven to aid performance by boosting self-regulatory efficacy.

To my knowledge, Sergey Bubka never completed the Hogan Personality Inventory, but if he had, I'm confident he would have set yet another world record with his mastery orientation score. Only an athlete with such a mindset would have said (to repeat another previously cited quotation), "I want to be an artist of the pole vault." Seeking perfection in both training and competition, Sergey fussed over every little detail of his craft, leaving nothing to chance in his pursuit of better performance. On meet days, he arrived at the stadium two hours before his first vault to get the lay of the land, studying the runway, the conditions, the vaulting area—"every possible thing that could influence my result," as he put it on one occasion.

Another personality trait that Sergey has in abundance is the one Hogan calls "dutifulness." Like conscientiousness, dutifulness aligns with the concept of having one's shit together. If your friends describe you as "loyal, respectful, and conforming," Hogan Assessments might describe you as *one standard deviation above the mean in dutifulness*. And if you're an athlete, your coach might describe you as coachable. Like conscientiousness again, this other "shit together" trait is salient in elite athletes, particularly those involved in team sports. In the study of NFL draft prospects I mentioned earlier, the average score for dutifulness landed in the 91st percentile. When presenting these findings on the *Science of Personality* podcast, Ryne Sherman noted that it's hard to get an average score above 90 for *any* trait in a group of such size, and the fact that only dutifulness did so in this group of elite athletes is revealing.

There's a clear overlap between conscientiousness and dutifulness. The first of these traits enables athletes to exert self-discipline in pursuit of big goals, while the second enables athletes to submit to the discipline of outside help in the same pursuit. Both, as such, are facets of having one's shit together, and both were evident in Sergey Bubka's approach to the pole vault. His decision to seek expert coaching at the age of ten was right in character, and he remained eminently coachable throughout his career.

In his speech in Budapest, Sergey told the story of his experience at the European Championships eleven years earlier, where he felt oddly weak and listless and struggled to eke out a victory. Afterward, he consulted psychologist Rudolf Zaginoff, who hypothesized that Sergey had given out too much of his energy in interviews and appearances in the lead-up to the competition and advised him to refrain from the practice in the future. Heeding this counsel wasn't easy for Sergey, who enjoyed interacting with the public, but he did it nevertheless. "Now," he told his audience, "during a major competition I relax with a book, or I go to a park or other quiet places, or make conversation with my coach, family, and very close friends. But I avoid stress."

Pole vaulting isn't thought of as a team sport, but Sergey made it one, surrounding himself with an array of trusted experts whom he willingly depended on to reach new heights. "My results are due not only to my character and preparation," he said at the conclusion of his Budapest speech, "but to the contributions of my first coach, my current pole vault coach, my running coach, my weightlifting coach, my psychologist, my doctor, my physiotherapist, my masseur. We must combine all our knowledge to improve the final result."

LET'S REVIEW

Our aim in this chapter has been, in essence, to rewrite my theory of athletic greatness in the language of personality. And I think we've succeeded. Dweck's theory of personality, coupled with Sergey Bubka's case study, has shown us that the "screw loose" part of the two-sided mental makeup we see in great athletes corresponds to the traits of competitiveness and boldness, which impel the athlete who possesses them in abundance to make deeper sacrifices, take bigger risks, and endure greater suffering than others do in pursuit of victory. The "shit together" part, meanwhile, maps to conscientiousness, mastery orientation, and (in many cases) dutifulness.

These paired constellations of personality traits—competitiveness and boldness on one side; conscientiousness, mastery, and dutifulness on the other—are starkly unalike. When combined in a gifted athlete, they yield a Jekyll-and-Hyde type of performer who will quietly submit to a coach's orders Monday through Friday and then bite the heads off their opponents on Saturday. The oddness of such internal contradictions is resolved, however, when we recognize that personality traits are rooted in basic psychological needs, which are themselves diverse. In this sense, great athletes like Sergey Bubka appear to be more than one person because, well, they are.

What's more, any one person can change—in some cases drastically—over the course of their lifetime. An athlete might, for example, go from *really* not having their shit together at sixteen to surpassing their wildest ambitions at thirty-two, offering hope to basket cases everywhere, as you're about to see.

CHAPTER SEVEN

Get Your Shit Together

**It is never too late to be what
you might have been.**
—GEORGE ELIOT

Philosophers going back as far as the ancient Greeks have observed that all creatures capable of feeling pleasure and pain possess strong instinctive drives to seek pleasure and avoid pain. But do we really need Epicurus to tell us we strive to feel good most of the time? More than an "inalienable right," the pursuit of happiness is simply *what we do* with our life and liberty.

If happiness came easily, there wouldn't be much to say about it. But it doesn't. The problem is not only that pain finds us routinely in a variety of forms despite our best efforts to escape it. Putting pain aside, learning how to feel good most of the time takes real effort. Eating, having sex, and getting high bring immediate pleasure, but a life devoted to these things does not bring happiness. The happiest people, typically, are those who enjoy their work, have healthy relationships, find meaning in their lives, and have an attitude of acceptance toward themselves and the world, and unless I'm mistaken, you can't buy these things at Walmart.

The happiest people are also the best self-regulators. After all, self-regulation is the means by which we pursue goals, and happiness is the goal behind all goals. Research has shown that self-regulatory ability strongly predicts life satisfaction in a variety of populations. A 2018 study involving 8,143 female Iranian high school students, for example, found that higher scores on a standard index of self-regulation strongly predicted self-rated happiness.

This doesn't mean that good self-regulators always start off happy, however. As we saw with Andre Agassi, childhood trauma will cause even the most promising self-regulators to struggle to get their shit together. But no matter how messily they begin life, folks like Andre tend to get their shit together increasingly as they grow and learn from experience what they truly need to be happy. In direct contradiction to the set-point theory of happiness, which holds that each person's baseline level of life satisfaction resists change in either direction, data from the multi-decade German Socio-Economic Panel suggests that as many as three in ten people experience significant and lasting changes in happiness, for better or worse, over the course of their lives. And you can be certain that among those who enjoy the biggest gains in happiness are folks who, like Andre Agassi, suffered bad breaks in their early years but got their shit together eventually by tapping into their innate self-regulatory resources.

This book is about athletic greatness, not happiness. But the two are linked. After all, what makes great athletes great—largely—is that they feel their happiness depends on being the best at their sport. Does the monomaniacal pursuit of winning truly make them happy? No, but it very often makes them happi*er*, because (A) enjoyable work, as mentioned, is a pillar of happiness, and (B) chasing excellence in athletics rewards and strengthens self-regulatory ability, which is the wellspring of happiness. Hence, what you often find with athletes who commit to a sport in search of happiness is that doing so is a crucial step, but not the last step, in getting their shit together. Just ask Clara Hughes.

ENTER CLARA

If Clara Hughes were a *Jeopardy!* question, the answer would be, "She holds the distinction of being the first Canadian to win Olympic medals in both the Summer and Winter Games." But our interest in her goes beyond trivia. Through no fault of her own, Clara did not have her shit together early on in life. In fact, as she makes quite clear in her memoir, *Open Heart, Open Mind,* she's still working on getting her shit together to this day. But it's this very work, as well as its effect on both her athletic achievements and her happiness, that makes her story so compelling.

The main cause of Clara's not having her shit together in her younger years was—you guessed it—a terrible father. Clara herself describes the man in more generous terms, writing, "My dad, Kenneth James Hughes, didn't know how to be a father." In all fairness, Hughes was a remarkable fellow for all his flaws. Raised hand to mouth in a hardscrabble mining town in England's Midlands region, he somehow developed a taste for opera and canonical literature as a teenager despite receiving minimal exposure to highbrow culture at home. A short stint in the

Royal Air Force was followed by emigration to Canada, where Hughes met and married Clara's mother, Maureen McBride, who encouraged her husband to go after his long-repressed literary ambitions. To his credit, Hughes took her advice, completing high school at the age of thirty, followed by four years of undergraduate study at Concordia University, a two-year master's program at McGill, and a year of doctoral work in Durham, England. By the time Clara was born on September 27, 1972, her father held a distinguished faculty position in the English department at St. John's College in Winnipeg and bore little resemblance to the benighted coal digger's boy he'd once been.

At a distance, Hughes's story read like a fairy tale. But Clara lacked the privilege of living at a distance from her father. Combative and erratic by disposition, he became volatile under the influence of alcohol, which he imbibed to the point of stupor seven nights a week. Clara and her older sister, Dodie, lived in perpetual fear of his wrath, which could be provoked by offenses as small as giggling or failing to finish a serving of lima beans. The perpetrator was punished most often with a torrent of verbal abuse that left wounds far deeper than the belt lashings Hughes inflicted on special occasions. But as bad as Clara and Dodie had it, their mother had it worse. Night after harrowing night, the sisters listened helplessly from their shared bedroom as their father berated and belittled the woman who had believed in and supported him as no one else had, including his own parents, who'd scoffed at his hifalutin fancies.

When Clara was nine years old, her long-suffering mum decided she'd had enough. The final straw was her husband's eighth (eighth!) drunk-driving accident, in the aftermath of which the esteemed professor moved out of the family home and into a bachelor apartment. Around the same time, Clara and Dodie started acting out in various ways: truancy, shoplifting—the usual wayward kid stuff. Lacking her big sister's aptitude for thievery, Clara soon got caught, and so ended her criminal career. But she'd only just begun to lose her shit, and years would pass before she reversed course and entered the long and winding path toward getting her shit back together.

By age thirteen Clara was drinking, smoking, and sleeping around. She found little pleasure in any of these recreations, but she did find oblivion, and that was good enough for the time being. Tall for her age, Clara could—with the help of makeup and a fake driver's license—pass for eighteen and purchase alcohol, always the hard kind, which she drank straight from the bottle, stopping only when she threw up or blacked out, whichever came first. She skipped class routinely to hang out in parking-garage stairwells with other ne'er-do-wells—fellow truants initially, then local gangbangers. She inhaled a pack of cigarettes a day plus the occasional joint, her drug use limited not so much by temperance as by a fortunate tendency to hallucinate when high. She felt nothing more for her various sex partners than a mild curiosity that invariably turned to disgust after a few weeks, at which time she'd ditch the latest loser for another just like him.

In short, Clara was a prototypical teenage waster, a classic disaffected pubescent party animal on a road to nowhere. Except for one thing: sports. In Canada, every kid can ice skate, and in this respect Clara was no different from her fellow Canucks, despite her substance abuse and promiscuity. In the first grade she took up ringette, a tame version of ice hockey meant for girls, and when she outgrew that, she played a season of the real thing on a boys' team, scoring three goals in the one opportunity she was given to play forward instead of defense. Later on, Clara entered and won a speed-skating competition wearing a stubby old pair of hockey blades.

It's amazing how often stories of rising to greatness can be traced back to a single moment of inspiration. For Clara, the moment came on

February 20, 1988, when her customary Saturday afternoon channel surfing brought her to CBC's coverage of the men's 1500-meter speed skating event at the Winter Olympics in Calgary. Clara sat mesmerized as Canadian legend Gaétan Boucher glided around the track with a seamless blend of grace and power that redefined her young notions of human possibility. The next day, Clara declared to her mom, "I want to speed skate in the Olympics."

History tells us that Clara did skate in the Olympics, not once but twice, winning medals both times. But even if she hadn't, the quickening she experienced while witnessing greatness in action on the frozen oval would have been an inflection point in her life, a galvanizing first glimpse of the timeless truth that real happiness lies in stretching oneself, not in momentary ecstasies. Seizing on her daughter's declaration, Maureen Hughes contacted the Winnipeg Speed Skating Club, whose coach, former Olympian Peter Williamson, agreed to take Clara on. The training was hard—way harder than Clara had imagined it would be—but she loved it. A fire had been lit, rousing Clara to sell her car and use the proceeds to purchase a proper pair of speed skates, to cut back on her smoking and drinking, and to apply herself in school. These baby steps of self-control were rewarded with a silver medal in the 800-meter race at the 1989 junior national speed skating championships. She was on her way!

Sort of. Given her troubled background, Clara was predisposed to accept her male coaches as father figures, irrespective of merit. With Williamson, whom she describes in her autobiography as "a wonderful human being, a leader who demanded our best but who was always ready to break tension with a laugh," she got lucky, investing her trust in a man worthy of it. But her luck ran out when Williamson took a new job in Winnipeg, a second paternal abandonment that Clara took hard, deflating her Olympic aspirations. The void created by Williamson's departure was quickly filled by Mirek Mazur, a cycling coach who had seen Clara skate and thought she had potential as a bike racer. Alas, he was no Peter Williamson.

Things started out okay. Mazur was certainly right about Clara's two-wheeled prospects. In her competitive debut, the 1990 Western Canada Summer Games, Clara won three events. Weeks later, she claimed another brace of gold medals at the Canadian Road Championships. But the very next year, history repeated itself, Mazur receiving and accepting an offer to serve as the provincial cycling coach in far-away Hamilton, Ontario, threatening the loss of another male mentor. This time, however, Clara refused to let go. An adult now (technically), she asserted her agency as a grown-up and followed Mazur, for better or worse. To get her shit together, Clara needed to break free from her dysfunctional family and her toxic living environment, and in tagging along behind her coach, she did so. Only later would she recognize that the specific escape route she chose indicated how far she had to go still in getting her shit together.

Like all too many coaches—male coaches especially—Mazur believed in joyless hard work, negative reinforcement, and absolute control. His tyrannical approach to developing Clara's talent made her physically fit, no doubt about it; but fitness should feel good, and Clara didn't feel good. Ever. Fear-based motivation and conditional approval were Mazur's methods of choice, intended to foster total dependency, yet despite his best efforts, he did not so fully paralyze Clara's self-regulatory faculties that she failed to recognize—eventually—the wrong turn she'd taken on the road to happiness.

It's unlikely that Mazur intended to ruin Clara's relationship with food and cause her to despise her own body. But if he did, he made all the right moves, calling her "fat" and critiquing her food choices and portion sizes. The effects on Clara were entirely predictable. "I would fill page after page with my calorie counts" she writes in *Open Heart, Open Mind*, "wanting to stay below 800. Then, I would hide food and binge, creating a loop of self-hatred and guilt, causing me to eat more. I wanted to be light and small and unburdened . . . Instead, I felt like I was carrying around an enormous heaviness, both physically and emotionally."

Mazur wanted Clara to believe she couldn't succeed without him, and because she lacked a sense of self-worth, she submitted to her dependency—mostly. More than once, she decided she'd had enough and sent Mazur packing, only to lose heart and go crawling back to him. Her greatest hope was that achieving the success he promised would permanently wash away her inner torments. When at last that gleaming package arrived, however, she found inside it only bitter disillusionment, not the sweet release she'd naively envisioned. More in spite of Mazur's coaching than because of it, Clara placed second in the time trial at the 1995 UCI Road World Championships in Colombia. The following year she took bronze in both the time trial and the road race at the Olympics in Atlanta. But instead of engendering the self-acceptance her soul craved, recalls Clara in her memoir, "My medals deepened my depression, because now I knew I was the same worthless person after Atlanta as I had been before."

As painful as this discovery was, it marked another important step forward in Clara's journey toward happiness, teaching her to look elsewhere for inner peace. Additional steps quickly followed. Clara made a final break with Mazur, whose parting words to her were (I'm not making this up): "Burn in Hell!" She quit cycling and exploited her newfound freedom from the grind of training to begin a romantic relationship with Peter Guzmán, her future husband. Clara could not have picked a more ideal partner for the hard journey ahead. In stark contrast to the other major male figures in her life, Guzmán was a patient, grounded person who wanted nothing more than the simple and nomadic life he'd created for himself, a life of minimal possessions and responsibilities and maximal time spent hiking and riding bikes in pristine natural environments all over the world. A person who already knew what it meant to be happy and whose appreciation and love for Clara in all her messiness offered a first hint of the possibility of self-acceptance, on which happiness depends.

In the summer of 1998, Clara and Guzmán spent six weeks touring the Baja peninsula by bicycle. The experience showed Clara a healthier way to relate to her sport, and she decided to give bike racing one more go. Resolved to do things differently this time, she hired a new coach, Eric Van den Eynde, who had a more balanced approach to elite performance, allowing Clara a day of rest every week and telling her, "To improve, you have to do one thing you like, and two you don't like, every day"—a radical departure from her prior routine of never resting and doing a thousand or more things she didn't enjoy for every one she did.

Weeks before the 2000 Olympics in Sydney, Clara came down with a bad case of whooping cough. Not yet fully recovered when she raced the time trial, she finished sixth, but because she had prepared and raced with a healthier mindset, she took greater satisfaction in this losing performance than she had in her medal-winning rides in Atlanta four years before. "It confirmed that how I felt depended on whether I accepted myself," she reflects in her autobiography, "and how I defined success and failure."

Upon returning home from Australia, Clara promptly quit cycling a second time. But this time was different. Whereas her previous retirement had been an act of retreat, this one was an act of pursuit, a positively motivated effort to resuscitate her childhood dream of becoming an Olympic speed skater. Older and wiser than she'd been on that February afternoon in 1988 when this vision first implanted itself in her mind, Clara insisted on having more control over her training than she had as a cyclist (even under Van den Eynde), so she hired unheralded Xiuli Wang, a Chinese expatriate, to coach her, with the understanding that Wang would provide just enough guidance to keep Clara from straying off course in the process of doing things her own way. Aware also that her greatest strength was her almost superhuman tolerance for physical suffering, which she would later recognize as a not entirely healthy distraction from her ever-present emotional pain, Clara dispensed with the tried-and-true approach to racing the longer events she specialized in, treating each contest as a sprint while everyone else held back and keyed off the clock. "To me," she writes, "if you're skating to lap times, you'll never know how hard you could have gone. I started as fast as I could, and I ended as fast as I could, and I blew up in almost every race."

Clara still wanted to win, naturally, but above all she wanted to enjoy being an athlete, so she focused less on outcomes and more on the pursuit of outcomes, aiming to do well by feeling good. She arrived in Seoul, South Korea, for the 2004 World Championships in a Zen-like state of mindful acceptance of everything she experienced—even the ill-timed case of laryngitis she picked up en route. "I felt so aware," she recalls, "so ready for anything, that if someone had thrown marbles on the ice, I could have skated on them, telling myself they belonged there."

As it turned out, the ice at the competition venue was of such poor quality that the athletes might as well have been skating on marbles. Unfazed, Clara embraced the adverse conditions—and her opponents' grumbling—as a personal advantage. In the 5000-meter race she skated so hard that she lost count of how many laps she'd completed. Expecting to hear the bell signaling the start of the final circuit, she heard instead a dreadful silence indicating she must somehow stretch her hollowed-out legs an extra 400 meters. The instant she breached the finish line, Clara's knees buckled, sending the new champion of the world crashing into her own team bench, too woozy to realize she'd won but already knowing something far more valuable—that she had found her absolute limit, her way.

If Clara's performance at the 2004 World Championships demonstrated how far she'd come in getting her shit together, her behavior afterward revealed how much farther she had to go to get where she wanted to be as a person. Her first mistake was failing to anticipate the mental comedown that was bound to shadow the afterglow of her near-perfect race in Seoul, a mistake she compounded by reverting to old habits—specifically, bingeing on alcohol and junk food—in a misdirected effort to soften the landing. She became suddenly prone to explosive temper tantrums and sloppy conduct, such as oversleeping and missing flights, that were all too reminiscent of her father's old ways and strained her relationships with Wang and Guzmán. In Clara's defense, she knew as well as those around her that she needed to get a grip, and to this end she traveled to Arizona with Guzmán for another cycling tour, only to become violently ill as a result of drinking tainted water. For her next trick, Clara came down with pneumonia upon returning to Canada for a mandatory pre-Olympic training camp. A badly needed bit of good news came on the eve of her scheduled flight to Italy for the 2006 Winter Games in Turin, when she received medical clearance from the team doctor to compete. But also bad news: her body fat was measured at 23 percent—the highest level of her career.

Clara watched the Opening Ceremony on television, too weak to participate. Her first race, the 3000-meter event, was held the following day. She finished ninth. On the plus side, Clara had two full weeks to rest up and get ready for her forte, the 5000. When the day came, Clara found herself paired against three-time and defending Olympic champion (and convicted drug cheat) Claudia Pechstein of Germany.

Bad blood ran between them, justifiably on Clara's side, not so much on Pechstein's. Clara knew she wasn't fit enough to beat the world record holder, but she didn't care. Having discovered in Seoul how to completely empty herself, she found a way to dig even deeper—and to hurt even more. Tears of pain blurred her vision as she churned through the last hard laps, her mighty thighs pleading under the weight of an invisible anvil on her back. But by then she was ahead of Pechstein, and she stayed ahead to win her first Olympic gold medal at the age of thirty-three.

Back home, the Canadian team doctor who had given Clara the bad news about her body composition pulled her aside. "You have proven everything I believe in to be wrong," he confessed. "You have a focus that I've never seen before that allows you to do anything, no matter what."

That focus came at a cost, however, and Clara wasn't sure how much longer she could sustain it. The next Olympics seemed impossibly distant, the prospect of training for four more years as daunting as a prison sentence of the same duration. Had the 2010 Winter Games taken place anywhere else but Canada, Clara might have given them a pass, and she nearly did. In the end, however, she couldn't resist the once-in-a-lifetime opportunity to showcase her gifts in front of her compatriots, justifying the sacrifices required with an internal appeal to patriotic duty. It was a choice she wouldn't regret, culminating in a bronze-medal performance in her signature event at Richmond Olympic Oval in Calgary, after which Clara was "mobbed in the street" everywhere she went, a surreal experience for an athlete who had toiled in relative obscurity most of her career.

At thirty-six, Clara knew for sure she'd had her fill of speed skating. But she wasn't yet ready to leave behind the life of a world-class athlete. She still needed closure as a cyclist—or so she convinced herself—and she got it, qualifying for and competing in the 2012 Olympics in

London, where she placed fifth in the time trial—not bad for a woman about to turn forty. Only then did Clara bid a final adieu to professional sports, having participated in six Olympics in two sports over a span of eighteen years, winning six Olympic medals, seven world championship medals, and an astounding thirty-five national championship titles.

THERE'S A LESSON HERE

With her last race behind her—for real this time—Clara Hughes discovered the true reason she'd kept striving for six arduous years beyond her greatest triumph. Something frightful lay hidden behind the all-consuming goals that had dominated her attention for so long. Something she didn't want to face. Something that, deprived of such goals, she now *had* to face: herself.

Other pro athletes put off retirement for fear of boredom. This wasn't Clara's concern. In the latter part of her racing career, she got involved in the IOC's Right to Play program, which supports sports participation in poverty-stricken regions, and she also became a spokesperson for a mental health awareness initiative funded by Bell Canada—commitments that gave her a sense of purpose long after she hung up her skates. But as much as they meant to her, these causes lacked the distractive power of her prior ambitions, leaving her with too much time inside her own head, the result of which was a swift plunge into depression and self-loathing.

Clara had made a lot of progress in getting her shit together during her time as an athlete—progress that, without question, was facilitated by her pursuit of greatness in sport. But this same pursuit ultimately held her back from taking the crucial last steps toward happiness. "My warrior self had served me well while I was competing in the arena," she writes of this transitional period in her life. "Now, I needed to have the courage to accept my wounded self."

We have seen that skillful self-regulators employ a "whatever works" approach to achieving their goals. When challenges hit, they get resourceful, willingly experimenting with different tools until they find the right one for the job rather than stubbornly applying the same familiar tool to every challenge. We have also seen that self-regulatory processes are not entirely internal, despite what is implied by the term's prefix. Outward actions, including social actions like seeking help, can be as effective as inward thoughts and feelings as self-regulatory tools. Together, these two facets of self-regulation—resourcefulness and action—explain how Clara took the next step forward in getting her shit together, which was by taking the novel step of seeking help in accepting her wounded self.

Another thing we've learned about self-regulation is that it feeds on itself. The better a person is at self-regulating, the better they get at self-regulating. Of course, this also means you need to have your shit together—at least to some degree—to get your shit together. A rough childhood made it impossible for Clara to get her shit together without help. But having her shit *somewhat* together naturally (in other words, having a strong innate capacity to self-regulate) enabled her to not only seek help when she needed it but also choose the right helpers, as she did with Owen Schwartz, a physician, and Hap Davis, a clinical psychologist. Schwartz came into Clara's life while she was still racing, and his influence laid a foundation for the self-work that awaited her in retirement. After gaining her trust, Schwartz persuaded Clara to try a session of regression therapy, which produced a tearful catharsis involving a vision of a smiling bird with loving eyes (and no, there were no drugs involved), and which helped her make peace with the idea that she could love her father without fixing him, and love her mother without rescuing her, and be okay with herself despite her unchangeable past.

Hap Davis offered a more mainstream and pragmatic form of assistance. In her first appointment with him, Clara wept nonstop, an emotional outpouring that paved the way for an overdue verbal unbosoming. Never before had she put it all out there with someone ("issues with food, my sense of failure, guilt over my successes, and so on"), and by doing so with Davis, Clara came to appreciate the full measure of the trauma she had suffered, and the normalness of her ongoing emotional struggles, as well as the importance of focusing on progress versus perfection in working through her struggles. It is notable that, in the concluding pages of her memoir, Clara does not write as one who has arrived at some "happily ever after," but rather as one who is still getting her shit together, confessing that "I still struggle with what I see in the mirror" and describing her marriage as "an eighteen-year work-in-progress." I would argue that only a person who has her shit in fairly decent order could be so frank in assessing her remaining issues.

Clara's story teaches us a number of valuable lessons. Above all, Clara is living proof that it's possible to go from really not having your shit together as a teenager to having it mostly together later in life. Her story also demonstrates that, in athletes, success does not equal happiness, and that the true path to both of these things—success and happiness—is self-regulatory development. And finally, we find in it a kind of blueprint for getting your shit together.

HOW TO ACTUALLY GET YOUR SHIT TOGETHER

You might be surprised to learn that there are credible, sober-minded psychologists and psychotherapists all over the English-speaking world who use the phrase "get your shit together" in their clinical work, regarding it as an accurate and relatable description of the goal they bring to their work with patients. Among them is Mary Hoang, head psychologist at The Indigo Project, one of Australia's largest psychotherapy practices, who distilled her clinical work into an online course in self-development, insight, and personal growth called (drumroll, please) "Get Your Shit Together." The course guides students through a six-step process that mirrors Clara Hughes's journey and marks the way for other athletes looking to get their shit together for the sake of their performance and overall well-being. Here, briefly, are those six steps:

1. Identify what's holding you back (and discover the beliefs and thoughts that you struggle to change).

Sports are essentially a concentrated form of life. As such, they have a way of highlighting the self-regulatory limitations that hold us back in life. If a person has room for improvement in their capacity to self-regulate, they are likely to experience the same self-limiting thoughts, feelings, and behaviors in both life and sport and may even experience them most acutely within the sporting environment. Recognizing these limiters (i.e., recognizing that the athlete doesn't have their shit together) is an important first step toward overcoming them.

We see Clara Hughes doing this throughout her athletic career. A major limiter for her, which stemmed from her feeble sense of self-worth, was a tendency to allow others to define her. It held her back both on and off the racecourse, but it was in the cauldron of competition that Clara became aware of it as something she could control. It happened during a cycling race that came down to a duel for victory between her and a sprint specialist for whom Clara was no match in a final surge to the line—at least not on paper. Her first thought, knowing this, was reflexively defeatist: *Well, she's going to win*. Exactly what Mirek Mazur would have said. But Mazur was elsewhere, and a second voice broke in, challenging the first: *Why not attack and see what happens?* So Clara attacked—and won! "As a competition, it had meant little," Clara reflects in her book. "However, psychologically, it meant everything. I'd managed to put [Coach] Mirek's belittling voice out of my head, and from that day forward, I decided I would strive to win every single race, whether I was 'suited' for it or not."

2. Deal with your emotions and manage your mind (for a calmer and more self-aware you).

This second step makes the challenge of dealing with emotions and managing the mind sound easy, like taking out the trash on trash day. In reality, of course, it is far from easy, as Hoang understands, and as the following except from Clara's diary, dated June 3, 1997 (eleven months after her first Olympics), makes clear: "Why do I despise my body so? Why do I feel trapped under these layers of flesh? I cannot accept this physical being as it is. I am disgusted by my lack of self-control, disgusted at the rolls of flesh that cover my body. It hurts me, and I feel guilt for my lack of self-worth, hinging on my body-fat count. LET THESE FEELINGS GO so I can feel the freedom of being. I want to live. Perhaps it is time to begin to try."

These are the words of a young woman who wants to deal with her emotions and manage her mind and who understands that doing so will free her, but she's just not able. Yet. The self-awareness she needs to succeed in these efforts is present, but much work remains to be done. Clara was wise to use a journal to perform this self-work. Studies have shown that journaling is an effective tool for cultivating self-awareness and empowering change, and it is a big part of Hoang's "Get Your Shit Together" program. There's no wrong way to do it: journaling on paper or digitally, daily or as inspired, privately or publicly, will all achieve the same effect.

3. Let go of the shit that's holding you back (so you can feel free).

Although Clara may never let go of all the shit that's holding her back—something she readily admits—she has succeeded in letting go of bits and pieces throughout her life. Her first major act of letting go was her escape from Winnipeg in 1991 to pursue a cycling career. Six years later, she let go of her cycling career (albeit temporarily) for the sake of her mental well-being, an act she memorialized by donating all of her cycling clothes and gear to charity. Clara still had a lot of letting go left to do after these events, but in each case she demonstrated an inner wisdom that boded well for the future. Letting go of shit that's holding you back is hard, but it can be made easier through symbolic gestures such as relocating and parting with objects weighted with dark significance.

4. Understand your needs and learn how to set boundaries (for healthy, balanced relationships).

A person's mental health is only as good as the health of their relationships. Show me a person whose relationships are a mess and I'll show you a person who doesn't have their shit together. Clara's regression-therapy epiphany left her with a renewed appreciation for this important truth, and she used it to set boundaries with her family. One such boundary was a new rule of visiting her mother, her father, and her sister individually in each trip back to Winnipeg instead of seeing everyone together as before, which always ended disastrously.

Clara could have spared herself years of grief had she made this self-protective move sooner, but she had to build up to it. She did this by managing other important relationships, becoming increasingly confident in her ability to set healthy boundaries as she gained a better understanding of her personal needs. Key steps in this process were firing Mirek Mazur, hiring Eric Van den Eynde and Xiuli Wang, and marrying Peter Guzmán. It is notable that three of the four people just mentioned are coaches. For athletes, coaches offer ready opportunities to practice managing healthy relationships as a means to getting their shit together.

5. Align your values and priorities (so you're living more in line with your desires).

On the morning of her gold-medal performance at the 2006 Olympics, Clara watched a television documentary about the Right to Play program's work in Uganda and was deeply moved by the capacity of the children it showcased to forget their own poverty, their experiences of war, and the ravages of the AIDS epidemic and lose themselves in sport. That same evening, Clara competed with the word "Joy" inscribed on her right hand, vowing to donate her $10,000 prize to Right to Play if she won, which she did. She left Italy having learned that, "For medals to mean something to me, they must stand for something more than my having crossed the finish line faster than anyone else."

This awakening marked the beginning of step five in Clara's journey toward getting her shit together. Her exposure to Right to Play, with which she became deeply involved after Turin, revealed to her a previously unseen desire to be a joyful athlete who not only trained and competed with joy but spread this feeling to others, particularly the disadvantaged. Instead of detracting from her performance, this shift in focus from results to values, from self to others, raised her game to a new level. Here again we see that athletes need not choose between feeling good and doing well. In getting their shit together, they both feel better and perform better.

6. Integration (for sustainable change).

The sixth and final stage in Mary Hoang's course is similar to the top two levels of Athanasios Drigas and Chara Papoutsi's pyramid of emotional intelligence, which we discussed in Chapter 5. Hoang borrows the concept of integration from ethnographer Arnold van Gennep, who studied rites of passage in various cultures. Although the specifics differ from one culture to the next, Van Gennep found that these rituals serve a common purpose everywhere, which he called integration. In her book, *Darkness Is Golden: A Guide to Personal Transformation and Dealing with Life's Messiness,* Hoang explains that "Integration allows the individual to recognize that an old identity has been let go and a new identity is emerging."

Many of the traditional rites of passage that Van Gennep studied (vision quests, adult circumcision) are no longer available to most of us. But sport can and does fulfill the same function for those who, consciously or otherwise, recognize its potential as a vehicle for personal transformation, as Clara Hughes did. Life is indeed messy, and for this very reason few of us reach adulthood with our shit fully together. This is bad news for people who just plain suck at self-regulating. But the good news in Clara's story is that a sufficient quantity of inborn self-regulatory potential and a growth-minded approach to sports can eventually transform a self-limiting hot mess of an athlete into one who finds her absolute limit—and finds joy in getting there.

Nor is having one's shit together the only component of later talent that an athlete can acquire after lacking it initially. There are also a variety of ways to procure a loose screw, as you're about to find out.

CHAPTER
EIGHT

Find Your "Crazy"

**You need a little bit of insanity
to do great things.**
—HENRY ROLLINS

Gareth Thomas is regarded as one of the finest rugby players ever produced by the rugby-mad country of Wales. In a professional career spanning seventeen years, he scored 655 points for six different clubs, led the French Toulouse squad to victory in the prestigious Heineken Cup, made a record-setting one hundred appearances for the Welsh national team, and retired as one of the top ten scorers in the history of international rugby competition.

Impressive stuff. Yet these summary statistics barely hint at how much Gareth Thomas meant to his people during his lengthy prime. In a place where, according to the *Encyclopedia of Wales*, "rugby is seen by many as a symbol of Welsh identity and an expression of national consciousness," Gareth became the very embodiment of Welsh masculinity. Nicknamed "Alfie" (on account of a supposed childhood resemblance to a certain 1980s sitcom puppet-alien), he stood six feet three inches tall and weighed 227 pounds, his chiseled bald head perched stonelike atop a prison-yard physique, all tatted and shredded.

Over the course of his career, he broke his nose five times. Had eight teeth knocked out. Fractured one shoulder, then the other. Broke a hip, a forearm, a thumb, and his palate. (His palate!) He lost count of how many concussions he'd incurred after about the tenth. Suffered a *stroke* after taking a punch to the jaw on a scoring play.

As they say, though, you should see the other guy. Gareth gave as good as he got on the rugby pitch—and sometimes off it. In 2005, he was charged with assault and suspended from competition for a month for his role in a drunken brawl at a nightclub after a match in southern France. His countrymen gobbled it up, seeing in Gareth the epitome of Welsh virility. He was gritty, like the miners who dominated Wales's male workforce; fearless, like a pub crawler five pints in; and resilient, like the people as a whole—a nation of no-quit grinders who just couldn't catch a break economically but kept on keeping on.

Unless you were there yourself, you can't possibly fathom how much rugby mattered to Wales, and how much Wales mattered to its rugby players, when Gareth took up the game as a tweener. Like Ireland and Scotland, Wales spent much of its history under the imperial boot of England, but unlike its ethnopolitical cousins, which enjoyed a measure of geographical and cultural separation from England, Wales struggled to create a cohesive identity that set it distinctly apart from its domineering next-door neighbor. Rugby afforded it a way to do so. Between 1899 and 1909, Wales defeated England ten times in eleven contests, the mismatch deriving largely from class differences in the makeups of their respective teams. Whereas English rugby was a sport of the elite, occupying the same rarified stratum as cricket and polo, in Wales rugby was the workingman's pastime, and it remained so when Gareth came to it as a teenager. Historians have noted that, over the decades, the economic fortunes of Wales have tended to rise and fall in lockstep with those of the Welsh national rugby team. "Sceptics can dismiss it as a game for muddied oafs," Gareth writes in his memoir, *Proud*, "but I know it matters. It lightens the load, addresses the inequalities of everyday existence; it can justify prejudices, right wrongs and put things on an even keel."

When you dig into the biography of any great athlete, you invariably uncover marks of destiny, an origin story that makes you say, "Of course!" and Gareth Thomas is no exception. Born to excel in a sport of hard collisions, he was in fact born *via* collision—specifically, a headfirst impact between his mother and a privet hedge in the backyard of the family home in the town of Bridgend. Nearly nine months pregnant at the time of the mishap, Yvonne (who'd been chasing a rogue puppy) went into sudden labor, and two days later out came Gareth, weighing nine pounds, twelve ounces—nearly big enough already to play fullback.

Another thing you'd expect to see in a lad anointed for greatness on the rugby pitch is a disdain for sitting, and Gareth had that also. According to Thomas family lore, an exasperated teacher once ripped a ruler from young Gareth's hand to stop the boy's fidgety desk tapping. Confiscation achieved nothing, however, for the instant the disruptive instrument was snatched away, the tapping continued on the floor by way of his foot. When Gareth did pay attention in school, he paid attention not to the teacher's droning but to the verdant row of playing fields visible outside the classroom window, quietly beckoning as the teacher yammered and his fellow pupils learned. He loved any sport played on grass, but above all rugby, which suited his unusual combination of size, speed, and agility.

Gareth's physical gifts and his love of the game were more than equaled by his work ethic (or his conscientiousness, as the personality experts would label it). He became known by teammates in his first junior club as that weird kid who trained alone, behavior that was almost unheard of in an era when the sport remained nominally amateur even at the highest levels. Gareth ran alone, lifted weights alone, and spent hours alone at Pandy Park, messing around with his ball. "It didn't matter how hard the rain fell," he writes in *Proud*, "or how painfully the hailstones stung . . . I was oblivious to everyone, and everything."

At fifteen, Gareth quit school to focus on his burgeoning rugby career. Four years later, he made his senior debut for Bridgend RFC, his hometown team. The local stud distinguished himself immediately, and he was soon invited to try out for the Welsh national team that would compete in the 1995 Rugby World Cup in South Africa. Despite showing up to training camp two days late, having been waylaid by a bad case of cold feet, he made the cut, scoring three tries in his first cap in red and white, sending the Welsh sporting press into a frenzy.

The World Cup itself went poorly for Wales, who lost two of their three games in the rounds and failed to advance, but despite his team's lackluster performance, twenty-year-old Gareth received a hero's welcome on his return home. He was slapped on the back until his back was sore and treated to drinks until he could drink no more. Then, when the backslapping and drinking were done, Gareth slouched back to his parents' house alone, dropped face-first onto the single mattress in his childhood bedroom, and wept into his pillow.

It was around age ten that Gareth began to realize he was different from other boys. For example, he loved *The Fall Guy*, a TV show about a Hollywood stuntman moonlighting as a bounty hunter, which in itself did not set him apart from his male peers. But unlike most, he had a huge crush on Lee Majors, the program's handsome leading man. This wasn't a problem, initially. Why would it be? We like who we like. By the time he reached sixteen, however, Gareth felt a growing pressure to conform, and to hide a part of his authentic self from everyone but himself.

It doesn't take a genius to understand why. To spend any amount of time in a boys' or men's locker room is to hear a lot of homophobic chatter, and Gareth heard his share. Worse, though, was the sport-specific messaging contained in much of this chatter, the chief perpetrators of which equated being a "bender" (British slang for queer) with athletic ineptitude. "You'll be able to guess the standard of conversation," Gareth tells his readers. "'Don't worry about him, he's a fucking bender and he can't tackle to save his life.'"

Put yourself in his situation. The hopes of your nation—a nation you fiercely love—rest on your shoulders. Your countrymen adore you. In your strong body lies the power to make their lives a little better, which is pretty incredible. But you're gay. And if your countrymen knew it, they (enough of them, anyway) would no longer adore you, and your power to make their lives a little better would be lost. That's a hell of a pickle.

Gareth's way of coping was, in essence, to overcompensate. He took the work-hard, play-hard rugby ethos to the extreme, hoping to pass off this hypermasculine version of himself as the real Gareth Thomas, succeeding less often than he imagined. "You're trying to be one of the wild boys," his friend and teammate Ian "Compo" Greenslade told him once, "and overdoing it a bit." Compo sensed the truth, and although few others did, Gareth lived in constant fear of discovery, a fear that transformed into blind rage whenever the "bender" epithet was directed at him, as it was bound to be every now and again in the furnace of competition.

In 1997, Gareth left Bridgend for rival Cardiff, branding himself a turncoat in the eyes of the more rabid partisans of his hometown club. When the two sides next met at Bridgend's Brewery Field, a local fan shouted out from the bleachers, "Eh, Thomas. You're a fucking bender!" Big mistake. Gareth sprinted off the field of play and bore down on the offending ignoramus, whose eyes bulged in futile regret as the hulking object of his abuse prepared to vault over a boundary fence. Lucky for everyone, the Bridgend team's water carrier intervened just in time to save the fan's jaw and Gareth's career.

On another occasion, an opposing player took the opportunity of being pinned to the turf with his mouth in Gareth's ear to hiss, "You're bent." *Really* big mistake. Gareth spent the rest of the match hunting down and brutalizing his insulter, favoring him with such gratuitous violence that Gareth's teammates tried to rein him in, reminding him that the goal was to score more points than the other team, not to murder an individual member of that team, but to no avail. The vendetta went on for years, in fact, the stronger man terrorizing the weaker every time the poor fellow was unlucky enough to find himself in the same stadium as his unforgiving avenger.

Gareth did eventually come out, albeit in stages. The first person to learn his secret was Jemma, his wife of fourteen years. Of all the "Honey, we need to talk" conversations that couples have in bedrooms around the world, this one has to be among the most awkward and consequential. Gareth was not and had never been sexually attracted to Jemma, but he did love her, and when she left him three months after his confession, he fell apart. He began drinking heavily, and on more than one occasion he tried to kill himself. His teammates and coaches couldn't help but notice Gareth's unraveling—the suddenly erratic shaving habits, the thousand-yard stare, the no-shows—which led him eventually to a second confession, this time in the locker room instead of the bedroom. Gareth had nursed his fear of being discovered for so long that he considered the worst-case scenario—total rejection by his fellow players—the only scenario, but that's not what happened.

"Bud, don't worry about it," was one teammate's response to the big reveal. "Let's have a beer."

The press were next to learn Gareth's secret, though not from the man himself. On the eve of a Saturday match against England, Gareth received a tip that a major London tabloid planned to expose his sexual orientation publicly in Sunday's edition. Panicked, he silenced the paper as only he could, leading his team to a decisive victory that robbed his would-be outer of an expected opportunity to pile on. "In essence," he writes, "I was telling the tabloids: 'Come and have a go, if you think you're hard enough!'"

Having bought himself the time he needed to take the final step voluntarily, Gareth went ahead and took it, granting a no-questions-barred interview to the *Daily Mail* that was printed on December 18, 2009. The next day, Gareth's Cardiff Blues club played his French former team in Toulouse. Braced for jeers and abuse from the 30,000 ardent fans packed inside Stade Toulousain, he instead received a standing ovation when introduced before the match.

Despite such welcome surprises—and there were others—Gareth remained on high alert, and justifiably so. At a match in Castleford, a rowdy faction of spectators saw fit to treat him to a chant of "Gareth Thomas takes it up the arse." When would they ever learn? Like a harpooned shark, Alfie drew strength from injury—and from the pressure he felt to avoid validating prejudicial expectations. "I trained like a demon, worked harder than I thought possible," he recounts in *Proud*. "Failure, at this stage of my life, was not an option."

The need to prove himself continued to drive Gareth until the very end of his playing days. In March 2010 he changed allegiances once again, this time jumping not only from one team to another but from one sport to another. Having spent his whole career pursuing the fifteen-man game of rugby union, he elected at age thirty-five to try his hand at rugby league, which features thirteen players per side, a move he describes as "a conscious attempt to stretch myself." And stretched he was. To the outsider, the two rugby codes look about the same, but in fact rugby league is a faster, more open game, demanding a higher level of conditioning. Always known as one of the fittest athletes on the pitch in rugby union, Gareth got a rude awakening on his first day of training with the Castleford Tigers, whose mostly younger members ran circles around him. In response, he doubled his solo workout regimen, "determined to defy the doubters."

Fittingly, Alfie broke his arm in his final match. Although he recovered in time to represent Wales one last time in the Four Nations tournament, he graciously ceded his spot on the team to a rookie. At last, Gareth Thomas had nothing left to prove.

THERE IS NO FORMULA. OR IS THERE?

Great athletes are willing take bigger risks, make deeper sacrifices, and endure greater suffering in pursuit of winning than seems reasonable to most people. That's what makes them great. And in every case, this "unreasonable" drive is fueled by an unmet need. You can look high and low for an exception to these universal patterns, but you won't find one. What differs from one athlete to the next is the specific nature of that driving need.

For Gareth Thomas, rugby satisfied a need for acceptance. Well, sort of. According to Carol Dweck's theory of emotions, which we discussed in Chapter 6, acceptance is one of three basic psychological needs, an imperative for all humans from the very beginning of life. And in Wales, there's no better way to fulfill this need than to be awesome at rugby. Because Gareth didn't fully accept his own sexuality, however, and because he believed the people around him would also not accept it, he needed the acceptance he got from rugby a lot more than his peers did, and this, over and above his physical talent or anything else, drove him to greatness.

Trouble was, until Gareth came out, fulfilling his need for acceptance came at the expense of other critical needs, most notably his need for self-coherence. Throughout his memoir, he writes of having a split personality—a public self, Alfie, who epitomized the macho rugby lad, and a private self, Gareth, a unique individual who defied stereotyping. A divided self is not sustainable. Gareth's duality was either going to kill him—and it nearly did—or be resolved by coming out, at whatever risk to his rugby career. Considering how well his eventual uncloseting was received where it mattered, which was inside the locker room, you might assume that Gareth now regrets having not come out sooner. But in a letter to his sixteen-year-old self that he penned when he turned forty, he wrote, "Instinct tells me to gloss over the reality that if you come out at 19 . . . your career will shrivel and die. I want to allow you to enjoy the blissful innocence of your dreams." Painful as it was to live a lie for so long, it really couldn't have happened any other way, and Gareth knows it.

Let me be clear: Gareth Thomas achieved athletic greatness neither because of nor despite his sexuality. He achieved it because, for him, the pursuit of greatness in rugby fulfilled a need for acceptance that was intensified by the pressure he felt to hide his sexuality. The important thing to understand is that, although Gareth might well have been born gay, he wasn't born with a screw loose. Instead, he had a screw loosened by life experience. Now, if being queer in an intolerant world were the *only* way to meet the screw-loose requirement for athletic greatness, straight athletes would be S.O.L. Happily, there are other ways.

We've seen that some athletes, including Jack Johnson, really do seem to have been born with a sort of "craziness" that facilitates greatness, whereas others, like Gareth Thomas, earn their "crazy" in the school of hard knocks. When we focus on the second category—athletes whose loose screw appears to have come mainly from the nurture side of the nature/nurture divide—we see tremendous variety in the types of experiences that trigger the drive to risk, sacrifice, and endure beyond reason in pursuit of victory. In this sense, there is no formula for meeting the "screw loose" requirement for athletic greatness. But when we look deeper, a pattern emerges.

Let's go back to Jack Johnson. What distinguished him from other boxers of his day? Lots of things, but most of all his preternatural fearlessness, which was often perceived by those around him as insanity. Jack took tremendous risks, made extraordinary sacrifices, and endured ten long years of dogged peripatetic scrapping and scraping to earn his title shot, all *because he wasn't afraid.* Fear is the ultimate human limiter. The essential difference between athletes who are "crazy" enough to risk, sacrifice, and endure more than anyone else in pursuit of winning and those who aren't is that, for the former, losing is scarier than any risk, any sacrifice, or any amount of suffering they might endure in the name of victory. When a person truly needs something that others merely want, fear is not a barrier. Sure, Jack Johnson was fearless by nature, but the main reason he never blinked in the boxing ring was that he feared nothing more than being a man who blinked.

The good news for athletes not named Jack Johnson is that certain types of life experience destroy the fears that stand in the way of giving everything to fulfill one's potential. Some of these experiences work by creating a genuine need to find the absolute limit of one's ability, while others presuppose this need and destroy fear in other ways. Taken together, such experiences constitute a formula of sorts for acquiring the loose screw that athletes need to be great. The most common fear-reducing phenomena in the lives of athletes are the following: *sweet redemption, healthy regret, gaining by losing, triumph over tragedy, the old shoulder chip, the nemesis factor,* and *the inspiration effect.* Let's have a look at them.

Sweet Redemption

American snowboarder Lindsey Jacobellis arrived in Turin, Italy, for the 2006 Winter Olympics as the reigning world champion in snowboard cross at just twenty years old. As expected, she qualified easily for the four-woman final and then dominated that race, slashing her way to an insurmountable lead over Switzerland's Tanja Frieden after the first few turns. A quick glance over her shoulder on the homestretch assured Lindsey she had the gold medal in the bag, so she decided to start her celebration early, performing a showy board-grab trick on the final jump. It was a terrible lapse in judgment, and she paid for it, landing ass first and spinning helplessly on her back like a capsized beetle as Frieden sped past her to victory.

Lindsey left Italy devastated and humiliated yet comforted by the knowledge that she was still plenty young and would have other chances. But how many more? At the 2010 Olympics in Vancouver, she fell a second time and finished out of the medals. At the 2014 Olympics in Sochi, she was leading her semifinal race when she wiped out on a turn, and again went home empty-handed.

It was all mental, Lindsey knew. Virtually unbeatable everywhere except the Olympics, she amassed five world championship titles and ten X Games gold medals before the 2018 Olympics in Pyeongchang. Haunted by the trauma she'd experienced in Turin, she choked like clockwork once every four years, when it mattered most. To break the cycle, Lindsey hired a performance coach, and it helped. In South Korea, for the first time in four Olympics, Lindsey made it all the way through the elimination round, the second round, the quarterfinals, the semifinals, and the final without crashing. But after leading the final race most of the way, she faded to last, missing the podium by 0.03 seconds.

Sports fans love redemption stories, as do the sports media. We love them so much, in fact, that we force redemption narratives on star athletes. Whenever a marquee athlete fails spectacularly as a consequence of their own immaturity, we enjoy a momentary frisson of schadenfreude that quickly gives way to a hopeful expectation that the athlete will learn and grow and claw their way back to the top, redeeming themselves ultimately by winning in the same venue where they previously lost. Athletes' awareness of these expectations has the potential to burden them in ways that actually increase the likelihood they choke again, resulting in even greater public pressure to get it right and redeem themselves—a classic vicious circle. Lindsey Jacobellis chafed against the redemption narrative foisted upon her after Turin, telling a newspaper writer ahead of the 2018 Olympics, "Wouldn't it just be nice if the media didn't harangue me for something that happened twelve years ago? I'm sure we can go into everyone's past twelve years ago and pick out something that they coulda, shoulda, woulda done. It's just mine was on a world stage that people have a hard time forgetting, or they just think that's the only thing that's happened or that it defined me as an athlete."

Fair point. But does this sound like an athlete who's in the proper headspace for optimal performance? Not to me. While Lindsey was right to want to control her own narrative, she was wrong to think she didn't need to redeem herself. She just needed to do it on her terms. As far as the public was concerned, redemption meant winning an Olympic gold medal. For Lindsey herself, however, true redemption meant *becoming an athlete who didn't let public expectations get to her.*

By the time the 2022 Olympics in Beijing rolled around, Lindsey understood this. "I definitely took a different tactic in these last Games," she told NBC after winning not one but two gold medals, finishing first in both the women's individual snowboard cross and the newly added mixed-team event. "I wanted it to be fun and memorable and not this circus. I wanted it to be my experience and not how the media wanted it to be." Fortified by this healthy new attitude, Lindsey raced fearlessly for the first time since her first Olympics, redeeming herself before she even crossed the finish line.

Admittedly, star athletes like Lindsey Jacobellis aren't the best examples of how redemption works because they operate in an artificial fishbowl that most athletes never experience. An example of how redemption works in an athlete whom no one has ever heard of is me. I mentioned in Chapter 1 that I quit running in high school because I couldn't handle the pain of racing, and I promised to explain in a later chapter how I later overcame this aversion. Well, here we are, and I will now tell you that it was through the power of redemption that I found my "crazy" and belatedly fulfilled my potential as an athlete. When I got back into running in my late twenties, I felt ashamed of the coward I'd been as a teenager and was deeply motivated to deliver myself from this shame by learning to train and compete bravely. Because this motivation came entirely from within me, I felt empowered by the internal pressure it created instead of crushed by environmental pressure as Lindsey Jacobellis was in her second, third, and fourth Olympics. I'd be lying if I said my quest for redemption transformed me overnight, but in time I did become the fearless runner I wanted to be, the kind who smiled on the starting line because he *couldn't fucking wait*!

If you've ever let yourself down as an athlete or in another aspect of life—I mean *really* let yourself down—know that this very experience, or rather how you interpret it and what you do with it, could be the very screw loosener you need to achieve your version of greatness.

Healthy Regret

In 2022, the *New York Times* ran an opinion piece by writer Lindsay Crouse that appeared under the title "A 63-Year-Old Runner Changed How I Think About Regret." In it, Crouse shared the story of Mariko Yugeta, a Japanese woman who had recently set an age-group world record of 2:52:13 in the marathon. Amazing, right? But here's the kicker: Not only was Mariko's time faster than any runner her age had ever run in the entire history of women's marathoning, but it was also faster than Mariko herself had run *in her twenties*.

True to the headline of Crouse's article, Mariko attributed her late-life heroics to regret. Specifically, she regretted putting her running career on ice during her physical prime to focus on career and motherhood. When she came back to the sport post-menopause, assuaging this regret became a deep psychological need that enabled her to run more fearlessly than her younger self. "I've always wanted to be number one," she told Crouse. And she meant it. On learning that the current number one marathoner in the world was Eliud Kipchoge—a man young enough to be her son—Mariko researched his training online and copied it. Which is kind of "crazy." But it's the right kind of "crazy" if you want to be great.

In his book *The Power of Regret: How Looking Backward Moves Us Forward*, science writer Daniel Pink explodes the myth that people who live correctly have "no regrets." Pink's research has shown that all of us regret things we did—or more often, things we didn't do—in the past. What matters is not whether we have regrets or not but whether, like Mariko Yugeta, we use our regrets positively or let them fester.

Do you have festering regrets, athletic or other? If so, congratulations! Look no further for the "crazy" you need to become the athlete—or person—you might have been.

Gaining by Losing

Australian cyclist Cadel Evans holds the distinction of having lost the Tour de France more times (six) than any other eventual winner of the event. When he rode his first Tour in 2005 at age twenty-eight, Cadel seemed destined to stand atop the podium one day. A two-time World Cup champion in mountain biking, he finished eighth that year, fourth the following year, and second the next two years. But then he stalled out, plummeting outside the top twenty-five in his fifth and sixth attempts to claim the biggest prize in cycling. And time was ticking—Cadel would be thirty-four in his next Tour.

Pundits agreed Australia's great hope had missed his chance. But the Cadel Evans who showed up for the 2011 Tour de France was not the Cadel Evans who'd cracked in Stage 10 the previous year, sobbing in the arms of BMC Racing teammate Mauro Santambrogio after bonking on a mountain climb and losing time to his key rivals. The knock on Cadel had always been that he was too cautious, too risk averse. Imagine the pundits' surprise when the thirty-four-year-old Cadel rode his seventh

Tour with a whole new attitude, an unshackled mix of recklessness and playfulness that signaled a man with nothing left to lose. He served notice by launching a surprise attack at the end of Stage 1, gaining three seconds on the main contenders. Three days later, he did it again, earning himself a stage victory. The aggression continued, and on the eve of the decisive Stage 20 time trial, Cadel ranked third in the general classification, 57 seconds behind yellow-jersey wearer Andy Schleck. At the BMC team dinner, Cadel was seen enjoying a glass of wine, smiling and laughing with his fellow riders as though he hadn't a care in the world. Andy Schleck didn't stand a chance.

"Freedom's just another word for nothing left to lose," goes a line in the song "Me and Bobby McGee." There's a lot of wisdom in this lyric, as any great athlete will tell you. Competing with a sense of having nothing to lose is powerfully liberating. Fear makes athletes tight and tentative, hindering performance. To compete as though there is nothing to lose is to compete without fear, hence loosely and boldly. And there's nothing quite like losing, or failing, to leave an athlete feeling they have nothing to lose. If defeat has already done the worst it can to you, what is there really to be afraid of?

When the recently retired Australian rules footballer Tom Williams handed over his number 12 jersey to rookie Zaine Cordy in a ceremony held in August 2015, he said in a speech to his former Western Bulldogs teammates, "You should play like you have nothing to lose." Excellent advice, but the "should" part is problematic. An athlete cannot play like they have nothing to lose simply because they've been told they should. It requires that they feel it in their heart. That's why NFL teams don't run their two-minute offense outside the last two minutes.

The flip side of this reality is that, when an athlete who has everything they need to succeed except a loose screw experiences the right kind of failure at the right time—a loss that constitutes the last straw—something snaps inside them, as it did in Cadel Evans, and their fear vanishes automatically. Who knows? You could be one failure away from finding your "crazy."

Triumph Over Tragedy

On July 30, 2016, during a summer visit to Martha's Vineyard, Noelle Lambert and Kelly Moran, both nineteen-year-old members of the UMass Lowell Women's Lacrosse team, rented a moped, as Cape Cod vacationers often do. Despite having never driven a moped before, Noelle took the pilot seat and Kelly wedged in behind her. At precisely 12:35 PM (according to the police report), Noelle lost control of the vehicle and veered into oncoming traffic, sideswiping a commercial truck. Turn away if you're squeamish.

Noelle's left leg was severed just below the knee. Otherwise unscratched, she remained conscious and all too alert in the aftermath, wondering if she would ever play lacrosse again as a witness to the accident applied a lifesaving tourniquet and another good Samaritan scooped up her detached and mangled shank with a blanket.

"That needs to come with me!" she called out to him, naively imagining a surgeon would be able to reattach the dead extremity.

As it turned out, not only was Noelle's left lower leg beyond saving, but so was the knee, which was removed on the operating table. Years later, in an interview for the *Mike Drop* podcast, Noelle recalled, "The few days I was in the hospital, I'm sitting there overlooking my life, and I'm thinking about the type of person I was and how I went at things, and I asked myself, 'Did I give it my all?' It was probably 12 or 1 AM, and I'm thinking to myself, *If I ever get the opportunity to play sports again, I swear to God I will give it my all.*"

Two-legged Noelle hadn't needed to give it her all. The new and improved one-legged Noelle did, and that need made her fearless. On April 7, 2018, Noelle returned to the lacrosse field, a carbon-fiber prosthesis in the role previously held by her left shin and foot, and scored a goal in a game against rival Hartford. But that was just the beginning. A three-sport athlete in high school, Noelle had never competed in track and field before her accident, but she took it up afterward, specializing in the 100-meter sprint. In 2019, she set an American record at the World Para Athletics Championship in Dubai, and at the 2021 Paralympic Games in Tokyo she did it again, clocking 15.97 seconds.

Noelle genuinely believes losing her leg was the luckiest thing that ever happened to her, a wake-up call inspiring her to become a better athlete and a better woman. This doesn't mean that *nothing short of* losing a limb will suffice to deliver a similar kind of wake-up call to others. A myriad of lesser or indirect calamities may also instill a second-chance mindset, catalyzing a fearless approach to sport or life. My friend Stephanie Bruce comes to mind. She was a second-tier high school runner until she lost her father to cancer. She then lopped twenty seconds off her mile time, won a state championship, and went on to enjoy a long and successful pro running career.

I doubt there has ever lived an athlete so utterly bonkers that they wished personal tragedy upon themselves for the sake of their sporting ambitions. But the reality is that, sooner or later, in one form or another, tragedy strikes all of us, and when it does, a fearless approach to sport is one good thing that may come out of it.

The Old Shoulder Chip

Triathlon debuted as an Olympic sport at the 2000 Games in Sydney, Australia. The host country's best hope for a gold medal on the men's side was Chris "Macca" McCormack, who'd dominated World Cup racing since going pro five years earlier. In 1997 alone he recorded nine top ten World Cup finishes and won the ITU Triathlon World Championship and the World Cup series title. When the time came for Australia to select its representatives for the first-ever Olympic Triathlon, Macca was ranked third in the world, ahead of all of his countrymen. Shockingly, however, he was left off the team, snubbed because his cocky personality rubbed some of the sport's domestic power brokers the wrong way.

"That put a giant chip on my shoulder," Macca writes in his autobiography, the aptly titled *I'm Here to Win*. If the best revenge is a life well lived, Chris McCormack got his and more. In 2001, he won the Goodwill Games Triathlon, beating both of the Aussies present who'd been chosen ahead of him for the Olympics. He then bid good riddance altogether to his ungrateful homeland, becoming unstoppable on the American triathlon circuit, where he won thirty-three consecutive races. When that got old, he moved up to the Ironman distance and found similar success, claiming five straight Ironman Australia titles and two Ironman World Championship victories.

As Chris McCormack's example demonstrates, having a chip on one's shoulder can be a potent driver of athletic performance. The underlying psychology is pretty straightforward. A chippy athlete is an angry athlete. Feeling wronged or disrespected, they are determined to make the party that insulted them pay. If a bar fight breaks out between two people of equal size, strength, and fighting ability, and one of them goes berserk, that person will probably prevail. Sports competition is not so different from a bar fight in this regard. Athletes with chips on their shoulders go berserk on the opposition, a fearless state that enables them to sacrifice, risk, and endure more than their physical equals in competition.

Any athlete who wants a chip on their shoulder can easily find one. There's a certain type of athlete—we've all seen them—who's always spoiling for a fight. "Tell me I can't!" they challenge their doubters, real and perceived. They *want* you to doubt them, openly, so they can devote their lives to proving you wrong and shoving the proof in your face.

Chris McCormack was this type of athlete. While he certainly didn't want to be left off the Australian Olympic Team, he made the most of the snub, and if it hadn't been this particular slight that put a giant chip on his shoulder, he'd have found another. You can tell by the way Macca reacted. "I would go to races and say, 'I'm going to smash it today and I hope my Federation is watching,'" he writes. *"Not good enough?* I thought. *Take that!"* In short, he went berserk.

Not every athlete has the makeup to genuinely want a chip on their shoulder, and that's okay. If you feel more hurt than angry when someone doubts your ability to achieve something, the old shoulder chip is not the screw loosener for you. But if instead of feeling hurt you get angry when this sort of thing happens—and if you enjoy your anger, like the hero in a revenge movie—then it just might be.

The Nemesis Factor

Chris Evert faced Martina Navratilova for the first time in competition at the Virginia Slims of Akron tournament in 1973. Despite winning the match in straight sets, Chris said afterward that she felt "threatened" by Navratilova, who at sixteen was already a hell of a player and only going to get better. Just eighteen herself, Chris was on a meteoric rise, poised for a long reign at the top of women's tennis, and the sudden appearance of a younger and equally gifted rival provoked a big-sisterly jealousy in her.

Two years later, Navratilova delivered on the threat she'd presented in Akron, defeating Chris—now ranked number one in the world—in the pair's sixth meeting. Still, Chris maintained the upper hand for some time, winning fifteen of the next eighteen showdowns with the Czech expatriate before a fully matured Navratilova turned the tables, becoming almost unbeatable in the early 1980s. The record books show that, of the eighty singles matches Chris Evert and Martina Navratilova played against each other, Navratilova won forty-three, including ten of their fourteen face-offs in major finals. But what the record books don't show is that Chris became a far better tennis player than she ever would have become if not for the threat posed by her nemesis.

There were really three phases to the Evert-Navratilova rivalry, widely considered the greatest in sports history. We've covered the first two phases, which were lopsided in either direction. Phase three spanned the last four years of Chris's career and featured relative parity between the two athletes, not because Navratilova had lost a step, but because Chris had raised her game. A stronger serve and more powerful forehand and backhand shots were part of it, but the biggest change was that Chris no longer played scared against Navratilova, adopting a riskier style of tennis in their final ten duels, of which Chris won four, including the 1987 Wimbledon final. Fittingly, both players retired with eighteen Grand Slam singles titles on their resumes.

Research has shown that rivalry improves performance in sport. A 2022 paper published in *Organizational Psychology Review* looked at eighteen past studies on the effects of athletic rivalry and concluded: "When rivalry is present, the competing actors have an increased desire to win and invest extra effort into the competition, leading to enhanced performance." The psychology of athletic rivalry is rooted in family dynamics. Our first rivals in life are often our siblings, whom we compete against for parental approval. Intense jealousy is commonly felt when a brother or sister receives the favor we covet, a gnawing negative emotion we seek to avoid by outshining our filial competitors.

Athletic rivalries sublimate these family dynamics, replacing siblings with opponents and parental approval with victory. In certain athletes, the personalization of competition via rivalry transforms a mere desire to win into a bona fide need to win. When this happens, as it did with Chris Evert, a fear-driven hope that one's rival fails gives way to an agentic determination to be the deserving cause of the rival's failure, and greatness ensues.

The Inspiration Effect

The six screw-loosening experiences we've looked at so far—sweet redemption, healthy regret, gaining by losing, triumph over tragedy, and the old shoulder chip—work in similar ways. Specifically, they generate negative emotions that overpower athletes' fear in a manner similar to how stubbing a toe distracts a person from a headache. In the case of sweet redemption, that negative emotion is shame. With healthy regret, it's (surprise!) regret that overpowers fear. Gaining by losing uses frustration to the same effect. With triumph over tragedy, it's grief, and with the old shoulder chip, it's anger. Jealousy serves the same function vis-à-vis the nemesis factor.

Are there no positive emotions that empower athletes to channel their "crazy" into performance? I can think of one: inspiration.

Before Muhammad Ali was Muhammad Ali, he was Cassius Clay. In 1961, young Cassius met professional wrestler Gorgeous George in Las Vegas. Impressed by George's histrionic showmanship, he decided to emulate it, becoming the winkingly brash human spectacle we remember so fondly. But it's arguable that, although Ali borrowed

Gorgeous George's act for commercial purposes mainly, it contributed to his athletic greatness as well.

Prizefighting is a high-pressure vocation. To lose a heavyweight title fight is to receive a very public ass whupping. Yet Ali willingly quadrupled the pressure he was under by mouthing off and clowning around before his fights. It's humiliating enough to be knocked flat before an audience of millions, far worse to meet this fate after having predicted—in rhyming couplets—the exact round in which you would knock your opponent flat. Gorgeous George was what is known in pro wrestling as a heel, generating interest in his matches by provoking fans and making them want to see him lose. Ali used the same playbook, pitting the entire boxing world against him ahead of his first title shot by predicting an eighth-round knockout of undefeated champion Sonny Liston. Such immense self-imposed pressure will either weigh an athlete down or lift them to otherwise unattainable heights. In Ali's case, we know the result. Sonny Liston quit on his stool after six rounds.

I'm not suggesting that, if not for Gorgeous George, Cassius Clay would not have become Muhammad Ali. What I am suggesting is that inspiration is powerful. Psychologists have demonstrated that much of human learning occurs through emulation of role models, and the philosopher Linda Zagzebski has written persuasively on the special efficacy of admiration as a motivational trigger for emulation, and emulation for achievement. A young Cassius Clay looks at a Gorgeous George and says, "I want to be like that guy," then transforms into a Muhammad Ali.

Gareth Thomas understands the inspiration effect, and it's a big reason he wrote *Proud* and created the Gareth Thomas Rugby Academy and has been outspoken on issues related to sexual orientation and tolerance. More than one great athlete will have him to thank, at least in part, for their own greatness. As for you, only your heart can decide who, if anyone, inspires you to pursue your sport fearlessly. And if your heart stays mum, no problem—as we've seen, there are other ways to find your "crazy" and channel it into achievement.

We've said enough for now about how to release inner potential by focusing inwardly, removing barriers to greatness either by getting your shit together or by acquiring a loose screw. Let's now turn our attention outward and see if it's possible to achieve greatness by changing the world around you—or at least your immediate environment. (Spoiler alert: it is.)

CHAPTER
NINE

Context Is Everything

**Those who succeed at anything and don't
mention luck are kidding themselves.**
—LARRY KING

It sounded like a collision between two automobiles, not two bodies. With just over five minutes left in the fourth quarter of game two of the 2001 NFL season, the New England Patriots offense was bogged down at their own 19-yard line, facing third and ten against a stout New York Jets defense. Quarterback Drew Bledsoe took the snap and dropped back to pass, but his protection broke down immediately, forcing him to scramble right. A lumbering runner, Drew eked out a

191

respectable yet insufficient gain of eight yards without being touched, and he was on the verge of stepping safely out of bounds when Jets linebacker Mo Lewis flattened him with a perfectly timed hockey-style shoulder check delivered at full speed, producing a pad-on-pad *clap!* that echoed into the nosebleed seats at Foxboro Stadium, drawing a collective "*Oh!*" from fans. Drew's head whipped one way as his body flew the opposite way, concussing his brain. The jolt of impact penetrated deep inside the quarterback's torso, shearing an artery behind a rib, resulting in unchecked internal bleeding. Drew was now literally drowning in his own blood, and he would be dead within hours if he didn't receive proper medical attention. He knew none of this, however, and more important, the game wasn't over.

The Patriots elected to punt, but their own defense held firm, and they got the ball back less than a minute later. Having assured coach Bill Belichick that he was okay, Drew returned to the field, but he just didn't look right. Intense shoulder pain (a telltale sign of a hemothorax—the potentially fatal type of injury he'd suffered) made it difficult for him to throw, and his breathing was labored. When the Patriots offense returned to the sideline after losing the ball on a second-down fumble, fullback Marc Edwards (who'd committed the turnover) informed Belichick that Drew "wasn't all there" and had been unable to remember his play calls. When New England regained possession one last time, backup quarterback Tom Brady took his place, and the rest, as they say, is history. Unless you're Drew Bledsoe.

Few NFL players of Drew's era were more likely to lose their life on the playing field. His four-night stay at Massachusetts General Hospital—where *three liters* of leaked blood were drained from his abdomen—was not the first instance of an internal injury sustained during a game sending him to the emergency room. A similar incident occurred during his sophomore year at Walla Walla High School in southern Washington State, when Drew absorbed a brutal hit and played on, but "didn't seem right" afterward and was rushed to the hospital, where he was diagnosed with a badly bruised liver.

To play professional football is to put your health at risk. Some players risk more than others, however, and Drew Bledsoe sacrificed his body to the cause of winning with an extraordinary willingness. Statistics prove it. Drew absorbed more hits than any other quarterback of his generation, finding himself on the receiving end of one hundred sacks in a span of just two seasons preceding the Mo Lewis incident. A porous Patriots offensive line was partly to blame for the punishment he took from opposing pass rushers, but he also tended to hold on to the ball too long, waiting patiently for a teammate to give him an open target downfield instead of throwing the ball away to avoid getting drilled—*because he wasn't afraid of getting drilled.*

Granted, Drew was a lunker of a man—a 238-pound slab of lean, all-American beefcake—so he could take a licking. Even so, he got hurt sometimes, and he played hurt most of the time. In 1998, Drew broke a bone on his throwing hand during a game against the Miami Dolphins. He stayed on the field, and a few plays later he threw a game-winning touchdown pass. The following week he played with a medical pin sticking out of his right index finger. Only when throwing the ball was physically impossible did Drew miss a game, like when he sat out against the Atlanta Falcons after suffering a separated shoulder the Sunday before. In all, he missed only six games during his eight-year tenure as the Patriots' starting quarterback.

Drew's win-or-die-trying mentality was untaught, revealing itself in toddlerhood. He started skiing at age two, when most kids are still in diapers, and fell instantly in love with the adrenaline rush he got from bombing down the slopes of the Cascade Mountains, a rush that he would later describe as the next best thing to the thrill of "taking the field in front of 70,000 screaming fans and having an entire organization trying to stop you and some of the biggest, baddest athletes on the planet trying to run you over." When he turned pro in 1993, Drew bought a home in Whitefish, Montana, where he could ski to his heart's content at nearby resorts during the offseason. Aware of his daredevil extracurriculars, Patriots owner Robert Kraft attached a clause to the $103 million contract he offered Drew in 2001, which required him to return a portion of his earnings in the event that he broke his neck on a black diamond run. More than willing to take his chances, Drew agreed to the condition, using a slice of his nine-figure windfall to purchase special accident insurance from Lloyd's of London.

Entwined with Drew's insatiable lust for physical risk-taking was a maniacal need to win that went back just as far. We've seen that some great athletes are born with a screw loose, while others acquire a loose screw through life experience. Drew belongs to the first category, safe to say. In a 2005 *Seattle Times* profile, a former babysitter described him as the type of kid who loved to compete and was determined to win, no matter the game—backyard football, skiing, table tennis, foosball, you name it. As evidence, she cited the time she caught him cheating in a three-legged Easter egg hunt, stealing victory by surreptitiously reconnoitering the course ahead of the competition.

Drew's lust for dominance and his craving for danger supplied him with the hungry ghost required to achieve athletic greatness, driving him to take bigger risks, make deeper sacrifices, and endure greater suffering as a football player than a "normal" person would. But even with all his physical talent (and he had talent aplenty, hurling the ball at higher velocity than all but a few quarterbacks in NFL history), Drew could not have become the great athlete he was through boldness and competitiveness alone. He also needed to have his shit together, and he did. Indeed, Drew Bledsoe might be even more sane than he is "crazy."

We see this in the way he handled himself after recovering from the damage he sustained in his collision with Mo Lewis. Doctors cleared Drew to return to football on the twelfth of November, 2001, fifty-one days after his injury. While he was away, Tom Brady had played well but not spectacularly, doing just enough to keep the Patriots in contention to make the playoffs but not enough, in the view of talk radio pundits, to steal Drew's job as the team's first-string QB. Instead of restoring the starting role to Drew, however, Coach Belichick told him he'd have to compete for it, a real slap in the face to a man who'd just been valued at $103 million. Nevertheless, Drew swallowed his pride and competed, only to get slapped again less than a week later, when Belichick, having evidently seen enough at practice, sat down with both quarterbacks and informed them that Brady would remain the starter for the rest of the season.

Drew was livid. He'd been sidelined by *injury*, for Christ's sake, not benched for poor performance! And he was healthy now—good as new—with a doctor's note and everything! In the eight years Drew had been with the team, the Patriots had ended a seven-year playoff drought, qualified for the playoffs four times, won their division twice, and made it all the way to the Super Bowl in 1997. Drew was a three-time Pro Bowl selection and already the franchise's all-time leader in completed passes and passing yards. At twenty-nine, he was in the prime of his prime, and did I mention he'd just signed a ten-year, $103 million contract?

Some players in Drew's position—not many, but some—would have made a stink, airing their dissatisfaction publicly and being as unhelpful as possible to their usurper. Others might have expressed their anger in subtler ways, saying the right things in the wrong tone and "supporting" the wearer of their rightful crown without making him *feel* supported. Drew did none of these things. Instead he put a lid on his simmering resentment and mentored Brady to the best of his ability, putting the team first—a feat of emotional self-regulation that was every bit as impressive as the tight spirals he threw. Brady never forgot what a class act Drew was in this critical moment, stating in an ESPN documentary twenty years later, "What I respect so much about him is he never let any of those emotions negatively impact me in any way."

With Brady under center, the Patriots won five of their remaining six regular-season games and clinched a playoff berth. Then Brady got hurt, spraining his ankle late in the second quarter of an AFC Championship matchup against the Pittsburgh Steelers. Drew came off the bench and, showing no signs of rust, led his team to victory and a trip to the Super Bowl. Talk radio went nuts. The sporting media loves nothing more than a quarterback controversy, and here was one for the ages. You could flip the channels all you liked, but you couldn't escape the question on everyone's lips: Who would get the ball two weeks later when New England faced the heavily favored St. Louis Rams—the promising upstart with a bum ankle or the proven veteran who had gotten the job done when it mattered most?

Belichick chose Brady, smacking Drew's still-smarting cheek for the third time in as many months. But this one *really* stung, seeming almost unreal in its gratuitous cruelty. And yet, as with his many physical injuries, you wouldn't have known by his behavior how much Drew was hurting inside. Before kickoff, he was seen on the Patriots sideline hyping up his understudy, pounding his shoulder pads and barking in his face the way football players do. Keep in mind, Tom Brady wasn't *Tom Brady* yet. At twenty-four, he was, in essence, a rookie still, having spent his entire first season in the NFL on the bench, awaiting his opportunity. History tells us Brady was more than equal to the moment, but until that moment came, even he couldn't have known this, and Drew, who'd been there before, demonstrated an unfeigned desire to do whatever he could to help his team win, even if it meant giving confidence to the man who'd taken his place.

The Patriots did win, of course, despite an unexceptional performance from Brady, who completed sixteen of twenty-seven passes for a piddling total of 145 yards. By eleven o'clock the next morning, Drew was in Montana, at his favorite ski resort, sitting alone on a chairlift, sobbing. "I just sat there," he recalled in the aforementioned ESPN documentary, "and it was the first time I let it all come crashing down on me."

What a picture! I get a little choked up myself just thinking about it. No words could better express what it took for Drew to sacrifice his personal interests to those of his team, for as long as he needed to, than the image of this hulking grown man weeping alone on a desolate mountain less than twenty-four hours after Super Bowl XXXVI, the biggest win of his career, and also the biggest loss.

UNANSWERED QUESTIONS

There are two important questions this book has implicitly raised but has not explicitly answered. First, we know that, for great athletes, the pursuit of mastery in sport addresses an urgent psychological need, and this is why they are willing to take bigger risks, make deeper sacrifices, and endure greater suffering than most people would in pursuit of winning. But that being the case, what happens on the inevitable day when the athlete retires and moves on from the sport they've counted on to feed the hungry ghost inside them for so long?

The second question, which I'll bet has crossed your mind at some point, concerns whether the "screw loose, shit together" formula for greatness applies in domains outside of sports. In other words, *must* a person have a screw loose and their shit together to achieve greatness not only in the athletic arena but also in business, science, the arts, and elsewhere?

These two questions are linked in the sense that, when an athlete retires, they need to find an alternative means to meet the need that drove them to greatness in their sport—a new way to self-actualize. If having a "screw loose, shit together" mental makeup is *generally* useful in feeding the hungry ghost within a person and facilitating self-actualization, then we would expect most great athletes to cope reasonably well with retirement, at least after an initial adjustment period. Do they?

Let's pick up Drew Bledsoe's story where we left it. In a 2021 appearance on *The Herd* television show, Drew told host Colin Cowherd, "I love Tom Brady, but it feels like my career has been treated like a footnote to his." The reason Drew feels this way, of course, is that his career *has* been treated as a footnote to Brady's. Not even Drew himself would deny that the two men's professional trajectories moved in very different directions after Super Bowl XXXVI. Brady went on to play in an astounding ten more Super Bowls, winning six. Drew, meanwhile, was traded to the Buffalo Bills, who just two years later shipped him to Dallas, replacing him with a young hotshot taken in the first round of the 2004 NFL draft (the now-forgotten J. P. Losman). Drew played twenty-two games for the Cowboys before being demoted in favor of the younger Tony Romo. When the season ended, the Cowboys released Drew, who promptly retired.

"There are a million wonderful, amazing things about playing professional football," Drew told The Ringer's Katie Baker in 2017. "But one of the downsides is just, you know, it generally doesn't end in storybook fashion."

What does a retired thirty-five-year-old multimillionaire do with himself? If he has his shit together, he plans for his life after football well ahead of time, and that is precisely what Drew did. His vision for a second career began to take shape in the late 1990s, during a visit to California's Napa Valley. Having grown up next door to a winery in Walla Walla, Drew developed a taste for reds after college, which is why he chose to vacation in wine country, and it was there that he became fascinated with the winemaking process.

It checked a number of boxes. Drew loved the outdoors, and winemaking is rooted (so to speak) in nature. He relished a challenge, and the wine industry is uniquely challenging, straddling the domains of agriculture, culture, and capitalism. He thrived on risk, and there is no shortage of risks in the life of the vintner, whose survival is threatened by climatic and economic vagaries in the same way quarterbacks are endangered by "some of the biggest, baddest athletes on the planet." Could he operate a winery of his own one day? It wasn't hard to picture.

Within weeks of hanging up his cleats for good, Drew founded Doubleback wines, releasing his first vintage, a Cabernet Sauvignon, before the year was out. Today Doubleback occupies four vineyards in the Walla Walla Valley, producing cabs, merlots, and red blends, all of them estate wines, meaning the entire production process, from planting to bottling, happens in one place. The label's offerings have landed as high as number fifty-four on *Wine Spectator*'s coveted Top 100 list. If you'd like to sample them, your best bet is to visit the tasting room located inside the company's state-of-the-art, 14,000-square-foot winery, built in 2018. You can also order online at Doubleback.com, but there's a waiting list for allocations, and it's a long one.

I forgot to mention that the wine business is also competitive—glutted with brands vying for better scores, higher ratings, and stronger reputations. It is unsurprising that Drew has wholeheartedly embraced this element of his second career, bringing to it the same ferocious will to win that he'd previously brought to football (and to three-legged

Easter egg hunts). Making *Wine Spectator*'s Top 100 list is good, but not good enough for Drew, who, according to Doubleback's marketing material, is pursuing "the goal of crafting America's best Cabernet Sauvignon." Not *one of* the best, mind you—*the* best. Drew's relationship with Josh McDaniels', his handpicked CEO and director of winemaking, is described in the same marketing material as "a competitive partnership that pushes them to continue the pursuit of perfection in Cabernet Sauvignon every day." It sounds almost like a pair of pro football quarterbacks competing for their team's starting job, doesn't it?

Drew's football career might not have ended in storybook fashion, but he's found a way to live happily ever after, more or less. "I haven't had any days where I've gotten out of bed and wondered what I was going to do," is how he put it to The Ringer. If you're looking for proof that great athletes can find alternative ways to feed the hungry ghost inside them after retirement, or that the same "screw loose, shit together" mental makeup that makes them great at a particular sport can serve them well in other sorts of undertakings, look no further than Drew Bledsoe's transition from quarterback to Doubleback. And you needn't look much further to find other examples of great athletes who have found fulfillment in second careers. There's Kerri Strug, who after winning an Olympic gold medal in gymnastics made it all the way to the White House as an education policy expert; Michael Strahan, who has attained even greater fame as a morning television show host than he did in his Hall of Fame football career; and Mo Vaughn, who reinvented himself after a legendary baseball career as a real estate mogul specializing in

---

* No relation to the Josh McDaniels who served as an assistant coach for the New England Patriots during Drew's final season with the team, and who was later elevated to offensive coordinator and became instrumental in Tom Brady's success. Life is funny sometimes.

rehabilitating buildings in low-income neighborhoods to provide safe and affordable living spaces to local residents—just to name a few.

This is hardly shocking when we remind ourselves what it really means to have a screw loose and your shit together. A loose screw, as we've defined it, is a willingness—and not just a willingness, but an addiction-like compulsion—to work harder than anyone else is willing to work to achieve a goal. We like to think of hard work as an expression of discipline, and up to a point it is. But it takes more than discipline to be the last person still working when everyone else has quit. This is true not only in sports but in every other competitive field. Show me an all-time great in science, the arts, humanitarianism, or industry, and I'll show you a person who outworked their competitors because they couldn't help it. Even rock 'n' roll greats conform to this rule. Nirvana frontman Kurt Cobain wrote, "Thank you for my tragedy, I need it for my art." Fans remember Kurt as a guitar-smashing slacker dude hooked on heroin, but his bandmates knew him as an indefatigable workhorse who wanted to rehearse way more than anyone else did, a haunted perfectionist forever striving to transcend the tragedy inside him by mastering his art. Producer Butch Vig claims Nirvana practiced ten hours a day for six straight months prior to recording their breakout album *Nevermind*, which is perhaps hyperbolic, but folks are never more likely to embellish than when a deep impression has been made.

Having your shit together, meanwhile, means you are a skillful self-regulator with excellent control of your thoughts, emotions, and actions. We've seen how useful this capacity is in sports, courtesy of Lynne Cox, Clara Hughes, and Andre Agassi, in particular. But let's remember, most of the research on self-regulation has been done outside the athletic arena, and it has shown that the ability to control one's thoughts, emotions, and actions predicts success in all domains of life, including professional life. This isn't to say that the Isaac Newtons and

Florence Nightingales of the world have their shit completely together on every level. They just have their shit together a bit more than the average person—or just enough to harness their "crazy" productively.

Further evidence that the "screw loose, shit together" formula undergirds greatness of all kinds, not just the athletic kind, can be found in examples of individuals who excelled in something other than sport before they made their mark athletically. Because sport is so physically demanding, it favors the young, so there aren't as many examples of this kind as there are of people who, like Drew Bledsoe, excelled first in sport and later in something entirely different. But there are some, and Chrissie Wellington is one.

In a professional career that lasted just five years, Chrissie cemented a legacy as the most dominant long-course triathlete in history. She won all of the thirteen iron-distance triathlons she contested, including four Ironman World Championships. She broke the women's world record for this distance on three occasions and eclipsed a seventeen-year-old course record in Hawaii. Had Chrissie been male, she would have earned a share of the men's prize purse in a number of her races, finishing second overall—just 83 seconds behind the men's winner—at the grueling Alpe d'Huez Triathlon in 2008, and seventh overall at the highly competitive Challenge Roth triathlon later that same year.

The reason Chrissie's triathlon career lasted only five years—one reason, anyway—is that she discovered the sport quite late, completing her first race at twenty-seven and turning pro at thirty. And the reason she discovered the sport so late was that she had other interests, in which she also excelled. Chief among these was international development, a passion that took seed when, as a young girl growing up in Norfolk, England, Chrissie was moved to tears by televised images of famine in Ethiopia. She studied geography at the University of Birmingham, earning the highest grade in the history of her department, then put her degree to use with extensive travels in Africa and Asia, which inspired Chrissie to make it her life's work to address global poverty, in pursuit of which mission she got a master's degree in development studies at the University of Manchester. This was followed by stints at the United Kingdom's Department for Environment, Food, and Rural Affairs and at Rural Reconstruction Nepal, where she managed a community-led rural sanitation project in Salyan. Only after she left Nepal to explore Oceania and South America did Chrissie, who'd been a casual athlete in her school days, discover triathlon—and her gift for it.

It is clear to anyone who's read Chrissie Wellington's autobiography, *A Life Without Limits*, that—physical gifts aside—her successes in academics, international development, and triathlon sprung from the same source. "If there was one thing that marked me out as unusual," she writes, "it was my drive. I would go so far as to describe myself as obsessive-compulsive. I have, and always have had, the most powerful urge to make the best of myself . . . My early sporting career might have been modest, but my academic career was more impressive. I attribute that to my determination, as I do the success I enjoyed as a civil servant in my career before triathlon."

Elsewhere in her memoir, Chrissie describes herself as "perfection-istic" and "fueled by a ferocious competitiveness." Without question, she had a screw loose. But as we know, even the most gifted athlete with a loose screw cannot achieve the level of greatness Chrissie did without also having their shit together, and it's also clear to readers of Chrissie's memoir that the success she found in her various pursuits had as much to do with her capacity to self-regulate as it did with the hungry ghost inside her. Like Clara Hughes, Chrissie kept a diary that she used as a tool to examine and improve herself. "I need to address some flaws in my personality," she wrote during her post-collegiate sojourns. To have your shit together is to have the ability to set goals that align with your deepest values and to do whatever it takes to achieve them. In these unsparing words from Chrissie's diary, we see a young woman very much capable of both. Had the screw-loose part of her nature lacked this counterforce, she would have remained mired in the eating disorders that plagued her late adolescence and early adulthood, but in the end she found the wherewithal to control her own excessive need for control, later reflecting that "in time you get to know yourself, and with a better understanding of yourself comes the ability to modulate the highs and lows. More of the control, less of the freak."

It takes a supremely skilled self-regulator to achieve true perfection on the racecourse despite being burdened with a bone-deep conviction that "anything short of perfection is weakness," which in most athletes guarantees *under*performance, as we saw in Chapter 6's discussion of perfectionistic strivings and perfectionistic concerns. And only an athlete who really had her shit together would choose to walk away from her sport at the zenith of her perfection simply because, as Chrissie puts it, "I knew only that the world was full of wonderful things and that I must embrace as many of them as possible."

Long story short, if you want to be great at just about anything, it helps to have a screw loose and your shit together. But this is different from saying that if a person has a screw loose and their shit together they can be great at anything, or they can find fulfillment in something other than the one thing they're great at. It's common knowledge that a lot of great athletes struggle after giving up their sport, coming up empty in their search for something else that fits their makeup as wholly as their sport did. A 2012 study by researchers at the University of Texas found that one in ten retired NFL players had been diagnosed with depression. Drew Bledsoe was very much aware of these numbers during his playing days, and they got him looking ahead. "The statistics are pretty terrifying when you look at what happens to players when they retire from professional sports," he said in a 2017 Boston.com interview. "I was pretty concerned about figuring out what I was going to do while I was still playing. So when I decided to retire, it wasn't because I didn't want to play football anymore. It was because I had a plan and I was ready to go execute that plan."

Good for him. He defied the odds. But the fact remains that a lot of great athletes have a hard time writing a second act for their working lives that equals the satisfaction they found in the first. The reason, I believe, has to do with an ingredient in the recipe for athletic greatness we've given scant attention until now: context.

FINDING YOUR FIT

If you're as into wine as Drew Bledsoe is, you know about *terroir*, a French word that refers to everything outside the grape itself—the soil it grew in, the climate that surrounded it, the specific weather conditions it was subjected to—that affects the flavor of the wine made from it. Grapes grown in different places and at different times from the same seeds will produce wines that taste noticeably different. To make a truly great wine, therefore, you need the right grapes *and* the right terroir.

It's the same with people. Each of us is influenced profoundly by all aspects of our environment, as has been shown time and time again in studies of twins. Identical twins separated in early childhood and raised in different environments become very different people—eerily similar in some of their behavioral tics, sure, but more unalike than you would expect if you thought that genes ran the show. This is another reason why talent, whether physical or mental, doesn't guarantee greatness. I'm no longer talking about nature versus nurture here; I'm talking about nature versus nurture versus *circumstances*.

"Be not afraid of greatness," goes a famous line from Shakespeare's *Twelfth Night*. "Some are born great, some achieve greatness, and some have greatness thrust upon 'em." That hits the nail on the head. To be born great is to be born with one or more gifts, such as strength or intelligence, that facilitate success in any context. To achieve greatness requires that your God-given potential be nurtured to the utmost degree. And to have greatness thrust upon you is to get lucky, finding yourself at the right place at the right time to take maximum advantage of your potential. In reality, greatness always requires all three, with only the relative contributions of each factor differing from case to case. No person becomes great, in other words, unless they are born with a gift that is then nurtured by life experience and aided by "terroir," or circumstance—the lucky accidents that are a bigger part of life than we like to acknowledge.

Another thing about twins is that they are never truly identical, even when they are monozygotic, meaning they possess the same genes (nature), and when they are raised in the same household (nurture). When a pair of identical twins happen to be world-class athletes, the nongenetic, nonenvironmental differences between them become measurable. In the 1980s, when Dave Scott and Mark Allen were dominating Ironman racing on the men's side, two of the top performers on the women's side were identical twins Sylviane and Patricia Puntous of Canada. As you would expect, the sisters were near equals in performance, yet they weren't exact equals, Sylviane earning five podium finishes to Patricia's two at the Ironman World Championship, where Patricia never finished ahead of Sylviane (except once, only to be disqualified for illegally drafting on the bike).

Animal research offers further confirmation that nature and nurture do not alone determine individual characteristics. Evolutionary biologist Benjamin de Bivort has shown that houseflies with matching genomes bred in the same environment exhibit widely varying behaviors, including the housefly equivalents of left- and right-handedness. The reason is that *different things happen* in the lives of these would-be clones, and even tiny differences in what happens lead to significant differences in behavior and (in the case of humans) personality.

When I say tiny, I mean tiny. Circumstantial differences in life experience begin before birth, at the biochemical level, inside the developing embryo. When the human brain develops in utero, genes orchestrate the processes of cell division and synaptic wiring, but they do so in a loose way that allows the self-organizing nature of biochemistry to handle the rest. This allows a certain amount of randomness to shape the "final" outcome, such that two identical twins who develop in the same womb are born with slightly different brains.

Post-birth, external events take over. Among twins there is a well-known phenomenon called self-differentiation whereby each twin fashions a unique identity in contrast to the other. For example, a five-year-old twin might crack a joke that gets a positive response from an adult. Seeing this, the other twin begins to see the first as "the funny one," and to fashion a contrasting identity that is more serious. It might have been purely a matter of chance that the one twin and not the other cracked a joke that got a response that made an impression on both; nevertheless, this chance event could function as a developmental wedge resulting in easily distinguished personalities in adulthood.

The random element in life influences the biographical trajectories of not just twins but everyone, including athletes. A 2006 study found that active players in four major sports leagues—the NBA, the NHL, the MLB, and the PGA—hailed disproportionately from small cities rather than large cities or rural areas. Although the authors of the study were not able to determine exactly what it was about the terroir of small cities that favored athletic achievement, we can be sure it had nothing to do with talent.

Being born at the right time is another form of luck that affects the likelihood of achieving athletic greatness. I remind you again of Dave Scott and Mark Allen, the rival triathletes we first met in Chapter 1. The sport of triathlon didn't even exist when Dave and Mark were in college, where they tried and failed to make it to the Olympics as swimmers. Had swim-bike-run racing come around any later, Dave likely would have remained a swim coach, as he was when he discovered triathlon, and Mark might have heeded his father's wish that he become a doctor, for it is certain that neither of them could have achieved greatness in any other sport.

Sometimes the contextual shift required to unleash greatness is subtle. Hope Solo is considered one of the finest goalkeepers in the history of women's soccer. But she started out playing forward, and she played it well, scoring 109 goals in high school and earning All-American status twice. But her college coach persuaded her to change positions, and it turned out she was even better at stopping goals than she was at scoring them. We'll never know what would have become of Hope had she remained a striker, but odds are she would have fallen somewhat short of greatness.

Warren Kennaugh, an Australian performance coach and author of the book *FIT: When Talent and Intelligence Just Won't Cut It*, has argued that "talent is nothing more than the accurate and consistent deployment of a behavior in an environment where that behavior is valued and creates the desired results." In other words, talent has no existence independent of context.* Not everyone has the potential to achieve greatness in a way that is valued to the degree that elite sports

---

* This is true not only for human athletes but also, according to evolutionary biologist Andreas Wagner, for nature as a whole. In his 2023 book *Sleeping Beauties: The Mystery of Dormant Innovations in Nature and Culture*, Wagner notes that "no innovation succeeds on its own merit. The value of a new gene does not come

are, but everyone does have an optimal environment somewhere in the multiverse in which their talent is best expressed. A few lucky people are almost born into their ideal terroir, like the Williams sisters, Venus and Serena, whose talent for tennis might have gone undiscovered had their father not been a tennis fanatic with a knack for coaching and little or none of the domineering psychopathy of Mike Agassi. Most of us aren't so lucky, however, and must go looking for our special niche—or else create it. That's much harder. But harder still is finding or creating a *second* special niche at age thirty or forty after aging out of the first one, which is the challenge that faces retiring elite athletes. Why do so many of them struggle after leaving their sport? There's your answer.

Not everyone cares to pursue greatness, and that's fine. But for those who do, my advice is to respect the contextuality of talent and to be persistent and resourceful in finding or creating your special niche. If at first you don't succeed, try another sport—or change the game, as James Lawrence did.

I met James in August 2015 in Lehi, Utah, where he spent the day completing an improvised Ironman triathlon—that's 2.4 miles of swimming, 112 miles of bicycling, and a marathon for dessert—for the fiftieth time in as many days *in as many states*. The road that led him to this almost superhuman undertaking was neither straight nor smooth, much less marked for him in advance. Raised in British Columbia, James skipped college, started a family early, and bounced around among various lines of work (bartender, golf equipment salesman) before landing in real estate just in time for the great recession.

The state of desperation James found himself in after the collapse of his mortgage-lending business felt oddly freeing to him—or perhaps

---

from some inner quality of the gene. It comes from the world into which the gene is born, a world beyond the gene's control."

not so oddly, knowing what we know about screw-loosening life expe-riences. A few years before he lost everything, James had discovered and fallen in love with the sport of triathlon. Competitive by nature, he yearned to be a contender, but try as he might, he was no Chrissie Wellington. James did, however, have one thing going for him: He never seemed to get tired or break down. He couldn't go fast, but he could go forever. So he decided to change the sport to suit his strength, and the Iron Cowboy was born.

Under this *nom de guerre*, James performed a series of endurance feats that began with a successful attempt to break the world record for the most half-Ironman races completed in a single year. By draw-ing attention to these exploits and using them to raise money for wor-thy causes such as children's education, James was able to turn them into a full-blown career, one that not only paid the bills and made him semi-famous but also allowed him to experience greatness, something he couldn't have done had he stuck to life's pre-paved roads.

After meeting James on the final day of his "50-50-50" challenge, I kept in touch with him, and I even wound up ghostwriting his memoir, *Iron Cowboy*. Our goal was to provide a truthful account of his journey that left every reader believing that they, too, could be great. I will be far from disappointed if *this* book does the same for you.

CHAPTER TEN

Nurturing Greatness

If you bungle raising your children, I don't think whatever else you do matters very much.
—JACQUELINE KENNEDY

I promise this will be last time I bring up terrible fathers. If I could avoid making yet another reference to paternal malpractice I would, but as it is, I feel duty bound to offer an important clarification before I let the subject drop once and for all. My concern is that, having read the many profiles of great athletes with terrible fathers in the preceding chapters, some readers will have been left with the impression that, if they want to raise a child to become a great athlete, their best course of action is to traumatize the child in their formative years. No doubt I'm letting paranoia get the best of me here, but if even one reader is thinking such thoughts, I want to put a stop to them now.

First of all, no parent should have it as their goal to raise a child to become a great athlete. Forcing a child to pursue dreams chosen for them isn't parenting, it's enslavement. The best parents afford their children the freedom to choose their own dreams and instill in them the wherewithal to pursue those dreams with some measure of satisfaction, if not outright success. It's important to understand that great athletes with terrible fathers are black swans—rare phenomena produced by a confluence of special factors that are impossible to replicate. I would be lying to you if I claimed that Frank Shorter, Clara Hughes, and others like them succeeded *despite* their terrible fathers. After all, these athletes have openly expressed their own belief that early mistreatment by their dads contributed positively to their future successes in sports (while also subtracting from their overall well-being). However, bad parenting alone did not make these athletes great; rather, it was the combination of bad parenting and something in their makeup (namely, an innate self-regulatory strength) that enabled them to not only survive their unenviable upbringings but emerge from them with an even stronger capacity to self-regulate and an unreasonable will to win, hence fully equipped mentally to win at the highest level of sport. But for every Sergey Bubka or Andre Agassi who gained something athletically from having a terrible father, there are dozens of unknown athletes whose potential for greatness was extinguished rather than fortified by bad parenting.

I'll say it again: No parent should even *want* to raise a child to become a great athlete, let alone try, except if their child chooses this path for themselves. But let's suppose, for the sake of argument, that you *do* want this for your child, and you want to play the percentages.

In that case, your best course of action will be to do everything in your power to be a *terrific* parent, not a terrible one. For although it is true that great athletes with terrible fathers are overrepresented in this book, there are innumerable examples available to us of great athletes blessed with fine parents—fathers and mothers who aided their child's success by doing all the things that fine parents do. To be clear, even with first-rate parenting, your child will need to possess early talent and a loose screw to actually become great in their chosen sport. But that doesn't bother you, because you don't really care whether your child becomes a great athlete! All that matters to you is that your child will benefit from your fine parenting in a myriad of ways beyond sports. Right?

ONE THING IN COMMON

To prove to you that first-rate parenting is preferable to bad parenting in nurturing athletic greatness, I'm going to tell you about two great athletes whose parents exemplify the right way to rear a promising young athlete but are otherwise radically different. First up is Lorena Ochoa, who earned her place in history by becoming the first Mexican golfer ever to achieve the rank of number one in the world. Born and raised in Guadalajara, Lorena got the childhood every kid deserves. Her father, Javier Ochoa, is described in Lorena's autobiography, *Dream Big*, as a man with "a huge heart"; her mother, Marcela Reyes, as "a woman of great strength, warmth and joy, with a great capacity for giving and for dedication to her children." Reyes was a successful artist, Ochoa a businessman specializing in real estate, the family well-off by Mexican standards. Their primary residence sat adjacent to the Guadalajara Country Club, where they were members, and for most of Lorena's youth, the Ochoas kept a second home in Tapalpa, a rural dreamland where Lorena and her brothers and sister and cousins and friends enjoyed endless days of playing in tree forts, riding mountain bikes and motorbikes and horses, and causing mischief.

Lorena was especially close to her father, an avid golfer who, in response to his five-year-old daughter's incessant pestering, allowed her to tag along on his rounds, and who soon thereafter—in response to her continued pleading—permitted her to play alongside him, going so far as to ruin a perfectly good set of clubs by sawing them down to a size befitting Lorena's diminutive frame. It was a sacrifice he wouldn't regret, for it was obvious from the very first swing that Lorena had a gift her older brothers lacked—a gift so exceptional that club pro Jesús Sandoval hailed her as the best child golfer he'd ever seen and volunteered to coach her. Had Señor Ochoa been a terrible father, he would have done either of two things at this moment: jealously quash his daughter's budding passion for golf, and with it the threat that her superior ability represented, or push her headlong into the sport so that he might reap the benefits that naturally accrue to the parents of athletic prodigies. But Ochoa was not a terrible father, so he did neither of these things, instead supporting his daughter's golfing exploits with unbridled gusto and zero pressure. "They never obligated me to train or compete, much less to win," Lorena reflects in *Dream Big*.

Research has shown that, contrary to our intuitions, early specialization in a sport lowers the likelihood of achieving greatness therein. Kids who get too serious about a sport too early, playing it year-round to the exclusion of all other sports, tend to burn out or stagnate in their teens or college years. Lorena was spared this fate by her parents' hands-off support of her golfing exploits and whatever else she chose to do, and also by Lorena's wide-ranging tastes in physical activity. Despite investing huge amounts of time in golf when she was very young, she made time to also compete in basketball, soccer, swimming, tennis, and track and field. The thing that finally got her to focus on golf exclusively was not outside pressure but defeat.

At thirteen, Lorena had won nearly every golf tournament she'd ever played in, including multiple junior national and world championships, but her involvement in other sports had created an opening for some of her domestic rivals to gain ground, and as a result she finished third in the 1994 junior national championship tournament. Another kid in Lorena's place would have been disappointed by the loss. Lorena, however, was not disappointed—she was devastated. "It was incredible what I felt," she writes. "I realized immediately that the experience of losing had been disagreeable, and that I would do everything I could to make sure it wouldn't happen again."

As I stated earlier, any parent who wants to nurture their child's potential for athletic greatness would be wise to raise them with textbook competence, doing all the things that lie within a parent's power to satisfy the basic psychological needs, as they will thereby strengthen the child's self-regulatory ability, and you won't find a great athlete who's not a master self-regulator. But to actually achieve greatness, the child of such a parent must have at least one core need that is *not* met by mommy and daddy, a hungry ghost inside that compels them to sacrifice, risk, and endure more than anyone else to succeed in sports. Whether they're born with a screw loose or acquire it through trauma outside the home, they simply must have it.

In her extreme reaction to defeat at the 1994 junior national golf championship, we see clear evidence of a loose screw in young Lorena Ochoa—a not-normal emotional response to losing, as she herself recognized. But was the hungry ghost that revealed itself in this moment inherited or somehow acquired, despite her good parenting? The answer lies in the fact that, although this seminal episode was Lorena's first taste of failure in high-stakes competition, it was not her first major display of hypercompetitiveness. That came much earlier, when a six-year-old Lorena started taking golf lessons from Jesús Sandoval. One of only two girls in a class of seventeen, she not only wanted but expected to outperform all of her fellow learners, including boys much older than her, and was outraged on the rare occasion she didn't. It's fair to say that anyone *this* competitive as a first-grader was probably born so, and likely to remain hypercompetitive in adolescence and beyond, and Lorena certainly did. At sixteen, she stalked former professional golfer Rafael Alarcón for weeks on the fairways and greens of Guadalajara Country Club before choosing a moment to approach him and, by way of introducing herself, declared her intention to beat him one day in match play.

To his credit, Alarcón was not put off by Lorena's chutzpah. Quite the opposite, in fact. Recognizing her potential, he offered to coach her. Not long afterward, and long before she made good on her promise to beat Alarcón in head-to-head match play, Lorena blindsided him with an even bolder declaration: "Rafa, I want to be world number one."

When I read these words in *Dream Big*, I couldn't help but think of that scene in *Swimming to Antarctica* where a twelve-year-old Lynne Cox, on her first day with Don Gambril's Phillips 66 club, voices her intention to one day join the Olympians in lane eight. In my mind's eye, I picture Alarcón reacting to Lorena's audacity the same way Gambril reacted to Lynne's, slack-jawed surprise giving way to a squint of reappraisal followed by a nod of recognition—and respect. In other words, the same behavior we all display when we're trying to decide whether the person talking to us is barking mad or very special before concluding that they are, in fact, both.

Boldness, you may recall from Chapter 6, is largely a matter of temperament, meaning that, unlike most personality traits, it does not express our psychological needs but exists independent of them. Lorena shot out of the womb like a cannonball, as bold as they come. At age three she earned the nickname "Voltereta" (Spanish for "Somersault") by performing forward flips off kitchen chairs, a year later woke her parents at dawn one morning by joyriding past the house in Tapalpa on a motorbike, and a year after that broke both arms in multiple locations after falling twenty feet in a failed attempt to execute a flying leap from a tree branch to a zip line.

It's easy to see how Lorena's wild side might have held her back from golfing greatness if she'd lacked another side that served to channel her boldness and competitiveness in the right direction. One can imagine this unbalanced version of her snapping putters over her thigh and flinging irons into water hazards like Happy Gilmore. But Lorena had her shit together, so she did none of these things. And for that she can thank her parents, at least in part. Her father walked every hole of every tournament at her side, holding her hand, from the day she started playing competitively until she left home to attend the University of Arizona on scholarship. One *cannot* easily imagine the child of such a parent becoming a self-sabotaging head case on the golf course, and of course Lorena did not. Is it possible that she possessed a sufficient quantity of innate self-regulatory capacity to have become great even without good parenting, à la Mark Allen, Frank Shorter, Sergey Bubka, Clara Hughes, and Andre Agassi? Sure. But Lorena herself thinks not.

"I've witnessed regrettable cases of parents who obligated their kids to play and train," she writes. "I saw dramatic scenes of parents shouting at their kids because they were losing the tournament, and even physically attacking them. It was very sad because the result is that they end up hating golf, and they never get to feel love or passion for the sport, but they play it with fear, like a sacrifice. Obviously it's difficult for them to stand out, and if they do it's only for a short time." These words ought to be taken at face value. If Lorena herself believes that without the support and nurturing of her family, she would never have fulfilled her dream of becoming the top-ranked female golfer in the world, who are we to disagree?

Throughout her childhood, people told Lorena she seemed older than she was. "I think I matured faster than was normal," she notes matter-of-factly in *Dream Big*. In an earlier chapter we saw that self-regulation is the engine that fuels emotional maturation, and that emotional growth in turn fuels athletic development. Poor parenting stymies emotional maturation, which is why it took Andre Agassi so long to get his shit together. And the inverse is also true: good parenting spurs emotional growth. A scientific review conducted by psychologist Alberto Alegre of East Stroudsburg University and published in *The Family Journal* in 2011 found that children who achieved high scores on measures of emotional maturity had parents who scored well on measures of "responsiveness, emotion-related coaching, and positive demandingness"—qualities that describe perfectly the parenting style of Javier Ochoa and Marcela Reyes. Again, it's possible that Lorena would have matured quickly with less spectacular parents, but it's certain she matured quicker with the parents she got, not only while she lived under their roof but long afterward. In fact, by the age of twenty-eight Lorena was so far ahead of her peers in overall maturity that she retired from golf, despite being at the absolute pinnacle of her unparalleled greatness, having held the world number one ranking for a record-shattering 158 consecutive weeks. Talk about quitting while you're ahead!

Supreme self-regulators like Lorena Ochoa have a way of zigging where others zag. Steered by their own internal compass, they choose the road not taken while others drift along the path of least resistance. No one—not even her parents—expected (much less wanted) Lorena to walk away from the game she loved, and from the wealth and fame it garnered, with so many prime years in front of her. Be that as it may, Lorena's loving, supportive, stable, trustworthy parents deserve at least some of the credit for raising a daughter capable of such bold and independent nonconformity.

DIFFERENT IN ALL WAYS BUT ONE

It goes without saying that the case study I've just presented does not qualify as science. A skeptical reader with an understanding of science might point out that the conclusions I've drawn from Lorena's story are vitiated by so-called confounding variables, which is to say, by the impossibility of disentangling the effects of the good parenting she received from the other advantages she enjoyed in her formative years, including good health and socioeconomic privilege. That's why I'm offering up a second case study—that of champion wheelchair racer Tatyana McFadden, whose *only* advantage during childhood was good parenting.

Tatyana was born with spina bifida, a congenital malformation of the spinal cord that left her without feeling or movement in her legs. In wealthier nations today, people with this condition have a better than 90 percent chance of surviving into adulthood and leading relatively normal lives. Tatyana, however, drew her first breath in St. Petersburg, Russia, in 1989, a time and place in which life expectancy for people like her was less than one week. Advised to leave the child in a government hospital and move on with her life, Tatyana's mother did so.

Still very much alive after several months, Tatyana was transferred to Baby House #13, an orphanage lifted straight out of a Dickens novel. In her autobiography, *Ya, Sama!* (Russian for "I can do it," which is Tatyana's personal motto), she describes the facility as "a place of long, empty hallways, dim, flickering lights, and cold, drafty rooms." Given porridge for breakfast, and seldom more than a thin soup for lunch and supper, she slept in a small bed in a dormitory crammed with about a dozen other children. Hygiene consisted of a daily, frigid sponge bath, and clothes (including cloth diapers) were shared communally. The all-female staff had no medical training and no clue how to care for Tatyana, the orphanage's only disabled resident, who remained frail and sickly despite defying predictions of an early demise. Left to fend for herself without the aid of a wheelchair, braces, or physical therapy, she discovered her own ways of getting around, which included walking upside down on her hands.

During the day, Tatyana and her fellow foundlings were deposited on plastic mats indoors or, weather permitting, in a fenced-in dirt yard, where they were expected to entertain themselves. There were no toys, few organized activities, and no lessons of any kind. Tatyana was not even taught to speak, let alone read, learning Russian word by word by eavesdropping while the staff conversed. Though not physically abusive, the caregivers at Baby House #13 were aloof and unkind, especially the night crew, who demanded absolute silence from the children and were quick to punish infractions as minor as getting out of bed to use the lavatory.

The hope of every orphan is to be adopted, and Tatyana was no exception. Whatever it was this hope was based on, it sure as hell wasn't statistics. Very few Russian couples adopt children, and fewer still adopt disabled children. The odds of finding a home decline steadily with each passing birthday, and by the time Tatyana turned six her future as a permanent ward of the state seemed a fait accompli. But then she caught a lucky break—her first, and the only one she would ever need. It came in the form of Deborah McFadden, an American woman who visited the orphanage in her role as head of the International Children's Alliance, a nonprofit adoption agency. Having previously served as the US commissioner of disabilities in the George H. W. Bush administration, McFadden had a soft spot for disabled persons, engendered by her own experience with the strange and terrible Guillain-Barré virus, which left her paralyzed for several years. And Tatyana wasn't just any disabled person. She had a happy, affectionate disposition and exuded positivity, despite the bleakness of her early years. McFadden found her irresistible.

"I couldn't get her off my mind," she told *People* magazine in 2016, after Tatyana won her fourth consecutive Boston Marathon. "I still can't explain the connection we had, but there was no question in my mind that she was supposed to be my child."

Within a year of that first meeting, Tatyana *was* McFadden's child, her cramped little world expanding vastly overnight. Her first-ever train ride brought her to Moscow, where she tasted ice cream for the first time before boarding her first-ever flight, bound for America, a place she'd never heard of, to begin life afresh with McFadden and her partner, Bridget O'Shaughnessy, in an affluent Baltimore suburb. As fate would have it, a local running race passed right in front of Tatyana's new home on the morning after her arrival, McFadden showing her how to high-five participants.

Here is where the parallels between Tatyana's and Lorena's stories become striking. Like Lorena's parents, Tatyana's adoptive mother supported her daughter without ever pushing her. Her role, as she saw it, was to create opportunities for Tatyana and then stand back, letting her puzzle out what to do with them. She started by opening up the yellow pages and phoning local swim instructors, who each in turn refused to give Tatyana lessons upon learning of her condition. Undaunted, McFadden outfoxed the last instructor on her list by withholding the fact of Tatyana's disability until she'd gotten the woman to boast that she could teach *anyone* to swim.

Later on, when it came to her attention that Tatyana was being held out of playground activities at school, McFadden shamed the phys ed teacher into relenting by challenging her daughter to scale a rope that had thwarted her classmates but was mastered in seconds by strong-armed Tatyana. Later still, when Tatyana joined the high school track team but was forbidden to compete alongside her teammates, McFadden stormed into the Maryland Disability Law Center and, with Tatyana's full participation, filed a lawsuit against the Howard County School District, which resulted in a change in state law that led to a domino effect in other states. "Had I said I was starting a rock band," Tatyana writes of her adoptive mother's supportiveness, "I am sure she would have bought me a set of drums."

Naturally, none of this skillful guardianship would have elevated Tatyana to athletic greatness if she hadn't shared certain of Lorena Ochoa's key mental traits. But she did. At the orphanage, Tatyana had scant opportunity to express her wild side. Under McFadden's roof, however, she was free to be her bold self. At her first swim lesson, Tatyana leaped into the water without any coaxing from the instructor (the very one McFadden had railroaded into accepting her daughter as a student), exhibiting none of the reluctance of most young beginners, and promptly sank to the bottom. "I would try anything," she recalls. "I swung from ropes, climbed up rock walls, bounced along on a raft behind a motorboat, and rode on a jet-ski."

As competitive as she was bold, Tatyana—like Lorena—reacted badly to her first taste of failure as an athlete. And it happened at almost the same age, coincidentally or otherwise. Tatyana discovered wheelchair racing at thirteen and enjoyed immediate success, setting a world record in the 100-meter sprint at the 2002 US Paralympic junior national championships and claiming two medals at the 2004 Paralympic Games in Athens. But at the 2006 world championships in the Netherlands, on the advice of others, Tatyana abandoned her preferred aggressive racing style in the 1500-meter event, choosing instead to ride in the slipstream of other athletes with the intent of passing them at the end. Lacking experience with the strategy, she got boxed in and finished out of the medals.

Nothing Tatyana had experienced in her brief life prior to this moment hurt as much. Not her birth mother's abandonment. Not the misery of her early poor health. Not even the bleak and loveless existence she endured at Baby House #13. "While the other racers all gathered around high-fiving and congratulating one another," she writes in *Ya, Sama!*, "I felt like the wind had been knocked out of me." Having learned her lesson, Tatyana went back to her aggressive racing style and was rewarded with victories in twenty-three major marathons, sixteen world championship races, and seven Paralympic events.

Tatyana won because she *needed* to win, and she needed to win because, well, she just did! Some people are born with hungry ghosts inside them—there's no explaining it. But what *is* explainable is the importance of good parenting (the most powerful force in the postnatal universe for getting a person's shit together) in actualizing the potential of naturally "crazy" athletes like Tatyana McFadden and Lorena Ochoa. Collectively, the parents of these two great athletes demonstrate the best way to raise a child who has both the potential and the desire—the physical talent and the unreasonable drive—to be great. Each in their own way allowed their gifted child to control the pace and direction of her athletic development, loved her unconditionally, encouraged her with perfect consistency through all the ups and downs she faced on the road to greatness, and sacrificed willingly to support their child's dreams.

When Lorena was fifteen, she sat her parents down to break the news that she intended to become the best woman golfer in the world. Her father's response, recorded verbatim in her memoir, was this: "Your mother and I are very happy with your decision, and you know that you have the support of all of the family."

Very happy.

Your decision.

Support of all.

Folks, you couldn't ask for a tidier summation of how to parent an athlete with the potential to be great. Or any athlete, for that matter. Or heck, even a nonathlete!

AN OPEN QUEST FOR MASTERY

We're almost done. There's just one more athlete I want to tell you about—an athlete who is unlike Lorena Ochoa and Tatyana McFadden and every other athlete we've studied thus far in one notable respect: she's never won anything, and she never will.

There's been a lot of talk about talent in this book. My goal in writing it—one of them, anyway—was to persuade you that later talent, which is mainly psychological in nature, is at least as important as early talent, which is mainly physical, in the recipe for athletic greatness. I'm confident that, if nothing else, I've succeeded in convincing you that the athletes profiled in the preceding pages had an abundance of later talent, which in each case manifested as an addiction-like need to excel in their chosen sport and an extraordinary capacity to control their actions, emotions, and thoughts in the pursuit of well-chosen goals. In making my argument, however, I've glossed over the important fact that these athletes also had no small amount of early talent, performing well, if not brilliantly, in their sport of choice when they first took it up. Which raises the following question: What role does later (mental) talent play for athletes who, unlike the greats, were not gifted with exceptional early (physical) talent?

I run no risk of insulting Diane Miller in stating that she was not gifted with exceptional talent for running. It's a truth that she openly acknowledges. Raised in Winona, Minnesota, Diane had scant interest in sports until her junior year of high school, when, for no obvious reason, she made a spontaneous decision to go out for cross country. She had no pretensions of branding herself the next Joan Benoit, and if she had, they'd have been laid to rest when she finished dead last in her debut race, and last again in each subsequent race, looking very much the also-ran she was in her off-brand sneakers purchased at Payless. Yet despite Diane's underwhelming results, her coach, a man with the enviable name of Jim Flim, lavished her with as much attention as he gave the faster runners—perhaps more. He stood waiting (and waiting) for her at the finish of each painful practice and every humbling race, his arms crossed in mock impatience, wearing a wry smile that made Diane smile back despite herself, and as she approached him, he called out to her (using a nickname he'd bestowed at the start of the season), "Bring it home, Lady Di!"

Coach Flim made Diane feel seen, understood, and valued, talent be damned. In a blog post she wrote some thirty-six years later, she reflected that "when I look back on how significant his influence was . . . I have come to the conclusion that he was matching the effort I was giving. It was a kind of circle, really. I never missed practice. I worked hard. I didn't complain. I didn't give up. I watched what he valued, and the example he set." Coach Flim, she continued, "saw beyond the quiet kid in last place—he saw that I had a little grit, and a little fire burning. And I wanted to be those things—gritty and fiery."

So, when the season ended, Diane kept on running, alone, without a soul to pull her along or await her at the finish, gritting her way through a brutal Minnesota winter, a soggy spring, and a muggy, buggy summer, swapping out her off-brand Payless sneakers for a pair of proper running shoes somewhere along the way. The result was that, come fall, Diane was no longer the slowest runner on the Winona High School cross-country team.

Nor was she the fastest. This is a true story, after all, not a Disney movie. Try as she might, the new Diane still fell short of making the varsity seven. But with her coach's help, Lady Di fulfilled as much of her natural potential as her more gifted teammates, probably more. By the end of her senior season, Diane had real momentum behind her running—or so it seemed—but when she left Winona for college she abruptly quit, and almost before she knew it, she was fifty years old, overweight, and unhealthy.

It's funny how often life's sudden turns are precipitated by nothing in particular. In much the same way the teenage Diane spontaneously decided to go out for cross country, the middle-aged Diane, on a day like any other day, got a notion to hire a personal trainer. She was thinking short-term, however, more interested in a quick fix than a deep trans-formation. Becoming a runner again was certainly the furthest thing from her mind when she walked into a Minneapolis gym with the goal of losing a certain number of pounds in eight weeks. But she didn't like the vibe she got from the trainer she spoke to there, nor that of the next three trainers she interviewed. On paper, all of these guys were per-fectly qualified to help Diane achieve her stated aim. So what was it she truly sought? Not until she crossed the threshold of Lions Gym and met Kirk DeWindt did Diane discover what she hadn't quite realized she'd wanted all along: not a trainer, but a *coach*.

From the moment she met him, Coach Kirk (as she calls him now, eight years after their first meeting) reminded Diane of Coach Flim, only younger and brawnier. Like Flim, DeWindt showed a genuine interest in Diane and took her seriously, defying her expectations as a plump, perimenopausal woman. Also like Flim, he inspired Diane to exceed her own expectations by showing a willingness to invest as much in her as she was willing to invest in herself, without limit.

By the time Diane reached her weight-loss goal, it was no longer her goal. For she had indeed become a runner again—an athlete—and athletes don't just achieve one goal and spend the rest of their lives celebrating. I met Diane at a three-day adult running camp in Austin, Texas, in 2022. Among the goals she had achieved in the several years that preceded this encounter were improving her 5K time (by thirteen minutes), completing an ultramarathon, racing with her daughter, and starting a running blog. But she was far from satisfied.

"I'm fifty-five years old and I'm slow," Diane wrote to me in an email message a few weeks after the camp. "Those are just the facts. But I think that's a cover, at least for me, for feeling like I might not even have a right to that kind of fantasy, let alone really considering it as reality." The fantasy Diane was referring to was an idea I'd cooked up for an extended residential adult running camp modeled after an experience I had in 2017 with the Northern Arizona Elite professional running team. Diane had lit up when I shared this vision with her in Austin, and now here she was expressing an irresistible pull toward the opportunity to go all the way with her running, just like the pros. Yet also some trepidation.

I assured Diane that the pro-style running camp I envisioned was designed with the express intent of exploding the myth that only gifted young athletes have a right to go all the way with their sport, making this opportunity available to any runner with an earnest desire to reach their full potential. Knowing how influential Coach Flim and Coach Kirk had been in her choice to take her running as far as she had already, I was confident Diane would overcome her reticence and go for it, and in the end she did.

It's exciting for any coach to have the chance to develop a young athlete blessed with off-the-charts early talent. But the best coaches don't really prefer such wunderkinds, because their true mission is to help athletes reach their full potential, and this mission can be accomplished with athletes at any level of early talent. Mind you, not every athlete has what it takes to make the most of their potential. It requires a mental makeup that is no less rare than elite physical talent. Yet this makeup is distinct and separate from physical talent, and it exists in less-gifted athletes as well as in the likes of Lorena Ochoa and Tatyana McFadden. And the best coaches are able to spot it in any athlete who happens to possess it, regardless of ability, as Flim and DeWindt did in Diane.

The unfortunate reality is that few athletes with less than elite-level physical talent feel it's worth their while to go all the way with their sport. The young and gifted are incentivized to do so by the promise of recognition and financial reward. Lacking these incentives, the Diane Millers of the world are left feeling vaguely ridiculous for even contemplating making a full commitment to sport. This irks me, because athletes who commit to the pursuit of greatness are rewarded with something far more valuable than fame and fortune: a personal journey that transcends sport.

In Chapter 2 I introduced the Buddhist concept of *dukkha,* a deep sense of dissatisfaction that lies at the core of the human condition. Let's face it: Life is hard, and we all struggle. Studying the lives and minds of great athletes exposes these truths in an interesting way. Sport is how these special individuals cope with a challenging existence. What makes them great, in large measure, is that they treat winning and losing as if they were life and death, which in a sense they are, because their entire personhood has been staked on the quest for greatness. But here's the thing: it works!

Like the rest of us, great athletes are a little bit "crazy." Yet in the pursuit of athletic greatness, these athletes find a productive use for their "craziness," transforming kryptonite into a superpower. What's more, in the same pursuit, they are required to get their shit together to a degree they never would in more modest undertakings, and the benefits of so doing spread far beyond the boundaries of the field of play. I believe that Diane Miller was glimpsing these rewards when she told me, "There must be some reason I have gone so deep with all this, and some reason, bigger than running, that running is such a driving force." In the several years Diane had been pursuing her version of greatness, she had learned more about herself, and had *changed* more, than she had in the thirty-plus years between her first and second incarnations as an athlete. But she sensed, rightly, that she could learn and grow even more if she just gave herself permission to allow running to be for her what it was for, say, Frank Shorter.

Great athletes are amazing people. I hope this book has given you a fuller appreciation for their amazingness. I'm under no illusion, however, that my theory of athletic greatness can be used to create a system for manufacturing great athletes, a breed of human that always has and always will come about in the accidental way of rare natural phenomena, like fogbows and sun dogs. But a version of greatness is available to all athletes and nonathletes alike, and here my theory may be of some practical use. And at the end of the day, I'd rather be impactful than right. While I've done my best to think and communicate scientifically in these pages, I'm a coach at heart. That's how I see my role in relation to *you*. And, like any coach, I measure success by the change I see in the people I touch, not by whether I'm agreed with.

I'm confident that the ideas I've shared with you are mostly true, and I'm certain that you can use them to your benefit, regardless of whether you're the next Lorena Ochoa, the next Diane Miller, or someone chasing your own version of greatness outside of sport. If, like the people you've encountered in these pages, you can be described as a human being with strengths and weaknesses and a striving spirit, then you can do something with the stuff you've learned and the emotions you've felt in receiving my "coaching." It doesn't have to be the same thing anyone else does with these learnings and feelings, but whatever it is, do it!

AFTERTHOUGHT

**Be perfect, therefore, as your
heavenly father is perfect.**
—MATTHEW 5:48 (NIV)

I'm old enough to remember when musical artists would sometimes hide a secret bonus track on the compact disc version of an album release. The one that haunts me still is "Endless, Nameless," a nightmarish cacophony buried behind ten minutes of silence on the Nirvana album *Nevermind*, which startled me out of an inebriated sleep in a Scottish dormitory late one night in a previous century. Anyhow, what you're reading now is sort of like the literary equivalent of this bygone practice.

My original outline for *The Other Talent* did not include an epilogue, or an afterword, or—as I've cheekily chosen to call this brief coda—an afterthought. No sooner had I completed the manuscript, however, than I realized I had more to say; not a lot more, but enough that I wasn't comfortable leaving it unsaid. Hence this "bonus track."

First, let's rewind. As you may recall, I prefaced the foregoing investigation into the minds of great athletes with a word about words—specifically, a preemptive defense of my use of fraught language such as "screw loose," "shit together," "addiction," and "crazy." Never one to miss an opportunity to come full circle, I'd like to conclude our journey with another word about words. One word in particular.

If an interviewer (I picture Anderson Cooper) were to ask me to summarize in a single word what this book is about, I would answer without hesitation: "talent." It has an interesting etymology, this little noun, deriving from the Latin *talentum*, which originally referred to a measure of weight as well as to a denomination of currency, similar to the English *pound*. If you know your Bible, you knew this already, courtesy of the parable of the talents. In the Gospel of Matthew, Jesus tells the story of a wealthy man who, prior to embarking on a long trip, deposits various sums of money with each of three servants. Upon his return, the wealthy man learns that the servant who was given five talents invested them and doubled his master's money, the servant given two talents did likewise, and the servant given one talent stashed it underground. Angered by this last report, the wealthy man excoriates the servant who did nothing with the little given to him and orders him to hand over his one talent to the servant with ten.

Some readers of this parable can't get past the fact that its protagonist is kind of a jerk. But keep in mind, it's a parable, and Jesus told it for a reason. The talents at the center of the story are meant to be interpreted not as literal coins but as gifts from God. This is why English dictionaries today define "talent" as "a special natural ability or aptitude." The message of the parable, then, is *do not waste the talents you are given, however few.* God judges us not by how much talent we start off with, Jesus infers, but by what we do with it. Not by early talent, as it were, but by later talent.

The conclusion I had originally intended for this book is the one you encountered at the end of Chapter 10, where I expressed my view that too many athletes possess the self-limiting belief that they aren't talented enough to bother making the most of their talent, and I wished aloud that passion, rather than ability, would determine how far each athlete went in pursuit of their full potential. But it occurred to me that this declaration doesn't go quite far enough, and in particular, that it ought to be broadened beyond sport to encompass the full spectrum of "talents," from botany to parenting.

At bottom, the message of this book is nothing more than a secular version of the message Jesus communicated in the parable of the talents. People forget what a hard-ass Jesus was during his brief tenancy on Earth. He held his followers to a high standard—an impossibly high standard, some might say—commanding them to love their enemies, admonishing them that a sinful thought was no better than a sinful deed, and expecting them to literally move mountains with the power of their faith. He cursed a fig tree for failing to bear fruit, a warning to his flock that the same judgment awaited them if they failed to bring forth the potential within them. He challenged us to "Be perfect . . . as your heavenly father is perfect."

I don't consider myself particularly religious, but I've sat in a lot of church pews on a lot of Sundays, and to the best of my recollection, I have never heard the man or woman at the pulpit adduce this particular line of scripture in the course of delivering their weekly sermon. Which is rather odd, because it's the grand finale of the famous Sermon on the Mount—a nine-word summation of Jesus's core teachings. The original mic drop, if you will (minus the microphone). Why, we might ask, would the most significant words ever spoken by arguably the most influential man who ever lived be so roundly ignored by those who profess to carry on his teachings? The answer is obvious: because nobody wants to believe that Jesus meant exactly what he said in verse 48 of Chapter 5 of the Book of Matthew!

The Sermon on the Mount is no parable. It's literal, earnest, and direct. Unequivocally, what Jesus meant when he told us to "be perfect" was that *we mortals ought to be nothing less than perfect*—as perfect as our creator—or at least try. That's a hell of a challenge, far too great a challenge for most people to accept—or even acknowledge. Which is why our esteemed preachers skip over this part and hurry ahead to Corinthians, where they linger, perhaps, on "God loves a cheerful giver."

In writing *The Other Talent*, I wrestled with a nagging awareness that there are already far too many books about the keys to worldly success. Stephen Covey opened the floodgates in 1989 with *The 7 Habits of Highly Effective People*, and we've been deluged ever since. The last thing I wanted to do in this book was contribute to the ongoing fetishization of high achievers. But have I not done precisely this in devoting 71,277 admiring words to high achievers in sport? Possibly. So I want to make it clear in this afterthought that I have never read *The 7 Habits of Highly Effective People* and I never will, and that Matthew 5:48 is among a select few quotations I would consider tattooing on the side of my neck. In other words, I wrote *The Other Talent* in the same spirit Jesus preached the Sermon on the Mount, far less in the spirit of Covey's blockbuster volume of self-help.

Oftentimes, the nagging awareness I mentioned a moment ago took the form of an imagined reader disgustedly casting aside my book and shouting, "What's so great about greatness, anyway?" (Or alternatively, "What's wrong with being ordinary?") The problem with such objections is that they presuppose a narrow view of greatness that is limited to productive labors such as sports, business, and the arts. But these are not the only ways to be great. Jesus himself had something else in mind entirely—namely, moral greatness—when he instructed us to be perfect. Judging by his words, the Son of Man didn't give a flying you-know-what about any form of greatness besides greatness of character (or "ordinary greatness," as some call it), about which he cared very much, making utterly plain his belief that none of us, however lacking in monetizable talents, has any legitimate excuse to give a mite less than our absolute best to be the absolute best we can be, as people.

ORDINARY GREATNESS

In the summer of 2022, while I was neck-deep in writing *The Other Talent* (then called *Screw Loose, Shit Together*), I traveled to Rhode Island to help my brother Sean clear out a third-generation family home that had been vacated recently by our elderly parents. It was a sentimental ritual, as you can well imagine—one step shy of organizing an estate sale. For such a tiny house, it contained an astonishing number of books, its erstwhile occupants having both been devout readers. I was especially struck by the vastness of my mother's collection on parenting. Granted, there were professional reasons for this profusion—specifically, Mom's decades of service as a social worker and family therapist—but I suspect she would have consumed much of this material regardless, for her career choice was far from arbitrary, born of an antecedent pull toward motherhood. The oldest title among the dozens Sean and I sorted through bore a copyright date of 1967, not coincidentally the year Mom became pregnant with our elder brother, Josh. We had a lot to do, Sean and I, and little time to do it, yet I couldn't resist pausing my labors to peer inside the musty volume, whose age-crispened pages, I discovered, were crowded with handwritten marginalia, underlinings, and other marks of a paperback that had been not only read, but absorbed. Internalized.

A complex emotion—two parts gratitude, one part awe, three parts grief—flooded my chest as I sifted this evidence of my mother's desire to be nothing less than perfect in her role as a parent. When I'd last seen her two weeks prior, at a memory care center in Vancouver, Washington, she had—for the first time since her Alzheimer's diagnosis—failed to recognize me, confirming her greatest fear. The reason I knew this was her greatest fear was that she'd told me, because I'd asked her, point blank—"What is your greatest fear?"—soon after her medical death sentence was handed down. Was it death itself, I wondered, that she feared most? Not death per se but dying? Not dying but suffering? Losing her independence? Her dignity? Medical expenses? What would I have feared most in Mom's place?

She answered quickly, as if the answer was already there, which—come to think of it—it probably was.

"I don't want to forget you," she rasped.

Laurie Elizabeth Sandeman Fitzgerald is—sorry, *was* (she died on December 13, 2022, six months after her worst fear was realized)—a great mother. As great as Jack Johnson was at boxing, or as Lynne Cox was at open-water swimming, or as any athlete has ever been at any sport. Case in point: When Mom found out I shoplifted one time, she sat me down and asked me if I needed a bigger allowance. Genius! She knew exactly what effect this unorthodox parenting move would have on me. Duly shamed, I refused the pay raise, returned the ill-gotten merchandise, and never stole again. My mother's maternal brilliance garnered none of the fame and fortune that accrue to great athletes, of course. It did, however, bless three grateful boys with beautiful lives—lives they wouldn't trade for any amount of athletic achievement. What made Laurie great was not any particular genetic endowment but her determination to be great. Not early talent, if you please, but later talent. Christlike, she saw no good reason why she shouldn't work as hard and as smart as humanly possible to be the best mother she could be, brooking no excuse for pursuing anything less than perfection in this role.

Take a moment to think about the people you know or have known who exceed all others in wisdom, or generosity, or innocence, or some other high virtue of negligible commercial value. We've encountered one such person in these very pages: Peter Guzmán, husband to Clara Hughes, a man who doesn't have to stop to smell the roses because he's already stopped and always sniffing, perennially immersed in the richness of the moment. What makes *these* people great? Is it that they were lucky enough to start life with five talents versus two, or two versus one? Or is it, rather, that they hold themselves to the highest of standards, taking to heart—either explicitly or implicitly—the command to "be perfect . . . as your heavenly father is perfect"?

What I'm getting at is the idea that greatness is there for the taking, available to anyone who truly wants it. Not everyone can be a great soccer player, or a great chemist, or a great author of books on the psychology of elite athletes. Early talent is real, and much depends on it. But everyone has something inside them that can become a kind of greatness with a full commitment to making the most of what was given to them.

Forget sports. The moral of the story of our journey into the minds of great athletes is much bigger: Don't settle. Don't make excuses. And above all, never assume you're not good enough to be great.

SELECTED REFERENCES

PREFACE

de Manzano, O., S. Cervenka, A. Karabanov, L. Farde, F. Ullén. "Thinking outside a less intact box: thalamic dopamine D2 receptor densities are negatively related to psychometric creativity in healthy individuals." *PLOS One* (2010); 5(5): e10670. doi: 10.1371/journal.pone.0010670. PMID: 20498850; PMCID: PMC2871784.

MacCabe, J. H., M. P. Lambe, S. Cnattingius, P. C. Sham, A. S. David, A. Reichenberg, R. M. Murray, C. M. Hultman. "Excellent school performance at age 16 and risk of adult bipolar disorder: national cohort study." *The British Journal of Psychiatry* (2010); 196(2): 109–15. doi: 10.1192/bjp.bp.108.060368. PMID: 20118454.

CHAPTER 1

Baker, Joe. *The Tyranny of Talent: How It Compels and Limits Athletic Achievement . . . and Why You Should Ignore It*. Toronto: Aberrant, 2022.

CHAPTER 2

Glasser, William. *Positive Addiction.* New York: Harper, 1976.

Lewis, Marc. *The Biology of Desire: Why Addiction Is Not a Disease.* New York: PublicAffairs, 2015.

Maslow, A. H. "A Theory of Human Motivation" (1943). *Psychological Review* 50, no. 4: 370–396.

Ward, Geoffrey C. *Unforgivable Blackness: The Rise and Fall of Jack Johnson.* New York: Vintage, 2006.

CHAPTER 3

Cox, Lynne. *Swimming to Antarctica: Tales of a Long-Distance Swimmer.* Boston: Mariner, 2005.

Hardy, L., M. Barlow, L. Evans, T. Rees, T. Woodman, and C. Warr. "Great British Medalists: Psychosocial Biographies of Super-Elite and Elite Athletes from Olympic Sports." *Progress in Brain Research* 232 (2017): 1–119. doi: 10.1016/bs.pbr.2017.03.004. Epub 2017 Jun 16. PMID: 28648228.

Inzlicht, M., K. M. Werner, J. L. Briskin, and B. W. Roberts. "Integrating Models of Self-Regulation." *Annual Review of Psychology* 72 (January 4, 2021): 319–345. doi: 10.1146/annurev-psych-061020-105721. Epub 2020 Oct 5. PMID: 33017559.

Jackman, P. C., A. E. Whitehead, C. Swann, and N. E. Brick. "Self-Regulatory Processes in Goal Striving During Excellent Distance-Running Performances: A Qualitative Study." *Psychology of Sport and Exercise* 70 (January 2024):102516. doi: 10.1016/j.psychsport.2023.102516. Epub 2023 Aug 25. PMID: 38065659.

Van Lange, Paul, E. Tory Higgins, Arie W. Kruglanski (eds). *Social Psychology: Handbook of Basic Principles*. New York: Guilford, 2022.

CHAPTER 4

Collins, D, Á. MacNamara, and N. McCarthy. "Super Champions, Champions, and Almosts: Important Differences and Commonalities on the Rocky Road." *Frontiers in Psychology* 6 (January 11, 2016): 2009. doi: 10.3389/fpsyg.2015.02009. PMID: 26793141; PMCID: PMC4707280.

Karlsson, Linnér R, T. T. Mallard, P. B. Barr, S. Sanchez-Roige, et al. "Multivariate Analysis of 1.5 Million People Identifies Genetic Associations with Traits Related to Self-Regulation and Addiction. *Nature Neuroscience*. 24, no. 10 (October 2021): 1367–76. doi: 10.1038/s41593-021-00908-3. Epub 2021 Aug 26. PMID: 34446935; PMCID: PMC8484054.

Libin, E. "Coping Intelligence: Efficient Life Stress Management." *Frontiers in Psychology* 8 (March 3, 2017): 302. doi: 10.3389/fpsyg .2017.00302. PMID: 28316579; PMCID: PMC5334319.

Maté, Gabor. *In the Realm of Hungry Ghosts: Close Encounters with Addiction*. Berkeley: North Atlantic, 2011.

Sarkar, Mustafa, David Fletcher, and Daniel J. Brown, "What Doesn't Kill Me . . . : Adversity-Related Experiences Are Vital in the Development of Superior Olympic Performance. *Journal of Science and Medicine in Sport* 18 (2015): 475–479. doi:10.1016/j.jsams.2014.06 .010.

Shorter, Frank. *My Marathon: Reflections on a Gold Medal Life*. New York: Rodale, 2016.

Skinner, E. A., and M. J. Zimmer-Gembeck. "The Development of Coping." *Annual Review of Psychol.* 58 (2007): 119–44. doi: 10.1146/annurev.psych.58.110405.085705. PMID: 16903804.

Werner, E. E. "Children of the Garden Island." *Scientific American* 260, no. 4 (April 1989): 106–11. doi: 10.1038/scientificamerican0489-106. PMID: 2928762.

Wilson, Mark, Vincent Walsh, and Beth Parkin (eds). *Sport and the Brain: The Science of Preparing, Enduring and Winning.* Amsterdam: Elsevier, 2017.

CHAPTER 5

Agassi, Andre. *Open: An Autobiography.* New York: Vintage, 2009.

Barrett, Lisa Feldman. *How Emotions Are Made: The Secret Life of the Brain.* Boston: Mariner, 2017.

Brown, E. Y., and C. N. Shaw. "Effects of a Stressor on a Specific Motor Task on Individuals Displaying Selected Personality Factors. *Research Quarterly* 46, no. 1 (March 1975): 71–7. PMID: 1056054.

Drigas, A. S., and C. Papoutsi. "A New Layered Model on Emotional Intelligence." *Behavioral Sciences* (Basel) 8, no. 5 (May 2, 2018): 45. doi: 10.3390/bs8050045. PMID: 29724021; PMCID: PMC5981239.

CHAPTER 6

Aidman, E. V. "Attribute-Based Selection for Success: The Role of Personality Attributes in Long-Term Predictions of Achievement in Sport." *Journal of the American Board of Sport Psychology* 3 (2007): 1–18.

Dweck, C. S. "From Needs to Goals and Representations: Foundations for a Unified Theory of Motivation, Personality, and Development. *Psychological Review* 124, no. 6 (November 2017): 689–719. doi: 10.1037/rev0000082. Epub 2017 Sep 21. PMID: 28933872.

Karp, Pamela. "Personality Assessment and the Prediction of Success and Achievement in Professional Hockey." (2000.)

McLeod, B. D., J. J. Wood, and J. R. Weisz. "Examining the Association Between Parenting and Childhood Anxiety: A Meta-Analysis. *Clinical Psychology Review* 27, no. 2 (March 2007): 155–72. doi: 10.1016/j.cpr.2006.09.002. Epub 2006 Nov 16. PMID: 17112647.

Perry, Joanne E., Michael J. Ross, Jeremiah Weinstock, and Jeffrey D. Gfeller. "Examining the Interrelationships between Motivation, Conscientiousness, and Individual Endurance Sport Performance." *Journal of Sports Sciences* 5 (2017).

Piepiora, P., and Z. Piepiora. "Personality Determinants of Success in Men's Sports in the Light of the Big Five." *International Journal of Environmental Research and Public Health* 18, no. 12 (June 10, 2021): 6297. doi: 10.3390/ijerph18126297. PMID: 34200739; PMCID: PMC8296103.

Schafer, Kevin. "Nurturing Dads Raise Emotionally Intelligent Kids, Helping Make Society More Respectful and Equitable." *UC Public Affairs.* June 17, 2022. https://www.ucpublicaffairs.com/home/2021 /6/17/nurturing-dads-raise-emotionally-intelligent-kids-helping -make-society-more-respectful-and-equitable-by-kevin-shafer.

Sergey Bubka. "Human Performance in Athletics: Limits and Possibilities." October 12, 1997. (Reposted in PoleVaultPower.com, December 3, 2003.) http://70.32.86.34/forum/viewtopic.php ?f=31&t=1553.

Sherman, Ryne and Blake Loepp. "The Science of Personality." Episode 45: August 23, 2022. https://www.hoganassessments.com/blog/personality-of-elite-athletes-nfl-football-players-personalities/.

Smith, Gary. "Coming Up Roses: Olympic Gold and 20 Feet Beckon as Pole Vaulter Sergei Bubka, Not Unlike the Flowers in Hometown of Donetsk, Burst Skyward." *Sports Illustrated*, September 14, 1988.

Stoeber, J., O. Stoll, O. Salmi, and J. Tiikkaja. "Perfectionism and Achievement Goals in Young Finnish Ice-Hockey Players Aspiring to Make the Under-16 National Team. *Journal of Sports Sciences* 27, no. 1 (January 1, 2009): 85–94. doi: 10.1080/02640410802448749. PMID: 19012074.

Zhang, G., X. Chen, L. Xiao, Y. Li, B. Li, Z. Yan, L. Guo, and D. H. Rost. "The Relationship Between Big Five and Self-Control in Boxers: A Mediating Model." *Frontiers in Psychology* 10 (August 8, 2019): 1690. doi: 10.3389/fpsyg.2019.01690. PMID: 31440177; PMCID: PMC6694765.

CHAPTER 7

Hamimi, T. "Prediction of Happiness Based on Self-Regulation and Self-Efficacy Among Female Students of Secondary High-Schools in Hamedan." *International Journal of School of Cognitive Psychology* 5, no. 4 (2018).

Headey, Bruce, Ruud Muffels, and Gert Wagner. "Long-Running German Panel Survey Shows That Personal and Economic Choices, Not Just Genes, Matter for Happiness." *Proceedings of the National Academy of Sciences* 107, no. 42 (2010): 17922–26.

Hoang, Mary. *Darkness Is Golden: A Guide to Personal Transformation and Dealing with Life's Messiness.* Neutral Bay: Pantera, 2021.

Hughes, Clara. *Open Heart, Open Mind*. New York: Touchstone, 2017.

Van Gennep, Arnold. *The Rites of Passage, Second Edition*. Chicago: University of Chicago, 2019.

CHAPTER 8

Lambert, Noelle. Interview with Sheehan Stanwick Burch. *The Stick Drop*, podcast audio, May 19, 2021. https://podcasts.apple.com/us /podcast/noelle-lambert-s1-e8.

McCormack, Chris. *I'm Here to Win: A World Champion's Advice for Peak Performance*. New York: Center Street, 2011.

Milstein, N., Y. Striet, M. Lavidor, D. Anaki, and I. Gordon. "Rivalry and Performance: A Systematic Review and Meta-Analysis." *Organizational Psychology Review* 12, no. 3 (2022): 332–61. https://doi.org/10 .1177/20413866221082128.

Thomas, Gareth. *Proud: My Autobiography*. London: Ebury, 2014.

Zagzebski, Linda. "Emulation." *Exemplarist Moral Theory*. New York: Oxford University Press, 2017. Online edition, March 23, 2017. https://doi.org/10.1093/acprof:oso/9780190655846.003.0005.

CHAPTER 9

Baker, Katie. "Vintage Bledsoe." *The Ringer*, January 27, 2017. https:// www.theringer.com/2017/1/27/16037408/nfl-drew-bledsoe-new -england-patriots-15-years-later-doubleback-wine-a24ef85c23f9.

Bird, Hayden. "Drew Bledsoe Recalls Being Drafted When the Patriots Were 'the Fourth Sports Team in Town.'" Boston.com, April 17, 2017.

Brodsky, Max, director. *Drew Bledsoe: Better with Age*. E:60 Pictures, 2020. 1 hour. https://youtu.be/HmBbqcpqTpg?si=G0pzULgOueS 6hotH.

Côté, J, D. J. Macdonald, J. Baker, and B. Abernethy. "When 'Where' Is More Important Than 'When': Birthplace and Birthdate Effects on the Achievement of Sporting Expertise." *Journal of Sports Sciences* 24, no. 10 (October 2006): 1065–73. doi: 10.1080/02640410500432490. PMID: 17115521.

Kennaugh, Warren. *FIT: When Talent and Intelligence Just Won't Cut It*. Brisbane: Wiley, 2016.

Kerr, Z. Y., S. W. Marshall, H. P. Harding Jr., and K. M. Guskiewicz. "Nine-Year Risk of Depression Diagnosis Increases with Increasing Self-Reported Concussions in Retired Professional Football Players." *American Journal of Sports Medicine* 40, no. 10 (October 2012): 2206–12. doi: 10.1177/0363546512456193. Epub 2012 Aug 24. PMID: 22922518.

Smith, M. A., K. S. Honegger, G. Turner, and B. de Bivort. "Idiosyncratic Learning Performance in Flies." *Biology Letters* 18, no. 2 (February 2022): 20210424. doi: 10.1098/rsbl.2021.0424. Epub 2022 Feb 2. PMID: 35104427; PMCID: PMC8807056.

Wellington, Chrissie. *A Life Without Limits: A World Champion's Journey*. New York: Center Street, 2012.

CHAPTER 10

Alegre, Alberto. "Parenting Styles and Children's Emotional Intelligence: What Do We Know?" *The Family Journal* 19 (2011):

56. doi: 10.1177/1066480710387486. https://www.researchgate.net/publication/258193465_Parenting_Styles_and_Children's_Emotional_Intelligence_What_do_We_Know.

Dodd, Johnny. "Meet My Two Moms: Wheelchair Racing Sensation Tatyana McFadden Reveals How She Was Saved from a Bleak Russian Orphanage." *People*, November 24, 2016. https://people.com/sports/tatyana-mcfadden-parents-and-upbringing-in-orphanage.

McFadden, Tatyana, with Tom Walker. *Ya, Sama! Moments from My Life*. InspiredEdge Editions, 2016.

Ochoa, Lorena. *Dream Big: My Life, Golf and How I Became World Number One*. Mexico City: Penguin Random House, 2014.

ACKNOWLEDGMENTS

I would like to express my heartfelt appreciation for my good friend Cait Chock, a well-chosen first sounding board for my theory of athletic greatness, whose enthusiasm encouraged me to undertake the immense effort required to turn it into a book. Joe Baker's subsequent validation of the ideas presented here gave me the confidence to continue the work, a blessing for which I am profoundly grateful. Eric Kussin added courage to my confidence through the example of his boldly nonconforming approach to mental health advocacy. My good friend Jake Tuber, along with Ryne Sherman of Hogan Assessments, assuaged my imposter syndrome as a psychological theorist by teaching me about personality science and helping me design and execute a proper study of personality in elite athletes. My longtime literary agent, Linda Konner, found the perfect publishing home for *The Other Talent* in BenBella, whose exceptional team of editors and other specialists made the final product much better than I ever could have made it alone. Thank you all.

ABOUT THE AUTHOR

 Matt Fitzgerald is the author of more than thirty sports-related books. A former editor at *Triathlete* magazine, he cofounded 80/20 Endurance, the world's largest online training resource for endurance athletes and coaches, and the Coaches of Color Initiative, an apprenticeship program that seeks to increase diversity in endurance coaching. He resides with his wife, Nataki, in Flagstaff, Arizona, where he operates Dream Run Camp, a pro-style training camp for runners of all abilities.